Marlow's Idaho Rock Hound

Marlow's Idaho Rock Hounding Guide Book 2024

The Definitive Tourist's Reference to Making the Best of Your Rock Hounding Trip to Idaho

Carlos B. Marlow

Marlow's Idaho Rock Hounding Guide Book 2024

DISCLAIMER

While every precaution has been taken in the preparation of this book, the publisher assumes no responsibility for errors or omissions, or for damages resulting from the use of the information contained herein.

Marlow's Idaho Rock Hounding Guide Book 2024: The Definitive Tourist's Reference to Making the Best of Your Rock Hounding Trip to Idaho

First edition.

COPYRIGHT © CARLOS B. MARLOW 2024. ALL RIGHTS RESERVED

Before this document can be legally duplicated or reproduced in any manner, the publisher's consent must be gained. Therefore, the contents within this document can neither be stored electronically, transferred, nor kept in a database. Neither in part, nor in full can this document be copied, scanned, faxed, or retained without approval from the publisher or creator.

Marlow's Idaho Rock Hounding Guide Book 2024

TABLE OF CONTENTS

Disclaimer 2
Copyright © Carlos B. Marlow 2024. All Rights Reserved 3
Table of Contents 4
Chapter 1 10
   Welcome to the Gem State 10
     Why Rockhound in Idaho? 10
     What Can You Find? 13
     Rock Hounding Ethics & Regulations in Idaho 16
Chapter 2 22
   Planning Your Idaho Rock Hounding Trip 22
     Getting Ready for Your Adventure 22
     Choosing Your Location 27
        Southern Idaho 27
        Central Idaho 30
        Northern Idaho 33
        Beyond the Regions 36
     Seasonality & Weather Considerations 37
        Spring 37
        Summer 38
        Autumn 39
     Rock Hounding on Public vs. Private Land 41
        Public Lands and Rock Hounding 41
        Exploring Private Lands 43
     Understanding Claim Sites & Fee Digging Operations . 46

Claim Sites 46
Fee Digging 47
Choosing the Right Path 48

Chapter 3 50

Essential Rock Hounding Techniques 50

Identifying Rocks & Minerals - A Beginner's Guide 50

Visual Traits 50

Additional Resources to Help with Gem and Mineral Identification 54

Simple Field Tests 55

The Scratch Test 56

The Streak Test 57

Safe Digging Practices 58

Using Basic Tools Effectively 59

Recognizing Gem Quality - What Makes a Find a Treasure? 63

Chapter 4 68

Northern Idaho 68

Priest Lake 68

Solo Creek 74

Pack River 80

Ruby Creek 84

Moyie River 89

Clark Fork 93

Talache 98

Vulcan Mine 103

Crystal Gold Mine 107

Sierra Silver Mine Tour 112

Marlow's Idaho Rock Hounding Guide Book 2024

    St. Joe River 117

    Big Carpenter Creek 122

    Emerald Creek 126

Chapter 4 132

    Central Idaho 132

        Betchel Mountain 132

        Fossil Bowl 137

        Mica Mountain 142

        Freezeout Ridge 146

        Crater Peak 151

        Orofino Creek 156

        Musselshell 160

        Lolo Pass 164

        Lower Clearwater 169

        Selway River 175

        Cottonwood 180

        Elk City 185

        White Bird 189

        Slate Creek 194

        Lucile 198

        Salmon River 204

        Ruby Rapids 210

        Florence 215

        Crystal Mountain 219

        Warren 221

        Stibnite 224

        Paddy Flat 227

- Goose Creek 230
- Big Creek, Valley County 233
- Big Creek, Shoshone County 236
- Mica Hill 238

Chapter 5 241

Western Idaho 241

- Little Weiser River 241
- Cuprum 243
- Mineral 246
- Fourth of July Creek 249
- Weiser 252
- Idaho City 255
- Dismal Swamp 258
- Sommer Camp Road 262
- Opalene Gulch 265
- McBride Creek 268
- Coal Mine Basin 272

Chapter 6 276

Southern Idaho 276

- South Mountain 276
- Reynolds Creek 279
- Bruneau River 283
- Rabbit Springs 286
- Clover Creek 290
- Big Wood River 294
- Croy Creek 297
- Little Wood River 301

Cold Springs Creek, Gem County 304

Cold Springs Creek, Elmore County 308

Muldoon Creek 313

Fish Creek Reservoir 318

Big Southern Butte 321

Acro Hills 325

Trail Creek (Salmon-Challis National Forest, Salmon River) 329

Trail Creek (Sawtooth National Forest, Boise River) .. 334

Chapter 7 338

   Eastern Idaho 338

      East Fork Salmon River 338

      Bayhorse 341

      Yankee Fork 344

      Napias Creek 349

      Meyers Cove 353

      Morgan Creek 357

      Challis 361

      Leanton Gulch 365

      Lemhi Pass 368

      Spencer Opal Mines 372

Chapter 8 376

   Snake River Region 376

      Cinder Butte 376

      Bitch Creek 381

      Conant Creek 385

      Caribou Mountain 388

Pelican Point 392
China Hat 396
Little Flat 400
Spence Gulch 404
Paris Canyon 408
St. Charles 412
Cedar Breaks National Monument 416
Bruneau Canyon 419
King of the Mountains Mine 423
Conclusion 427

CHAPTER 1
WELCOME TO THE GEM STATE

Craving an adventure that blends the thrill of discovery with the beauty of nature? Look no further than Idaho. This rugged and geologically diverse wonderland beckons rockhounds of all levels, offering a treasure trove of sparkling minerals, mesmerizing gems, fascinating fossils, and even a chance to pan for gold. But before you lace up your boots and grab your rock hammer, let's delve into the captivating world of Idaho rock hounding.

Rock hounding in Idaho is more than just collecting rocks. It's about connecting with nature, unraveling the geological story of a magnificent state, and experiencing the thrill of uncovering a hidden gem. Whether you're a seasoned collector or a curious newcomer, Idaho's diverse landscapes and hidden treasures promise an unforgettable adventure.

WHY ROCKHOUND IN IDAHO?

Idaho, aptly nicknamed the "Gem State," isn't just a moniker; it's a geological wonderland waiting to be explored by the adventurous rockhound. This diverse state boasts a treasure trove of minerals, gemstones, and fossils, each whispering tales of a dynamic past. But what exactly makes Idaho such a rockhounding paradise? Let's delve into the fascinating geological tapestry that sets this state apart.

Millions of years ago, where Idaho now stands, a vastly different landscape existed. Volcanic eruptions sculpted mountains, ancient seabeds deposited mineral-rich sediments, and powerful tectonic forces reshaped the land. These dramatic events, spread over eons, left behind a geological legacy that is a rockhound's dream.

Travel south, and you'll be greeted by a landscape sculpted by volcanic fury. The Owyhee Uplift, a vast volcanic plateau, is home to mesmerizing opal fields. Here, volcanic activity millions of years ago created pockets of silica-rich gel, which eventually transformed into the captivating opals we treasure today. These opals, known for their mesmerizing play of color, come in a variety of hues, from fiery orange to milky white, with flashes of blue, green, and purple. Exploring these opal fields is like stepping back in time, witnessing the remnants of a bygone volcanic era.

Venture north, and the landscape transforms into a majestic tapestry of towering mountains. This region, once a vast ocean floor, was uplifted and folded by powerful geological forces. The resulting metamorphic and igneous rocks became the perfect cradle for a variety of gemstones. Valley County, nestled in the heart of this mountainous region, is renowned for its sapphires. These captivating blue beauties, formed under immense pressure and heat, are a symbol of wisdom and truth. Unearthing your own sapphire in the shadow of these majestic peaks is an experience unlike any other.

Further north, lush forests cloak glacial lakes, hiding remnants of a prehistoric past. This region was once covered by a shallow sea teeming with marine life. Over time, as the sea receded and the landscape transformed, these creatures were fossilized, leaving behind a captivating record of life on Earth millions of years ago. Rockhounding in this region can reward you with fossilized shells, corals, and even the occasional dinosaur bone, offering a glimpse into a bygone era. The glacial activity that sculpted the landscape also played a role in creating breathtaking agate beds. These colorful stones, formed from layers of chalcedony, come in a variety of patterns and hues, making them prized possessions for rockhounds.

Idaho's geological bounty extends far beyond gemstones and fossils. The state is home to a wealth of fascinating minerals, each with its own unique story to tell. In central Idaho, explore the legacy of historic mining booms by searching for garnets, remnants of a time when the region was a major producer of these versatile minerals. Cassia County boasts thunder eggs, a geological marvel formed by layers of volcanic ash and minerals. These seemingly ordinary rocks split open to reveal a hidden beauty – a crystallized center that can be polished to reveal a breathtaking agate or jasper formation. And for those seeking a touch of history, central Idaho also offers the opportunity to pan for gold, a chance to relive the excitement of the Gold Rush era.

The beauty of Idaho's rock hounding scene lies in its diversity. Whether you're drawn to the fiery opals of the south, the captivating sapphires of the central mountains, or the ancient fossils and agates of the north, Idaho has something for everyone. Each region offers a unique geological puzzle to unravel, with stunning landscapes adding to the adventure.

Rock hounding in Idaho isn't just about collecting beautiful stones; it's about forging a deeper connection with nature. As you explore the state's diverse landscapes, you'll gain a newfound appreciation for the powerful forces that shaped our planet. Each rock you discover holds a story, a testament to millions of years of geological evolution. The thrill of unearthing a hidden treasure is amplified by the breathtaking scenery that surrounds you, making your rock hounding adventure an unforgettable experience.

WHAT CAN YOU FIND?

Idaho, the "Gem State," lives up to its name in a spectacular way. Venture into its diverse landscapes, and you'll be greeted by a treasure trove of sparkling gems, captivating minerals, fascinating fossils, and even the chance to pan for gold. But what exactly awaits the curious rockhound in this geological wonderland? Let's delve into the magnificent bounty that Idaho has to offer.

Undoubtedly, the crown jewel of Idaho's rock hounding scene is the sapphire. These captivating blue beauties, particularly concentrated in Valley County's Thunder Mountain region, hold a special allure. Formed under immense pressure and heat, sapphires symbolize wisdom and truth. Unearthing your own sapphire, nestled amidst the majesty of central Idaho's mountains, is an experience that transcends mere collecting. Beyond the iconic blue, sapphires can also occur in a range of hues, from pale yellow to a rare and coveted pink.

Fire enthusiasts will be captivated by opals, found predominantly in southern Idaho's Owyhee County. These mesmerizing stones, formed from volcanic silica-rich gel, are renowned for their play of color. Imagine holding a captivating gem that shimmers with flashes of red, orange, yellow, green, and blue – that's the magic of an Idaho opal. Opal varieties range from the precious "fire opal," ablaze with fiery hues, to the more common "opalized wood," where the play of color dances within fossilized wood.

Beyond sapphires and opals, Idaho boasts a wealth of other gemstones waiting to be discovered. Garnet hunters can rejoice, with central and northern Idaho offering a variety of these versatile minerals. From the deep red almandine garnets to the vibrant green tsavorite variety, these gemstones hold a rich history, as remnants of past mining booms. Idaho also offers a chance to unearth stunning garnets in a matrix, where the crystals are embedded in the surrounding rock, creating a captivating natural display.

For those seeking a touch of history and a unique gemstone, central Idaho beckons with star garnets. These rare beauties, often featuring a six-rayed star when viewed under a single light source, were prized by indigenous cultures and are still coveted by collectors today. And for a touch of whimsy, keep an eye out for Idaho's unique "moonstone opal." These translucent stones, found in Latah County, exhibit a soft play of color reminiscent of moonstones, with a touch of opal's signature fire.

Idaho's geological bounty extends far beyond gemstones. The state is a treasure trove of fascinating minerals, each with its own unique story to tell. History buffs will be drawn to central Idaho's old mining districts, where remnants of past mining endeavors can be found alongside intriguing minerals like galena (lead sulfide) and pyrite (fool's gold). These minerals, once mined for their economic value, offer a glimpse into the state's rich mining history.

For a touch of the exotic, explore northern Idaho's kyanite deposits. These vibrant blue bladed crystals are a unique find, often used in industrial applications but also prized by collectors for their striking appearance. And for those seeking a connection to the Earth's fiery past, obsidian, volcanic glass formed from cooled lava, can be found scattered throughout the state, particularly in southern Idaho. This jet-black, glassy material was used by indigenous cultures for tools and weapons, and its smooth, almost mirror-like surface continues to captivate collectors today.

Idaho's story isn't just about captivating minerals and gemstones; it's also about the fascinating creatures that once inhabited this land. Northern Idaho, in particular, offers a window into the prehistoric past through its rich fossil beds. Imagine uncovering a perfectly preserved trilobite fossil, a segmented arthropod that thrived in ancient seas millions of years ago. Or perhaps you'll stumble upon fossilized shells and corals, remnants of a vibrant marine ecosystem.

The thrill of unearthing a dinosaur bone, while rare, is a possibility in some areas of northern Idaho. These fossilized remains offer a tangible connection to the age of giants, allowing you to ponder the colossal creatures that once roamed this land. Fossil hunting in Idaho requires patience and a keen eye, but the rewards can be truly extraordinary, providing a unique glimpse into a bygone era.

Idaho's landscapes hold a treasure trove of natural wonders beyond the realm of traditional gemstones and fossils. Agate hunters will be delighted by the diverse varieties scattered throughout the state. Southern Idaho's deserts offer a chance to unearth colorful jaspers, a close relative of agate, with captivating red, brown, and yellow hues. These durable stones were often used by indigenous cultures for tools and weapons, and their beauty continues to be appreciated by collectors today.

For a truly unique find, keep an eye out for Idaho's thunder eggs. Predominantly found in Cassia County, these seemingly ordinary volcanic rocks hold a hidden surprise. When cracked open, they reveal a captivating center – a crystallized formation of agate or jasper. The anticipation of what lies within each thunder egg adds an extra layer of excitement to the rock hounding experience.

Central Idaho's rivers and streams are another treasure trove for the patient rockhound. With a bit of perseverance, you might uncover beautiful agates, tumbled smooth by the relentless flow of water. These agates come in a variety of colors and patterns, from banded varieties to stunning moss agates, where green inclusions resemble miniature moss formations.

For those seeking a taste of adventure and a connection to Idaho's historic Gold Rush era, central Idaho offers the opportunity to pan for gold. While large-scale gold mining is a relic of the past, recreational panning along rivers and streams can still yield small gold flakes. The thrill of finding even a speck of gold, a symbol of wealth and discovery, is sure to add a touch of excitement to your rock hounding adventure.

The beauty of Idaho's rock hounding scene lies not just in the treasures you unearth, but in the journey itself. As you explore the state's diverse landscapes, from the rugged mountains of the central region to the lush forests and glacial lakes of the north, you'll gain a newfound appreciation for the powerful forces that shaped our planet. Each rock, mineral, or fossil you discover holds a story, a testament to millions of years of geological evolution. The thrill of the hunt, the beauty of the surroundings, and the connection to nature's grandeur – these are the true treasures that await you on your Idaho rock hounding adventure.

ROCK HOUNDING ETHICS & REGULATIONS IN IDAHO

The thrill of unearthing a hidden gem or a captivating fossil in the heart of Idaho's wilderness is undeniable. But with this excitement comes a responsibility to respect the land and its resources. This section of Marlow's Idaho Rock Hounding Guidebook 2024 delves into the essential principles of ethical rock hounding and the regulations that govern this activity in the Gem State.

The "Leave No Trace" Ethic

Idaho's diverse landscapes, from its rugged mountains to its pristine rivers, provide a haven for rockhounds. However, it's crucial to remember that we are merely guests in these ecosystems. The "Leave No Trace" principles should be the cornerstone of every responsible rockhound's approach. Here's how to minimize your impact and ensure future generations can enjoy these treasures:

- **Stay on Designated Trails:** Resist the urge to veer off established trails. This helps protect fragile vegetation and minimize erosion.
- **Pack It In, Pack It Out:** Everything you bring in, from food wrappers to used toilet paper, must be taken out with you. Leave no trace of your visit.
- **Minimize Campfire Impact:** If you plan on camping, use designated fire rings and ensure your fire is completely extinguished before leaving the campsite. Consider using a camp stove to further minimize your impact.
- **Respect Wildlife:** Observe wildlife from a safe distance and never attempt to feed them. Leave their natural habitats undisturbed.
- **Respect Private Property:** Always obtain permission from the landowner before venturing onto private property. This includes respecting posted signs and boundaries.
- **Dig Responsibly:** If digging is permitted, fill in your holes before leaving the site. This minimizes trip hazards for future visitors and helps maintain the natural landscape.
- **Use Tools Wisely:** Use tools like hammers and chisels responsibly to avoid unnecessary damage to rocks and surrounding vegetation.

Understanding Regulations

Beyond the "Leave No Trace" principles, it's vital to understand the regulations that govern rock hounding on public lands in Idaho. Here's a breakdown of the key points to remember:

- **Federal vs. State Lands:** Rock hounding regulations differ between federal lands managed by the Bureau of Land Management (BLM) and the Forest Service (USFS), and state lands managed by the Idaho Department of Lands (IDL). Familiarize yourself with the specific regulations for the area you plan to visit. This information is often readily available on the respective agency websites.
- **Permits and Fees:** Certain areas may require permits for rock hounding, especially on federal land. Always obtain the necessary permits before embarking on your adventure. Some areas may also have associated fees to cover administrative costs.
- **Collecting Limits:** Most public lands have restrictions on the amount of material you can collect. Be mindful of these limits and avoid taking more than what's permitted.
- **Claim Sites:** Some areas may have designated claim sites where individuals or companies hold mineral rights. Rock hounding is strictly prohibited on these sites.
- **Protected Areas:** Certain areas, such as National Parks and Wilderness Areas, have stricter regulations or may even prohibit rock hounding altogether. Research the specific regulations for any protected area you plan to visit.

Protecting Cultural Resources

Idaho's landscapes hold not just geological wonders but also historical and cultural artifacts. Here's how to ensure you're a responsible steward of these resources as well:

- **Be Aware of Cultural Sites:** Some areas may contain archaeological sites or locations of cultural significance to indigenous tribes. These sites are often marked and protected by law. Leave them undisturbed and report any potential disturbances to the relevant authorities.
- **Respect Artifacts:** If you encounter historical artifacts like arrowheads or pottery fragments, leave them in place. These artifacts hold significant cultural value and should be left for professional archaeologists to study.

Becoming a Responsible Rockhound Ambassador

By following these ethical guidelines and regulations, you're not just protecting the land and its resources, but also setting a positive example for fellow rockhounds. Here are some additional ways to embrace responsible rock hounding:

- **Join a Rockhounding Club:** Connecting with local rockhounding clubs can provide valuable information on ethical practices and regulations in your area. You'll also learn from experienced rockhounds who can share their knowledge and best practices.
- **Educate Others:** Share your knowledge about responsible rock hounding with friends, family, and fellow explorers. The more people who embrace these principles, the better it is for Idaho's natural treasures.
- **Report Violations:** If you witness someone violating regulations or engaging in irresponsible behavior, report it to the appropriate authorities.

Responsible Collecting

Following regulations is crucial, but ethical rock hounding goes beyond the legal requirements. Here are some additional considerations for the responsible collector:

- **Rarity Matters:** Be mindful of the rarity of a particular rock, mineral, or fossil. For common finds, take only what you need and leave the rest for others to enjoy. For rare specimens, consider leaving them undisturbed, especially if they hold scientific or historical significance.
- **Focus on Quality, Not Quantity:** It's more rewarding to find a single, high-quality specimen than a collection of mediocre ones. Be selective and focus on unique or well-preserved finds.
- **Respect the Ecosystem:** Rock hounding often takes place in delicate ecosystems. Be mindful of your impact on plant and animal life. Avoid disturbing nesting areas, crucial habitats, or rare plant species.
- **Document Your Finds:** Take photographs of your finds in their natural setting, before collecting them. This helps document the location and context of your discovery, which can be valuable for scientific or historical purposes. Additionally, responsible documentation can help deter potential accusations of illegal collecting.
- **Knowledge is Power:** Educate yourself about the geology of the area you're exploring. Understanding the rock formations and mineral deposits will help you target your search efforts and increase your chances of finding unique specimens. Knowing what you're looking for also helps you avoid collecting protected or culturally significant artifacts.

The Importance of Sustainability

Rock hounding is a cherished activity, but it's important to remember that these resources are not limitless. By adopting sustainable practices, we ensure that future generations can enjoy the same thrill of discovery:

- **Practice "Recreational Collecting":** Focus on collecting for personal enjoyment and education, not for commercial purposes. Leave enough behind for others to experience the joy of discovery.
- **Replenish the "Treasure Chest":** Consider participating in organized "rockhounding clean-up" events, where responsible collectors help remove trash and debris from popular rockhounding sites. This helps maintain the beauty and health of these natural areas.
- **Become an Advocate:** Support organizations that work to conserve Idaho's public lands and geological resources. Your actions can make a difference in ensuring the long-term sustainability of this rewarding activity.

Rock hounding in Idaho isn't just about collecting rocks; it's about fostering a deep appreciation for the natural world and its wonders. By embracing responsible practices, you become a steward of this geological heritage. Let the thrill of discovery be coupled with a commitment to protecting these treasures for generations to come.

CHAPTER 2
PLANNING YOUR IDAHO ROCK HOUNDING TRIP

GETTING READY FOR YOUR ADVENTURE

Before you set off on your treasure hunt, a little preparation goes a long way in ensuring a safe, successful, and enjoyable experience. This section of Marlow's Idaho Rock Hounding Guidebook 2024 equips you with the essential knowledge on permits, tools, and gear to maximize your rock hounding adventure in the Gem State.

Understanding Permits and Regulations

Idaho's diverse landscapes offer a treasure trove for rockhounds, but venturing onto public lands comes with certain responsibilities. Familiarization with regulations and permits ensures you have a legal and ethical experience. Here's a breakdown of the key points to remember:

- **Know Your Location:** The first step is to identify the specific area you plan to explore. Rock hounding regulations differ between federal lands managed by the Bureau of Land Management (BLM) and the Forest Service (USFS), and state lands managed by the Idaho Department of Lands (IDL). Each agency has its own regulations and permit requirements.
- **Research Online:** Fortunately, the internet is a wealth of information. The official websites of the BLM (www.blm.gov/idaho), USFS (https://www.fs.usda.gov/fs-tags/idaho), and IDL (https://www.idl.idaho.gov/) provide comprehensive details on regulations and permits specific to each

region. Search for "rock hounding" on the respective agency website for your chosen area.
- **Contact the Local Office:** Don't hesitate to contact the local BLM, USFS, or IDL office for the most up-to-date information. They can answer any specific questions you may have and provide details on any potential closures or restrictions in your chosen location.
- **Permits and Fees:** Be prepared for the possibility of needing permits. Some areas have minimal or no permit requirements for casual rock collecting, while others may require permits for specific activities like digging or using motorized equipment. Always be prepared to pay any associated fees. These fees help manage public lands and support vital conservation efforts.

Essential Tools for the Rockhound

Now that you have the legalities covered, let's explore the tools that will transform you from a curious tourist into a resourceful rockhound.

- **Footwear:** Sturdy hiking boots are a non-negotiable. Rock hounding often involves navigating uneven terrain, and good ankle support is crucial for safety. Opt for boots with good traction to handle loose rocks, dirt, and potentially wet conditions.
- **Rock Hammer:** A good quality rock hammer is your primary tool for breaking open rocks and revealing potential treasures within. Choose a hammer with a comfortable grip and a sturdy head weight suitable for your needs. Geologists' hammers with a pointed pick on one end and a flat face on the other offer good versatility.
- **Chisel:** A sturdy chisel will come in handy for prying open small cracks and crevices in rocks where hidden

gems might be nestled. Choose a chisel made of hardened steel to ensure it can handle the task without breaking.
- **Safety Glasses:** Always wear safety glasses when hammering or chiseling rocks. Small rock fragments can fly unexpectedly, and protecting your eyes is essential.
- **Hand Lens:** A good hand lens, also known as a loupe, allows you to examine your finds in detail. This is vital for identifying minerals and appreciating the intricate details of your treasures. A 10x magnification lens is a good starting point.

Additional Gear for Enhanced Exploration

Beyond the essential tools, consider these additional items to enhance your rock hounding experience:

- **Backpack:** A sturdy backpack allows you to carry your tools, water, snacks, and any treasures you find. Choose a comfortable pack with enough space for your needs.
- **GPS Device:** A GPS device or a downloaded offline map application can help you navigate unfamiliar terrain and ensure you stay within legal boundaries.
- **First-Aid Kit:** A basic first-aid kit is essential for any outdoor activity. Be prepared for minor cuts, scrapes, or insect bites.
- **Sunscreen and Insect Repellent:** Protect yourself from the sun's harmful rays and pesky insects with sunscreen and insect repellent.
- **Water Bottle:** Stay hydrated throughout your adventure. Carrying a reusable water bottle is an eco-friendly option.
- **Snacks and Lunch:** Pack enough snacks and a lunch to keep your energy levels up during your exploration.

- **Notebook and Pen:** Jot down notes about your finds, including the location, any distinguishing features, and initial observations. This can be valuable for later identification.
- **Camera:** Capture the beauty of your surroundings and document your rock hounding adventure with a camera.

Specialized Gear for Specific Pursuits

Depending on your target finds, you may consider adding some specialized gear to your rock hounding arsenal:

- **Gold Panning:** For those seeking a touch of history and the thrill of panning for gold, a gold pan is essential. There are various pan styles available, but a basic 10-inch pan is a good starting point.
- **Sieve:** A fine-mesh sieve helps separate gold flakes from unwanted debris when panning.
- **Knee Pads:** If you plan on spending a lot of time kneeling while panning or sifting for gold, knee pads can provide added comfort and protection.
- **Flotation Bucket:** For exploring rivers and streams for agates and other gemstones, a flotation bucket can be a valuable tool. These buckets utilize water flow and specific gravity to separate lighter materials from denser gemstones.
- **Rock Classifier:** A rock classifier, also known as a sizing screen, is a set of nested screens with varying mesh sizes. This allows you to sort your rockhounding finds by size, making it easier to identify and organize your treasures.

Remember: When acquiring tools and gear, prioritize quality over quantity. Invest in durable items that will last for years of rock hounding adventures.

Clothing and Weather

While rugged and functional, your rock hounding attire should also be comfortable for navigating the outdoors. Here are some tips:

- **Comfortable Clothing:** Dress in layers to adapt to changing weather conditions. Opt for breathable, quick-drying fabrics like cotton or synthetic blends.
- **Long Pants and Long Sleeves:** Protect yourself from scratches, thorns, and insect bites with long pants and long sleeves.
- **Hat:** A wide-brimmed hat protects your face and neck from the sun.
- **Sun Protection:** Even on cloudy days, wear sunscreen to protect your skin from harmful UV rays.
- **Weather Awareness:** Always check the weather forecast before heading out. Be prepared for changing weather conditions and pack extra layers if necessary.

Leave No Trace Principles: Responsible Packing

Remember, rock hounding is about enjoying nature while respecting it. Here's how to pack responsibly:

- **Reusable Containers:** Pack your snacks and lunch in reusable containers to minimize waste.
- **Trash Bags:** Bring along a trash bag to collect any waste you generate during your exploration. Leave no trace of your visit.
- **Minimize Packaging:** When packing snacks and supplies, opt for items with minimal packaging.
- **Respect Wildlife:** Store your food and snacks properly to avoid attracting wildlife.

CHOOSING YOUR LOCATION

From the volcanic majesty of the south to the majestic peaks and glacial lakes of the north, each region boasts a unique geological tapestry waiting to be explored. But with such a vast and diverse landscape, where do you begin? This section will help you with matching your rockhounding interests with the ideal location in Idaho.

SOUTHERN IDAHO

The southern stretch of Idaho unveils a landscape sculpted by ancient volcanic activity, painted in fiery hues of red, orange, and brown. These sprawling deserts hold a captivating allure for rockhounds, offering a treasure trove of gemstones, minerals, and a glimpse into a fiery geological past.

Opals

Nestled in the southwestern corner of Idaho, Owyhee County beckons rockhounds with a dazzling prize – opals. Millions of years ago, volcanic activity left behind pockets of silica-rich gel, which transformed into captivating opals under immense pressure and time. These mesmerizing stones come in a dazzling array of colors, from fiery reds and oranges to cool blues and greens.

- **Blackjack Butte:** This iconic location, designated an Area of Critical Environmental Concern (ACEC) due to its ecological and geological significance, is renowned for its opal deposits. Prospectors can explore the rhyolitic tuff formations, searching for veins and nodules containing the precious stones. Remember to obtain the necessary permits before venturing onto

public lands and adhere to responsible collecting practices.
- **White Knob Mountain:** Another hotspot for opal hunters in Owyhee County is White Knob Mountain. Here, white to pale-yellow opalized rhyolite holds the potential to reveal hidden pockets of vibrant opals. The Bureau of Land Management (BLM) manages this area, so be sure to check for any closures or restrictions before your visit.

Jaspers and Thunder Eggs

Southern Idaho's volcanic past is further evidenced by the abundance of jaspers and thunder eggs found throughout the region.

- **Jaspers:** These captivating stones, formed from the microcrystalline quartz of volcanic rock, come in a dazzling array of colors, including red, brown, yellow, and even green. Southern Idaho's deserts offer opportunities to discover these durable stones, prized for their beauty and historical significance as tools and weapons used by indigenous cultures. Locations like Castle Creek State Park and Leslie Gulch are known for their jasper deposits. Always practice responsible collecting and follow park regulations.
- **Thunder Eggs:** A unique geological marvel awaits in Cassia County – thunder eggs. These seemingly ordinary volcanic rocks hold a hidden surprise within their unassuming exteriors. When cracked open, they reveal a captivating center, often composed of agate or jasper. Locations like Cow Creek and Little Jacks Creek are popular destinations for thunder egg enthusiasts. Remember to obtain permission from landowners before exploring private property.

Other Beautiful Finds

Southern Idaho's volcanic wonders offer a bounty beyond the most well-known finds. Here are some additional treasures to keep an eye out for:

- **Fire Agates:** These captivating agates, infused with volcanic minerals, display a mesmerizing play of color, often with fiery reds and oranges. Locations like Leslie Gulch and Bruneau Dunes National Monument hold the potential for uncovering these unique stones. Always adhere to park regulations and designated collecting areas.
- **Zeolites:** These fascinating minerals, formed in volcanic environments, come in a variety of crystal habits and colors. Zeolites like stilbite and heulandite can be found in locations like Castle Creek State Park, adding a unique element to your rockhounding collection. Practice responsible collecting and follow park regulations.
- **Fossilized Flora:** The volcanic activity that shaped southern Idaho's landscape also preserved remnants of ancient plant life. Locations like Bruneau Dunes National Monument offer opportunities to discover fossilized leaves and imprints of flora that once thrived in the region. Remember, most fossils on public lands are protected, so responsible collecting practices are crucial.

CENTRAL IDAHO

Gems in Central Idaho

Central Idaho's majestic mountain ranges, carved by glaciers and sculpted by volcanic forces, offer a captivating landscape for the adventurous rockhound. This region boasts a rich mining history, leaving behind a legacy of captivating gemstones, diverse minerals, and even a glimpse into the fossilized past.

Sapphires

Nestled amidst the breathtaking scenery of the central mountains, Valley County holds a treasure that has captivated prospectors for centuries – sapphires. These mesmerizing blue beauties, formed under immense pressure and heat millions of years ago, symbolize wisdom and truth. Exploring for sapphires in central Idaho offers a unique opportunity to combine the thrill of the hunt with a connection to the region's rich mining history.

- **Thunder Mountain:** This iconic location, steeped in mining lore, is a popular destination for sapphire hunters. Here, weathered gravel deposits hold the potential to reveal these captivating blue stones. Public access areas are managed by the BLM, so be sure to check for any closures or permit requirements before your visit. Always practice responsible collecting and respect designated collecting areas.
- **Independence Creek:** Another treasure trove for sapphire enthusiasts is Independence Creek. This scenic location, once a bustling mining operation, offers opportunities to explore placer deposits for sapphires and other gemstones. Remember to obtain the necessary permits before venturing onto public lands and follow responsible collecting practices.

Other Gemstones

While sapphires are a central draw, central Idaho offers a bounty for the discerning rockhound.

- **Garnets:** These captivating minerals, prized for their deep red hues, are found throughout central Idaho. From the almandine garnets discovered near Salmon to the vibrant green tsavorite variety unearthed in Latah County, garnets offer a diverse selection for collectors. Locations like Elk City and Emerald Creek are known for their garnet deposits. Always be mindful of regulations and obtain any necessary permits before exploring.
- **Amethysts:** For those seeking a touch of purple majesty, central Idaho offers opportunities to discover amethysts. These captivating quartz crystals, formed in volcanic environments, can be found in locations like the Seven Devils Mountains. Remember to check for access restrictions and responsible collecting practices before venturing into wilderness areas.
- **Opals:** While not as prevalent as in southern Idaho, central Idaho offers a chance to discover opalized wood. These fascinating fossils, formed when wood is replaced by silica, can be found in locations like the Bruneau-Jarbidge Craters National Monument. Remember, most fossils on public lands are protected, so responsible collecting practices are crucial.

Fossil Hunting in Central Idaho

Central Idaho's geological tapestry extends beyond gemstones. The ancient seabeds that once covered this region have left behind a fascinating record of life on Earth in the form of fossils.

- **Trilobites:** These fascinating marine arthropods, long vanished from the oceans, can be found in sedimentary rock formations throughout central Idaho. Locations like the Salmon River Mountains and the Clearwater Mountains offer opportunities to unearth these remnants of ancient life. Always follow responsible collecting practices and be mindful of regulations, as some fossils may be protected.
- **Leaf Fossils:** Volcanic activity in central Idaho preserved not only gemstones but also fossilized flora. Locations like the Bruneau-Jarbidge Craters National Monument offer opportunities to discover imprints of leaves and other plant life that once thrived in the region. Remember, most fossils on public lands are protected, so responsible collecting practices are crucial. Report any significant finds to the appropriate authorities.

Exploring Central Idaho's Historic Sites

Central Idaho's mining history is not just about gemstones and fossils; it's about the stories of the miners who braved the elements in search of riches. Several historic mining districts offer a glimpse into this bygone era, alongside potential rockhounding opportunities.

- **Silver City:** This once-booming silver mining town, now a ghost town, offers a chance to explore abandoned mine workings and potentially unearth remnants of the past. Remember to stay on designated trails and avoid entering unstable structures. Respect private property and follow responsible collecting practices on public lands.
- **War Eagle Mountain:** This historic gold mining district offers opportunities to explore old mining claims and potentially discover remnants of gold-bearing quartz veins. Always obtain permission from

landowners before exploring private property. Be mindful of regulations and responsible collecting practices on public lands.

NORTHERN IDAHO

Northern Idaho unfolds a captivating landscape sculpted by glaciers, carpeted in lush forests, and dotted with pristine lakes. This region offers a unique experience for the rockhound, with opportunities to unearth treasures polished by glacial movement, discover remnants of ancient marine life, and even encounter a rare gem in the rough. Marlow's Idaho Rock Hounding Guidebook 2024 delves into the heart of northern Idaho's forests and glacial lakes, highlighting the potential finds and locations that await the adventurous collector.

Agates and Fossils

The relentless flow of glaciers and the churning waters of glacial lakes have left behind a treasure trove for the patient rockhound – agates. These captivating stones, formed from layered chalcedony, come in a dazzling array of colors and patterns.

- **St. Joe River:** This scenic waterway, carving its path through the Selkirk Mountains, is renowned for its agate hunting potential. Explore riverbeds and gravel bars for these colorful treasures, smoothed and polished by the relentless flow of water. Remember to follow responsible collecting practices and be mindful of regulations, as some areas may be restricted.
- **Priest River:** Another prime location for agate hunters is the Priest River. Here, amidst the lush forests and cascading waterfalls, you might unearth a

variety of agates, including moss agates with their captivating green inclusions. Always respect private property and obtain permission from landowners before venturing onto their land.

Beyond Agates: Unveiling Northern Idaho's Diverse Treasures

While agates are a major draw, northern Idaho offers a bounty for the discerning rockhound.

- **Kyanite:** For those seeking a truly unique find, northern Idaho boasts deposits of kyanite. These captivating blue bladed crystals, often used in jewelry making, can be found in locations like the Selkirk Mountains. Remember to obtain permission from landowners before exploring private property and be mindful of regulations when exploring public lands.
- **Garnets:** The diverse geology of northern Idaho extends to garnets. Locations like the Scotchman Peaks Wilderness offer opportunities to discover these captivating minerals, prized for their deep red hues. Always check for access restrictions and responsible collecting practices before venturing into wilderness areas.
- **Metamorphic Rocks:** The forces that shaped northern Idaho's landscape also produced a variety of metamorphic rocks like schist and gneiss. These visually striking rocks, with their layered or banded appearances, can be interesting additions to a rock collection. Explore exposed rock faces throughout the region, but remember to respect private property and designated wilderness areas.

Fossil Hunting in Northern Idaho

The ancient seas that once covered northern Idaho left behind fascinating remnants of marine life in the form of fossils.

- **Trilobites:** These fascinating marine arthropods, long vanished from the oceans, can be found in sedimentary rock formations throughout northern Idaho. Locations like the Clark Fork River and the Coeur d'Alene Mountains offer a chance to unearth these remnants of ancient life. Always follow responsible collecting practices and be mindful of regulations, as some fossils may be protected.
- **Plant Fossils:** Volcanic activity and geological processes have preserved fossilized flora in certain areas of northern Idaho. Locations like the Kootenai National Wildlife Refuge offer opportunities to discover imprints of leaves and other plant life that thrived in the region millions of years ago. Remember, most fossils on public lands are protected, so responsible collecting practices are crucial. Report any significant finds to the appropriate authorities.

Gold Panning

History buffs can delve into the legacy of the Gold Rush era by trying their luck at panning for gold in select rivers and streams of northern Idaho.

- **Clearwater River:** This scenic waterway, with its rich history of gold mining activity, offers opportunities to pan for gold flakes. Remember, panning for gold is a recreational activity, and large-scale mining is no longer permitted. Always follow responsible collecting practices and obtain any necessary permits.
- **Lochsa River:** Another location with a gold mining past is the Lochsa River. Here, amidst the breathtaking scenery of the Clearwater National Forest, you can try

your luck at panning for a touch of history. Always respect wilderness regulations and practice responsible collecting.

BEYOND THE REGIONS

While this section provides a starting point for choosing your location based on specific interests, there are some additional factors to consider:

- **Accessibility:** Consider your physical fitness level and choose a location with trails and terrain that suit your abilities.
- **Time of Year:** Weather conditions can significantly impact your rock hounding experience. Research the best times to visit specific regions, considering factors like snowmelt, heat advisories, and mosquito activity.
- **Public vs. Private Lands:** Public lands offer more freedom for rock hounding, but regulations and permit requirements apply. Private property requires permission from the landowner before venturing onto their land. Respect all posted signs and boundaries.
- **Guided Tours and Rockhounding Clubs:** Consider joining a guided rockhounding tour or connecting with local rockhounding clubs. These can provide valuable insights into specific locations, regulations, and responsible collecting practices.

The beauty of rock hounding in Idaho lies not just in the treasures you unearth, but in the journey itself. As you explore the state's diverse landscapes, from the rugged canyons of the south to the majestic peaks of the north, you'll gain a newfound appreciation for the powerful forces that shaped our planet.

Each rock, mineral, or fossil you discover holds a story, a testament to millions of years of geological evolution. The thrill of the hunt, the beauty of the surroundings, and the connection to nature's grandeur – these are the true treasures that await you on your Idaho rock hounding adventure.

SEASONALITY & WEATHER CONSIDERATIONS

Idaho's diverse landscapes offer a treasure trove for rockhounds year-round. But to maximize your success and enjoyment, understanding the impact of seasons and weather patterns is crucial. Marlow's Idaho Rock Hounding Guidebook 2024 delves into the seasonal considerations for various regions, helping you choose the ideal location and timing for your rockhounding adventure.

SPRING

Spring paints a vibrant picture across Idaho, with melting snow revealing previously hidden treasures. However, some locations might still be inaccessible due to lingering snowpack.

- **Southern Idaho:** Spring brings warmer temperatures and melting snow, making high-elevation locations in southern Idaho more accessible. Explore volcanic landscapes for jaspers and thunder eggs, or venture to Owyhee County for opal hunting after the winter rains have subsided. Remember, spring can also bring unpredictable weather, so check the forecast and be prepared for rain or occasional snow showers.
- **Central Idaho:** While some higher-elevation areas might remain inaccessible, lower-lying regions in central Idaho start to thaw in spring. Explore riverbeds for agates tumbled by spring floods, or visit historic

mining districts as the snow melts, revealing remnants of the past. Be mindful of lingering mud and potential high water levels near rivers and streams.
- **Northern Idaho:** Spring arrives later in northern Idaho, with snowmelt slowly revealing the secrets beneath. This might not be the prime time for extensive rockhounding, but it's a good time to visit lower-elevation areas and plan your summer adventures. Research locations and obtain necessary permits for later exploration.

SUMMER

Summer paints Idaho with lush greenery and warm temperatures, making it the peak season for rockhounding enthusiasts. However, be prepared for potential heat and crowds in popular locations.

- **Southern Idaho:** Southern Idaho's deserts and volcanic landscapes are in full swing during summer. Explore for opals, jaspers, and thunder eggs, but be aware of the scorching temperatures. Early mornings and evenings offer the most comfortable exploration times. Always carry plenty of water, wear sun protection, and be aware of the risks of heatstroke.
- **Central Idaho:** Summer offers the most accessible conditions for exploring central Idaho's mountains and mining districts. Search for sapphires in Valley County, unearth garnets near Salmon, or explore historic mining sites for a glimpse into the past. However, be aware of potential afternoon thunderstorms, especially in higher elevations. Pack rain gear and check the forecast before heading out.
- **Northern Idaho:** Summer transforms northern Idaho into a rockhounder's paradise. Explore riverbeds and gravel bars along the St. Joe River and Priest River for a bounty of agates. Search for kyanite in the Selkirk

Mountains, or try your luck panning for gold in select rivers like the Clearwater. Mosquitoes can be a nuisance, so wear insect repellent and consider long sleeves and pants for added protection.

AUTUMN

Autumn paints Idaho in a blaze of color, offering pleasant temperatures and a unique opportunity for rockhounding.

- **Southern Idaho:** Autumn brings milder temperatures to southern Idaho, making it a comfortable time to explore volcanic landscapes. Search for fire agates in Leslie Gulch or Bruneau Dunes National Monument. Be aware of the potential for occasional rain showers and adjust your plans accordingly.
- **Central Idaho:** Autumn offers a final window to explore central Idaho's mountains before winter arrives. Search for amethysts in the Seven Devils Mountains or visit historic mining sites for a final exploration before the snow falls. Be aware of potential frost and freezing temperatures at higher elevations.
- **Northern Idaho:** Autumn can be a good time for a final exploration of northern Idaho before the winter snows arrive. Search for fossils in the Kootenai National Wildlife Refuge, or explore exposed rock faces for metamorphic rocks like schist and gneiss. Be prepared for potentially colder temperatures and the possibility of early snowfall, especially in higher elevations.

Winter

Winter transforms Idaho into a snowy wonderland, but rockhounding activities are generally limited due to snow cover and access restrictions. However, winter can be a productive time for planning and preparation for your next rockhounding adventure.

- **All Regions:** While rockhounding opportunities are limited during winter, use this time to research locations, acquire necessary permits, and invest in rockhounding gear and resources.

Weather Considerations

While seasonality provides a general framework, weather can be unpredictable, especially in mountainous regions. Here are some additional weather factors to consider:

- **Precipitation:** Heavy rainfall can cause flash floods, making riverbeds and low-lying areas dangerous. Always check weather forecasts before heading out and be prepared to adjust your plans if rain is predicted.
- **High Winds:** Strong winds can create hazardous conditions, especially in exposed areas. Avoid rockhounding during periods of high winds, as loose rocks and debris can become projectiles.
- **Lightning:** Afternoon thunderstorms are a common occurrence in some parts of Idaho, especially during summer months. Always be aware of the risk of lightning and seek shelter immediately if a storm approaches.
- **Heatstroke:** Summer temperatures in southern Idaho can be scorching. Plan your outings for early mornings or evenings, wear loose, breathable clothing, and stay hydrated by carrying plenty of water.

Planning for a Safe and Successful Rockhounding Adventure

By understanding seasonal variations and weather patterns, you can maximize your rockhounding success and safety in Idaho. Here are some additional tips:

- **Dress appropriately:** Layers are key for adapting to changing weather conditions. Wear sturdy footwear with good ankle support, and consider sun protection like a hat and sunglasses during the summer months.
- **Pack essentials:** Always carry a backpack with essential supplies like water, first-aid kit, snacks, a map and compass (or GPS device with downloaded maps), and a headlamp or flashlight.
- **Be prepared for emergencies:** Let someone know your itinerary and estimated return time. Carry a fully charged cell phone (if there is reception in the area you're exploring), and be aware of potential hazards like loose rock, wildlife encounters, and uneven terrain.

ROCK HOUNDING ON PUBLIC VS. PRIVATE LAND

Understanding the difference between public and private land is crucial for a responsible and enjoyable rockhounding experience. This section delves into the distinctions between these categories, highlighting the regulations and considerations for each.

PUBLIC LANDS AND ROCK HOUNDING

The vast majority of Idaho's rockhounding opportunities lie on public lands managed by various agencies. These agencies generally encourage responsible recreational rockhounding, but regulations and permit requirements can vary.

- **Bureau of Land Management (BLM):** The BLM manages millions of acres of public lands in Idaho, offering a wealth of rockhounding opportunities. Collecting for personal, non-commercial use is typically allowed on BLM lands, but specific regulations may apply in certain areas. Always check with the local BLM office for current restrictions and permit requirements before heading out. Remember, some areas may be designated as Wilderness Study Areas (WSAs) with stricter collecting guidelines.
- **US Forest Service (USFS):** National Forests managed by the USFS also offer rockhounding opportunities. Similar to BLM lands, collecting for personal use is generally allowed, but specific regulations and permit requirements can vary. Consult the local ranger district office for current information and any necessary permits. Be mindful of designated wilderness areas within National Forests, as collecting guidelines may be more restrictive.
- **Idaho Department of Lands (IDL):** Some state-managed lands administered by the IDL offer rockhounding opportunities. Always check with the IDL for specific regulations and any permit requirements before venturing onto these lands.

Essential Tips for Public Lands

While public lands offer exciting possibilities, responsible rockhounding requires following specific guidelines. Here are some key points to remember:

- **Know Before You Go:** Research the specific location you plan to visit. Consult the websites of the relevant

land management agency (BLM, USFS, IDL) to understand the regulations in place. Download maps and familiarize yourself with the area's boundaries.
- **Respect the Limits:** Most agencies have limitations on the amount of material you can collect. Be mindful of these restrictions and collect responsibly. Leave enough for others to enjoy the experience.
- **Minimize Your Impact:** Public lands are shared resources. Practice "Leave No Trace" principles by packing out all your trash, respecting wildlife habitats, and avoiding unnecessary damage to the landscape.
- **Permits and Fees:** Some areas may require permits or have associated fees for rockhounding. Be prepared to obtain the necessary permits and pay any applicable fees before venturing out.
- **Stay on Designated Trails:** Respect designated trails and avoid venturing off-road. This minimizes your impact on the environment and reduces the risk of getting lost.

EXPLORING PRIVATE LANDS

While public lands offer a vast array of rockhounding opportunities, some private properties may also hold hidden treasures. However, venturing onto private land requires permission from the landowner.

- **Seek Permission:** Always obtain explicit permission from the landowner before exploring private property. Trespassing is not only disrespectful but can also have legal consequences.
- **Respect the Owner's Wishes:** If the landowner grants permission, be respectful of their wishes. Ask about any limitations on collecting areas or types of materials you can collect.
- **Leave a Positive Impression:** Be a courteous guest. Leave the property as you found it, and express your

gratitude to the landowner for allowing you to explore their land.

Considerations for Private Lands

Even with permission, exploring private land requires additional considerations:

- **Liability:** When exploring private land, you are typically responsible for your own safety. Be aware of potential hazards and take necessary precautions.
- **Hidden Claims:** Some private lands may have active or historic mining claims. Be mindful of potential posted signs or boundaries, and avoid entering areas designated as off-limits.
- **Environmental Impact:** Even with permission, minimize your impact on the private property. Respect wildlife habitats and avoid causing any unnecessary damage to the land.

Choosing the Right Path: Public vs. Private Lands

The decision of whether to explore public or private lands depends on your comfort level, risk tolerance, and the specific rockhounding opportunities you seek.

- **Public Lands:** For beginners or those seeking a wider variety of locations, public lands offer a safe and accessible option. Research regulations beforehand and ensure you adhere to responsible collecting practices.
- **Private Lands:** Private lands can offer unique opportunities, but they require obtaining permission and come with additional considerations. Experienced rockhounds comfortable navigating landowner relations may find success exploring private properties,

but always prioritize safety and respect for the landowner's wishes.

Working with Local Clubs and Organizations

Local rockhounding clubs and organizations can be valuable resources for navigating the legalities of rockhounding on both public and private lands. Here's how they can help:

- **Knowledge Sharing:** Clubs often have experienced members familiar with local regulations and potential rockhounding locations. They can provide valuable insights and tips for responsible collecting.
- **Field Trips:** Many clubs organize field trips to public lands, offering a safe and informative way to explore new areas with experienced guides.
- **Landowner Relations:** Some clubs may have established relationships with private landowners, allowing them access to exclusive collecting locations. However, participation in such expeditions typically requires membership and adherence to the club's guidelines.

UNDERSTANDING CLAIM SITES & FEE DIGGING OPERATIONS

CLAIM SITES

Mining claims are designated areas on public lands where individuals or companies have the legal right to explore and extract minerals. These claims can offer a unique opportunity for experienced rockhounds to unearth valuable specimens, but understanding the legalities and responsible practices is crucial.

- **Types of Claims:** There are various types of mining claims in Idaho, each with its own regulations. Locater claims are the most common, allowing individuals to stake a claim on public lands for specific minerals. Placer claims focus on recovering loose, valuable minerals from streambeds or unconsolidated deposits. Always research the specific type of claim before venturing onto the land.
- **Claim Status:** Not all claims are actively worked. Some may be abandoned, while others might be held by individuals or companies. Always research the claim status before exploring the area. Active claims are off-limits to recreational rockhounding.
- **Bureau of Land Management (BLM):** The BLM manages most mining claims on public lands in Idaho. Their website provides a searchable database where you can check the status of specific claims and understand any associated regulations.

Considerations for Those Venturing onto Claims

While exploring active claims is prohibited, there can be opportunities for experienced rockhounds on inactive claims with the proper knowledge and permissions. Here's what to consider:

- **Obtaining Permission:** Even for inactive claims, it's crucial to obtain permission from the claim holder before venturing onto the land. Respecting private property rights is paramount.
- **Understanding the Risks:** Claim sites can be hazardous due to abandoned mine shafts, loose rock, or potential environmental contaminants. Only experienced rockhounds with proper safety gear and knowledge should consider exploring such areas.
- **Responsible Practices:** If granted permission, follow responsible collecting practices. Minimize your impact on the land, respect any existing infrastructure, and leave the area as you found it.

FEE DIGGING

Fee digging operations offer a structured alternative for rockhounds seeking a more predictable and family-friendly experience. These privately owned operations allow visitors to pay a fee to explore designated areas and potentially unearth a variety of treasures.

- **Variety of Options:** Fee digging operations cater to different interests and skill levels. Some focus on specific types of gems and minerals, while others offer a broader selection. Research different operations to find one that aligns with your interests.
- **Guaranteed Success (to an Extent):** Fee digging operations typically operate in areas with a high concentration of specific materials, increasing your

chances of finding something valuable. However, keep in mind that success is never guaranteed.
- **Amenities and Guidance:** Many fee digging operations offer amenities like restrooms, picnic areas, and basic tools for rockhounding. Some even provide on-site guidance or educational workshops for beginners.

How to Find Fee Digging Operations

With a growing number of fee digging operations in Idaho, finding the right one is easier than ever. Here are some resources to help you:

- **Rockhounding Clubs and Organizations:** Local clubs and organizations often have information on fee digging operations in their area.
- **Online Resources:** Several online directories list fee digging operations across the state. Look for websites dedicated to rockhounding in Idaho or fee digging operations specifically.
- **Considerations When Choosing:** Research the types of materials offered, pricing structures, amenities available, and any age restrictions before visiting a fee digging operation. Read reviews from other visitors to get a sense of the experience.

CHOOSING THE RIGHT PATH

The decision between exploring claim sites or participating in fee digging operations depends on your experience level, risk tolerance, and desired rockhounding experience.

- **Experienced Rockhounds:** For experienced individuals comfortable navigating claim legalities and potential hazards, exploring inactive claims with permission can be a rewarding adventure.

- **Families and Beginners:** Fee digging operations offer a safe, structured, and family-friendly environment for beginners and those seeking a more predictable experience.

CHAPTER 3
ESSENTIAL ROCK HOUNDING TECHNIQUES

IDENTIFYING ROCKS & MINERALS - A BEGINNER'S GUIDE

VISUAL TRAITS

While a rock's initial visual appeal might spark your interest, rock and mineral identification relies on a more nuanced approach. Geologists and experienced rockhounds utilize a combination of visual characteristics to differentiate their discoveries. Here, we delve into four key visual elements that hold valuable clues:

- **Color: A Spectrum of Possibilities**

Color is often the first aspect that draws us to a rock or mineral. However, it's crucial to understand that color alone is not a definitive identifier. Minerals can exhibit a wide range of colors due to several factors:

- Impurities: The presence of trace elements or minerals within a primary mineral can significantly alter its color. For instance, pure quartz is colorless, but the presence of iron oxides can turn it red (jasper), purple (amethyst), or even smoky gray.
- Defects: Structural imperfections within a mineral's crystal lattice can influence color. For example, some impurities or radiation exposure can create color centers in otherwise colorless minerals.

Despite these complexities, color can still provide valuable initial clues. Familiarize yourself with the typical color ranges of commonly found rocks and minerals in Idaho. Marlow's

Rockhounding Guidebook offers a starting point, but consider consulting regional field guides for more specific information.

- **Luster: How Light Interacts with the Surface**

Luster describes how light reflects off a mineral's surface. This characteristic plays a crucial role in differentiating between rocks and minerals. Here's a breakdown of some common types of luster:

- Metallic: This luster resembles polished metal, with a shiny and reflective appearance. Pyrite, often mistaken for gold due to its metallic luster, is a classic example.
- Vitreous: This luster is glassy and resembles glass. Many varieties of quartz, including clear quartz and amethyst, exhibit vitreous luster.
- Greasy: This luster appears oily or greasy, with a dull or subdued reflection. Nephrite jade, a prized gemstone material, is known for its greasy luster.
- Pearly: This luster resembles the iridescent sheen of a pearl. Muscovite mica, a common mineral in metamorphic rocks, exhibits a pearly luster.
- Dull: This luster appears earthy or lacking in any significant reflection. Chalk and some varieties of limestone often have a dull luster.

Observing the luster in natural daylight is crucial for accurate identification. Avoid relying on artificial light sources, as they can alter the perceived luster of a mineral.

- **Texture: A Tactile Exploration**

Texture refers to the feel of a rock or mineral's surface. While not always a defining characteristic, texture can provide valuable clues when used in conjunction with other visual properties. Here are some common textures to consider:

- Smooth: A smooth texture indicates a fine-grained mineral or a surface polished by weathering processes. Many varieties of quartz and agate have a smooth texture.
- Crystalline: This texture features interlocking crystals that can be visible to the naked eye or with a hand lens. Granitic rocks often exhibit a crystalline texture.
- Grainy: A grainy texture is composed of visible individual mineral grains. Sandstone, a sedimentary rock, is a classic example of a grainy texture.
- Fibrous: This texture features elongated, thread-like mineral grains. Asbestos, a hazardous mineral, exhibits a fibrous texture. (Important Note: Never handle suspected asbestos and always consult with a professional for identification.)
- Earthy: This texture feels soft and powdery, resembling soil. Chalk and some varieties of clay have an earthy texture.

Remember, texture can be subjective and can be influenced by the size and shape of the individual mineral grains. Utilize texture as a supporting piece of evidence alongside other visual characteristics.

- **Fracture: When a Mineral Breaks**

Fracture refers to the way a mineral breaks when it's not cleaved (a specific breakage pattern discussed later). Observing the fracture pattern can offer valuable insights into a mineral's internal structure. Here are some common fracture types:

- Conchoidal: This fracture resembles the smooth, curved surface of a seashell. Obsidian, a volcanicvolcanic glass, exhibits a conchoidal fracture.
- Uneven: This fracture results in a rough, irregular breakage surface. Many fine-grained rocks and some weathered minerals display an uneven fracture.
- Hackly: This fracture creates a sharp, jagged surface. Some metallic minerals, like fractured pyrite, can exhibit a hackly fracture.

It's important to note that observing a fracture pattern typically requires breaking a small piece of the mineral. This is generally not recommended for valuable specimens or for minerals found on public lands with collecting restrictions. Instead, rely on other visual characteristics and consult field guides or rock and mineral identification apps that showcase fracture patterns of various minerals.

By combining visual observations of color, luster, texture, and (when possible) fracture, you can significantly narrow down the possibilities of what you might have found. Remember, no single characteristic is definitive, and using a combination of these clues along with additional resources like field guides and mobile apps will enhance your identification accuracy.

Additional Considerations

While visual clues are a powerful starting point, other factors can contribute to rock and mineral identification. Here are some additional considerations:

- **Streak:** This refers to the color of a mineral in powdered form. To determine the streak, rub the

mineral across a streak plate (a rough, unglazed porcelain tile). The color left behind is the mineral's true streak and can be more consistent than its overall color.
- **Hardness:** The Mohs scale, a mineralogical scale from 1 to 10, measures a mineral's resistance to scratching. You can use common household items that correspond to different Mohs scale values to test the hardness of your finds.

Identifying rocks and minerals is a continuous learning process. As you gain experience in the field, your ability to recognize different visual properties and make accurate identifications will improve. Don't be discouraged if you can't identify everything you find right away.

Embrace the challenge, use the resources available, and don't hesitate to consult with experienced rockhounds or local gem and mineral clubs for help. With dedication and practice, you'll be well on your way to unlocking the secrets hidden within Idaho's treasures.

ADDITIONAL RESOURCES TO HELP WITH GEM AND MINERAL IDENTIFICATION

By combining these observations, you can begin to narrow down the possibilities of what you might have found. Here are some helpful tips for beginners:

- **Mobile Apps:** Several mobile applications can assist with mineral identification. These apps often allow you to input the observed properties and provide a list of potential matches with pictures for comparison. Follow the link below to download the Crystal Council app: https://thecrystalcouncil.com/app.
- **Online Resources:** Numerous websites and online databases offer extensive information on rock and

mineral identification. These resources often include detailed descriptions, high-resolution images, and interactive identification tools. The Mindat website (Mindat.org) is currently the largest open mineral, meteorites and rock database in the whole world. Among the information it provides includes the localities that minerals come from.

Gemstones

While many rocks and minerals hold beauty and intrigue, some are classified as gemstones due to their exceptional qualities. Here are some key characteristics of gemstones:

- **Beauty:** Gemstones possess a captivating visual appeal, often exhibiting a combination of desirable colors, luster, and transparency.
- **Durability:** Gemstones must be hard and resistant to scratching or fracturing to withstand cutting, polishing, and everyday wear.
- **Rarity:** The relative scarcity of a gemstone contributes to its value. More common minerals, even if visually appealing, wouldn't be considered gemstones.

Identifying rocks and minerals is a continuous learning process. As you gain experience in the field, your ability to recognize different properties and make accurate identifications will improve. Don't be discouraged if you can't identify everything you find right away. Embrace the challenge, use the resources available, and don't hesitate to consult with experienced rockhounds or local gem and mineral clubs for help.

SIMPLE FIELD TESTS

While color, luster, texture, and fracture provide valuable visual clues, additional tests can help narrow down your identification possibilities. These tests are designed to be conducted in the field with minimal equipment, empowering you to gain valuable insights on the spot.

THE SCRATCH TEST

The scratch test is a fundamental field test that utilizes the Mohs scale of mineralogy. This scale, ranging from 1 (softest) to 10 (hardest), measures a mineral's resistance to scratching. Here's how to conduct the scratch test:

1. **Gather Your Supplies:** You'll need a few readily available items:
   - The mineral you want to identify.
   - Common household objects representing different Mohs scale values. A fingernail (Mohs hardness 2.5), a penny (Mohs hardness 3), a steel knife (Mohs hardness 5.5), and a piece of unglazed porcelain (Mohs hardness 6.5) are good starting points.
2. **Conduct the Test:** Attempt to scratch the unknown mineral with each of the chosen objects. If the object scratches the mineral, the mineral's hardness is lower than the object's Mohs scale value. Conversely, if the mineral scratches the object, the mineral's hardness is higher.
3. **Interpreting the Results:** By using this comparative approach, you can eliminate a range of possibilities based on the scratch test results. For example, if a mineral scratches a penny (Mohs hardness 3) but not a steel knife (Mohs hardness 5.5), its hardness falls between 3 and 5.5 on the Mohs scale.

Important Considerations:

- **Exercise Caution:** While the scratch test is a valuable tool, perform it with care to avoid damaging valuable specimens. Use only a small, inconspicuous area of the mineral for testing.
- **Not All Minerals are Uniform:** The hardness of a mineral can vary slightly depending on its composition. The scratch test provides a general range rather than a definitive answer.

THE STREAK TEST

The streak test reveals the color of a mineral in powdered form. This color, often referred to as the mineral's true streak, can be more consistent than its overall surface color and can be a valuable identification tool. Here's how to conduct the streak test:

1. **Gather Your Supplies:** You'll need the mineral you want to identify and a streak plate – a rough, unglazed porcelain tile with a white surface.
2. **Conduct the Test:** Firmly rub the mineral back and forth across the unglazed surface of the streak plate. This creates a fine powder that reveals the mineral's true streak color.
3. **Interpreting the Results:** Consult a field guide or online resources to compare the observed streak color with known minerals. For example, a red streak is indicative of hematite, while a white or grayish streak might suggest quartz or calcite.

Important Note: Avoid using streak plates made of other materials, as they can contaminate the test results.

The Acid Test: A Word of Caution

The acid test, also known as the fizz test, is only applicable to carbonate minerals like calcite, dolomite, and aragonite.

These minerals react with hydrochloric acid (HCl) by releasing carbon dioxide gas, creating bubbles or a fizzing sound.

Important Considerations:

- **Safety First:** Hydrochloric acid is a corrosive substance. Only conduct this test with extreme caution and wear appropriate safety gear, including gloves and eye protection. 10% hydrochloric acid solution is the recommended concentration for field testing.
- **Limited Application:** The acid test is not a universal test and should only be used on suspected carbonate minerals. It can damage other minerals and should be used as a last resort after conducting the scratch and streak tests.
- **Environmental Responsibility:** Dispose of any leftover acid solution responsibly at a designated hazardous waste facility. Never pour acid on the ground or into waterways.

SAFE DIGGING PRACTICES

Once you're at the rockhounding site, remain vigilant and be aware of potential dangers. Here are some common hazards to keep in mind:

- **Loose Rock and Unstable Slopes:** Steep slopes and loose rock can be a significant risk. Avoid areas with loose rockfalls or crumbling cliffs. Be cautious when climbing or descending, and use designated trails whenever possible.
- **Abandoned Mine Shafts and Tunnels:** Abandoned mines can be incredibly dangerous due to unstable structures, hazardous gases, and potential collapses. Never enter abandoned mine shafts or tunnels.

- **Flash Floods and Dangerous Weather:** Flash floods can occur quickly in dry regions. Be aware of weather patterns and avoid areas prone to flooding, especially during heavy rains. Seek shelter immediately if a storm approaches.
- **Wildlife Encounters:** Idaho is home to a variety of wildlife. Be mindful of your surroundings and maintain a safe distance from wild animals. Do not approach or attempt to feed any wildlife.
- **Poisonous Plants and Insects:** Familiarize yourself with common poisonous plants and insects in the area you're visiting. Wear long pants and closed-toe shoes to minimize exposure.

Safe Digging Techniques: Respecting the Land & Your Safety

While the thrill of discovery is undeniable, responsible rockhounding requires respect for the environment and your own safety. Here are some key practices to follow:

- **Dig Responsibly:** Minimize your impact on the land. Dig small, manageable holes and refill them whenever possible. Use established digging areas if available.
- **Respect Claim Sites:** Never dig on active mining claims without explicit permission from the claim holder.
- **Use Tools with Caution:** Rock hammers and chisels can be dangerous if not handled properly. Wear eye protection and be mindful of your surroundings when using these tools.
- **Beware of Hidden Hazards:** Be aware of potential hazards like underground utilities, unmarked mineshafts, or loose rock overhangs before digging.

USING BASIC TOOLS EFFECTIVELY

While enthusiasm and a keen eye are essential, basic tools significantly enhance your rockhounding experience. Here's a breakdown of some fundamental tools and how to use them effectively:

- **The Rock Pick**

The rock pick is a multi-purpose tool ideal for prying loose rocks, breaking up moderately hard materials, and uncovering hidden specimens. Here's a closer look at its features and usage:

Types of Picks

There are various pick designs, but the most common is a geological pick. It features a pointed tip on one end for prying and a chisel-like edge on the other for breaking rocks. Other options include a mason's pick with a broader chisel end or a prospecting pick with a hooked tip for extracting loose material.

Choosing the Right Pick

Select a pick size and weight that feels comfortable in your hand. A typical geological pick is 12-18 inches long, but shorter picks can be easier to maneuver in tight spaces.

Using Your Pick Effectively

Use the pointed tip to pry loose rocks embedded in soil or break apart weathered rock faces. The chisel end can be used to break softer minerals or chip away at larger rocks to expose hidden treasures within. Strike the pick with a hammer for added force, but ensure you wear eye protection to avoid flying debris.

- ## The Rock Hammer

The rock hammer is another essential tool for breaking open rocks and accessing hidden minerals. Here's what you need to know about selecting and using this tool:

Types of Rock Hammers

Rock hammers come in various sizes and weights. A geologist's hammer, typically 14-22 ounces, is a good choice for most rockhounding applications. Heavier hammers (sledgehammers) are best left for experienced individuals working on very hard rocks.

Choosing the Right Hammer

Select a hammer weight that you can comfortably swing with one hand. A rubberized grip can enhance comfort and control.

Using Your Hammer Effectively

Always wear safety glasses when using a rock hammer. Position the chisel end of the hammer directly on the rock you want to break and strike it firmly with controlled force. Avoid hitting the hammer sideways, as this can damage the tool. For larger rocks, consider using a chisel and hammer in combination to create a breaking point.

- ## The Rock Chisel

The rock chisel is a specialized tool used for precise breaking and extracting valuable specimens from delicate rocks. Here are some key points to consider:

Types of Chisels

Rock chisels come in various sizes and tip shapes. A blunt chisel is ideal for splitting rocks along existing fractures, while a pointed chisel is better suited for prying or creating small cracks.

Choosing the Right Chisel

Select a chisel size appropriate for the rocks you'll be working with. A comfortable grip is essential for precise control.

Using Your Chisel Effectively

Wear safety glasses when using a rock chisel. Position the chisel tip on the desired breaking point of the rock and strike the chisel head firmly with the rock hammer. Use controlled force and aim for clean breaks to minimize damage to the desired specimen.

- **The Gold Pan**

While not exclusive to Idaho, gold panning remains a popular rockhounding activity, particularly in certain areas. Here's a basic introduction to using a gold pan:

The Pan's Design

A gold pan is a shallow, dish-shaped pan with slightly flared sides. Ridges or grooves on the bottom can aid in trapping gold particles.

The Panning Technique

Fill the pan about two-thirds full with loose material (dirt, gravel) suspected to contain gold. Submerge the pan in water and begin swirling it in a circular motion. The heavier gold flakes will tend to settle towards the bottom of the pan as lighter materials wash away.

Note: Gold panning regulations vary depending on location. Always research and obtain any necessary permits before panning for gold in Idaho.

RECOGNIZING GEM QUALITY - WHAT MAKES A FIND A TREASURE?

1. **Beauty: A Spectrum of Visual Appeal**

Color plays a crucial role in gemstone beauty. While some gemstones boast a single, vibrant hue (think emerald green or ruby red), others showcase a captivating interplay of colors. Sapphires, for example, can exhibit a range of colors from blue to yellow to pink, while opals are famous for their mesmerizing play of color.

Brilliance refers to a gemstone's ability to reflect light, creating a dazzling sparkle. The cut plays a significant role in brilliance, as it influences the way light interacts with the gemstone's facets. A well-cut gem will dance with light, captivating the eye.

Luster describes how light interacts with the gemstone's surface. Gemstones can exhibit a vitreous luster (glassy), adamantine luster (diamond-like), or a greasy luster (like opal). The desired luster varies depending on the gemstone, but it contributes to its overall visual appeal.

Transparency refers to the degree of light that passes through a gemstone. Some gemstones are completely transparent, allowing light to pass through unimpeded. Others are translucent, allowing some light to pass through with a diffused effect. Opaque gemstones don't allow light to pass through. The desired transparency varies depending on the gemstone; for instance, emeralds are typically valued for their transparency, while opals are prized for their play of color even in a translucent state.

Fire, also known as play of color, refers to the phenomenon where a gemstone exhibits a rainbow of colors as light interacts with its internal structure. Opals are renowned for their fire, while some diamonds can display a fiery play of color known as dispersion.

2. Durability: A Gemstone's Strength

A true gemstone must be tough enough to withstand the cutting and polishing process. It also needs to be durable enough for everyday wear in jewelry without significant risk of scratching or fracturing. The Mohs scale of mineralogy serves as a guide to a mineral's hardness. Gemstones typically fall within the 7 to 10 range on the Mohs scale. Diamonds, the hardest natural substance on Earth, rank a perfect 10, while sapphires and rubies rank 9, making them highly sought-after gemstones for jewelry.

3. Rarity: The Allure of the Scarce

The relative scarcity of a gemstone contributes significantly to its value. Common minerals, even if visually appealing, wouldn't be considered gemstones. For instance, quartz is one of the most abundant minerals on Earth and, while it can come in beautiful colors, it wouldn't be classified as a gemstone due to its widespread availability. Conversely, gemstones like emeralds or alexandrites, which are much rarer in nature, command higher prices due to their limited availability. It's important to note that rarity is a relative concept. While some gemstones are incredibly scarce, others may be relatively uncommon but still found in sufficient quantities to be accessible to collectors and jewelry enthusiasts.

4. Cut: The Art of Unlocking Beauty

The way a gemstone is cut has a profound impact on its overall beauty and value. A skilled lapidary (gem cutter) analyzes the rough gemstone to understand its internal characteristics like inclusions, color variations, and clarity. They then choose a cutting style that maximizes the gemstone's brilliance, fire, and color.

There are various cutting styles, each with its own advantages:

- **Brilliant Cut:** This classic cut is most commonly used for diamonds and features 58 facets designed to maximize brilliance and fire.
- **Step Cut:** This cut, often used for emeralds, features a series of flat, parallel facets that create a hall-of-mirrors effect, showcasing the gemstone's color and clarity.
- **Cabochon Cut:** This smooth, dome-shaped cut is often used for opaque gemstones like opals or certain varieties of jade, highlighting their natural beauty and play of color.

The quality of the cut significantly influences a gemstone's value. A well-cut gem will showcase its brilliance, color, and fire to their full potential, commanding a higher price than a poorly cut stone.

Beyond the Basics: Additional Considerations

While these core qualities define gem quality, other factors can influence a gemstone's value:

- **Size:** Larger, well-cut gemstones are generally more valuable than smaller ones of the same quality.
- **Clarity:** The presence of inclusions (internal flaws) can affect a gemstone's value. Generally, gemstones with fewer inclusions are considered more valuable.
- **Fashion Trends:** Certain gemstone colors or styles may be more popular at a given time, influencing their market value.

Now that you are armed with this information about rock hounding (which you would possibly have skipped if you are already conversant with them), let us go into the main purpose of the book; which is providing you with information about the hotspots that are available for you to rockhound in Idaho. We will also be providing information about some places that were formerly open for rockhounding but are now closed and rockhounding is prohibited.

These and lots more are going covered in the next part of this book. Please note that due to the fact that a lot of these locations are around the same places, certain information will be repeated among them.

Now, let's dig in.

PART 2

The Rock Hounding Hotspots of Idaho

CHAPTER 4
NORTHERN IDAHO

PRIEST LAKE

Nestled in the scenic northern panhandle of Idaho, Priest Lake offers breathtaking beauty alongside opportunities for rockhounding enthusiasts. This guide delves into the details of exploring Priest Lake for potential finds.

Detailed Route Description:

Reaching Priest Lake depends on your starting point. Here's a general route assuming you're coming from Spokane, WA:

1. Take I-90 E to Exit 43 for US-95 N towards Sandpoint.
2. Follow US-95 N for approximately 42 miles.
3. Turn left onto ID-56 W towards Priest Lake.
4. Continue on ID-56 W for approximately 22 miles to reach Priest Lake.

Land Type:

Priest Lake is surrounded by public forest lands managed by the Kootenai National Forest. Specific rockhounding locations may vary in land designation (National Forest, State Park, etc.), so research the specific site before heading out.

County:

Priest Lake is located in Bonner County, Idaho.

Marlow's Idaho Rock Hounding Guide Book 2024

GPS Location:

Priest Lake (general area): 48.7333° N, 116.7000° W (**Please note:** This is a general location for the lake. Specific rockhounding sites will have their own GPS coordinates.)

Best Season for Rockhounding:

Late spring, summer, and early fall (typically July-September) offer the most comfortable weather conditions for rockhounding at Priest Lake. Winter brings frigid temperatures and significant snowfall, limiting accessibility.

Land Manager:

Kootenai National Forest (https://www.fs.usda.gov/kootenai)

Materials that can be Found:

- Agates (variety of colors)
- Jasper
- Quartz crystals
- Garnet (less common)

Best Tools for Rockhounding:

- Rock hammer
- Rock pick
- Chisel
- Safety glasses
- Knee pads (optional)
- Hand trowel (optional)
- Magnifying glass (optional)
- Sifting screen (optional)

Marlow's Idaho Rock Hounding Guide Book 2024

Best Vehicles for Accessing and Traversing the Area:

A high-clearance vehicle (SUV, truck) is recommended, especially for accessing off-road trails leading to potential rockhounding sites. Some areas might be accessible with a passenger car, but check road conditions beforehand.

Accommodation Options:

Priest Lake offers a variety of lodging options, from campgrounds to resorts. Here are a few examples:

- **Island View RV Resort & Cabins:** (208) 443-2900, 38.7929° N, 116.6922° W. Offers RV sites, cabins, and tent camping.
- **Sandpoint West Resort Hotel & Marina:** (208) 263-2201, 48.6904° N, 116.5928° W. Full-service lakeside resort with various room options.
- **Elks Club RV Park:** (208) 263-3139, 48.6842° N, 116.5892° W. Offers RV sites and tent camping.

Recommended Stops and Attractions:

- **Priest Lake State Park:** (208) 443-2200, 48.7914° N, 116.7008° W. Offers camping, boating, and hiking opportunities.
- **Roundhouse Mountain Visitor Center:** (208) 263-5111, 48.7108° N, 116.6225° W. Scenic overlooks and interpretive exhibits about the area's natural history.

Directions to the Site:

- **Dollar Island:** Accessible by boat, this island is known for agates and jasper.
- **Indian Creek:** Located near the southern tip of the lake, this area might yield agates and jasper.

- **Evans Creek:** Located on the western shore, this area might have agates and jasper.

Sun Exposure and Availability of Shade:

Priest Lake experiences plenty of sunshine, especially during peak summer months. Sun protection is essential. Shaded areas can be found near forested areas or by seeking shelter near rock formations.

Points of Interest:

Here are some general tips for identifying promising rockhounding areas around Priest Lake:

1. **Look for exposed rock faces:** Areas with exposed bedrock, scree slopes (loose rock at the base of cliffs), or streambeds are more likely to reveal potential finds.
2. **Observe existing collections:** If you encounter other rockhounds in the area, politely inquire about their finds and the locations they explored.
3. **Consult online resources and forums:** Local rockhounding clubs or online forums dedicated to Idaho rockhounding might have discussions or posts about Priest Lake finds and potential locations.

Soil Type(s):

The soil types around Priest Lake vary depending on location. Generally, you might encounter:

- **Glacial till:** A mixture of deposited rock, sand, and clay left behind by glaciers.
- **Forest duff:** A layer of decomposing organic matter from trees and other vegetation.
- **Alluvial deposits:** Gravel and cobbles deposited by flowing water in streambeds.

Rock Type(s):

The bedrock underlying Priest Lake consists primarily of igneous rocks like granite and gneiss. These rocks can weather and erode, revealing potential finds like agates, jasper, and quartz crystals.

Popularity of the Site:

Priest Lake is a popular tourist destination, and rockhounding activity can vary depending on the location and time of year. More accessible areas near developed areas might see more traffic, while remote locations might be less crowded.

Where to Buy Essential Supplies:

- **Sandpoint True Value Hardware:** (208) 263-3158, 48.6833° N, 116.5792° W. Offers tools, gloves, safety glasses, and other basic supplies.
- **Les Schwab Tire Center:** (208) 263-1252, 48.6833° N, 116.5861° W. Offers basic tools and supplies.

Fuel Dispensing Units:

Several gas stations are located in Sandpoint, the closest major town to Priest Lake. It's recommended to fill up your gas tank before heading to the lake, as options might be limited near the lake itself. Utilize GPS navigation apps to locate gas stations in Sandpoint.

Public Toilets:

Public restrooms are available at designated campgrounds and recreational areas around Priest Lake, like Priest Lake State Park. Always check park websites or signage for restroom locations.

Car Parks:

Parking options vary depending on the specific location you plan to explore. Developed areas like Priest Lake State Park offer designated parking areas. For off-road locations, ensure you park in designated areas and avoid blocking trails or roadways.

Rockhounding Strategies at Priest Lake

Priest Lake offers a treasure hunt for rockhounds seeking agates, jasper, and quartz crystals. Here's a breakdown on optimizing your search based on the type of rock or soil you encounter:

Target Areas:

Before diving into specific techniques, remember to prioritize exposed areas. Look for:

- **Rock Outcrops:** These are areas where bedrock is visible at the surface. They can be cliffs, ledges, or areas recently exposed by erosion.
- **Scree Slopes:** These are slopes at the base of cliffs or rock faces where loose rock fragments have accumulated due to weathering.
- **Streambeds:** Flowing water can transport and concentrate rocks and minerals, making streambeds promising areas for searching.

Rock Types:

The bedrock around Priest Lake is primarily igneous, consisting of granite and gneiss. These rocks can weather and decompose, revealing the target materials:

- **Agates and Jasper:** These often occur as nodules or rounded masses within the weathered rock. They might also be found as loose pieces in scree slopes or streambeds. Look for areas with visible cracks or fractures in the rock, as these can hold hidden pockets of agate or jasper.

Soil Types:

The soil types around Priest Lake can influence your search strategy:

- **Glacial Till:** This dense mixture of deposited rock, sand, and clay can be challenging to sift through for smaller materials. However, larger agates or jasper nodules might be visible on the surface. Focus your search on exposed areas or areas where recent erosion has disturbed the glacial till.
- **Forest Duff:** This layer of decomposing organic matter isn't ideal for rockhounding. However, if you spot agates or jasper peeking through the duff, it might indicate a concentration of these materials underneath.
- **Alluvial Deposits:** These gravel and cobble deposits found in streambeds are prime areas for searching. Utilize tools like a rock hammer and chisel to break open promising cobbles that might contain hidden agate or jasper nodules. Additionally, sifting through the gravel deposits with a mesh screen can help you uncover smaller agate or jasper pieces.

SOLO CREEK

Solo Creek, Idaho, has long been a magnet for rockhounds seeking the beauty and value of quartz crystals. This guide equips you with the knowledge to navigate the area and potentially unearth hidden gems.

Detailed Route Description:

Reaching Solo Creek requires navigating through rural northern Idaho. Here's a general route assuming you're coming from Spokane, WA:

1. Take I-90 E to Exit 43 for US-95 N towards Sandpoint.
2. Follow US-95 N for approximately 42 miles.
3. Turn left onto ID-56 W towards Priest Lake.
4. Continue on ID-56 W for about 17 miles.
5. Turn right onto Forest Road 271 (marked as Squaw Valley Cutoff Rd).
6. Follow Forest Road 271 for approximately 6 miles until you reach a junction.
7. Take a sharp left onto Forest Road 659. Solo Creek is located along this road.

Land Type:

Solo Creek lies within the Colville National Forest, so most of the land is public forest land. However, always double-check the specific area you plan to explore, as land designations can vary.

County:

Pend Oreille County, Idaho

GPS Location:

Solo Creek (general area): 48.7167° N, 116.9000° W (**Please note:** This is a general location for Solo Creek. Specific rockhounding sites may have their own GPS coordinates.)

Best Season for Rockhounding:

Spring, summer, and early fall (typically July-September) offer the most favorable weather conditions for rockhounding at Solo Creek. Winter brings harsh conditions with significant snowfall, limiting accessibility.

Land Manager:

Colville National Forest (https://www.fs.usda.gov/colville)

Materials that can be Found:

- Quartz Crystals (primary target)
- Jasper (occasionally)

Best Tools for Rockhounding:

- Rock hammer
- Safety glasses
- Knee pads (optional)
- Hand trowel (optional)
- Rake (optional)
- Sifting screen (optional)

Best Vehicles for Accessing and Traversing the Area:

A high-clearance vehicle (SUV, truck) is strongly recommended due to the often unpaved and potentially rough terrain leading to Solo Creek.

Accommodation Options:

Since Solo Creek is a remote location, lodging options are limited. Here are some possibilities in nearby areas:

- **Priest Lake KOA Campground:** (208) 443-2800, 48.7414° N, 116.7664° W. Offers RV sites, tent camping, and cabin rentals.
- **Island View RV Resort & Cabins:** (208) 443-2900, 38.7929° N, 116.6922° W. Located on Priest Lake, offering RV sites, cabins, and tent camping.
- **Sandpoint West Resort Hotel & Marina:** (208) 263-2201, 48.6904° N, 116.5928° W. Full-service lakeside resort with various room options in Sandpoint.

Recommended Stops and Attractions:

- **Priest Lake:** (48.7333° N, 116.7000° W) This scenic lake offers stunning views and various recreational activities.
- **Roundhouse Mountain Visitor Center:** (48.7108° N, 116.6225° W) Scenic overlooks and interpretive exhibits about the area's natural history.

Directions to the Site:

Unfortunately, due to the closure of the main historical digging area and the dispersed nature of potential rockhounding locations, pinpointing a specific site is difficult. However, Forest Road 659 along Solo Creek is the general target area.

Sun Exposure and Availability of Shade:

The area around Solo Creek receives ample sunshine, especially during peak summer months. Sun protection is essential. Shade can be limited, so consider bringing a hat and breathable clothing.

Numbered Points of Interest:

As specific rockhounding locations can vary, identifying them with numbers is difficult. Here are some general tips for finding promising areas:

1. **Look for exposed areas:** Search for areas with exposed bedrock, scree slopes (loose rock at the base of cliffs), or streambeds.
2. **Observe previous diggings:** If you encounter other rockhounds, politely inquire about their finds and locations they explored. However, be mindful of respecting existing claims or designated digging areas.
3. **Consult online resources and forums:** Local rockhounding clubs or online forums dedicated to Idaho rockhounding might have discussions or posts about Solo Creek and potential locations for quartz crystals.

Soil Type(s):

The soil types around Solo Creek can vary depending on location. Generally, you might encounter:

- **Forest duff:** A layer of decomposing organic matter from trees and other vegetation.
- **Colluvium:** Loose rock and soil that has accumulated at the base of slopes due to gravity.
- **Talus:** A steep slope covered in large, angular rock fragments.

Rock Type(s):

The bedrock underlying Solo Creek is primarily composed of metamorphic rocks like schist and gneiss. These rocks can contain veins of quartz, which can weather and become exposed.

Popularity of the Site:

Solo Creek was once a popular spot for rockhounding quartz crystals. However, the main historical digging area is now closed. The dispersed nature of potential locations and the possibility of encountering existing claims can make rockhounding success more challenging.

Where to Buy Essential Supplies:

- **Sandpoint True Value Hardware:** (208) 263-3158, 48.6833° N, 116.5792° W. Offers tools, gloves, safety glasses, and other basic supplies.
- **Les Schwab Tire Center:** (208) 263-1252, 48.6833° N, 116.5861° W. Offers basic tools and supplies.

Public Toilets:

Public restrooms are scarce near Solo Creek. You might find some at designated campgrounds in nearby areas like Priest Lake KOA Campground. Always check park websites or signage for restroom locations.

Car Parks:

Parking options depend on the specific location you plan to explore. Developed areas near campgrounds might have designated parking areas. For off-road locations along Forest Road 659, park responsibly on the roadside shoulder, ensuring you don't block traffic or damage the environment.

Limited Success:

Due to the closure of the main historical digging area and the dispersed nature of potential locations, finding quartz crystals at Solo Creek might be more challenging than in the past. Persistence, a strategic approach based on rock and soil types, and responsible practices can still lead to a rewarding rockhounding experience.

PACK RIVER

The Pack River in Idaho offers a treasure hunt for rockhounds seeking unique finds. This guide equips you with the knowledge to navigate the area and potentially discover hidden gems.

Detailed Route Description:

Reaching the Pack River requires navigating through scenic northern Idaho. Here's a general route assuming you're coming from Spokane, WA:

1. Take I-90 E to Exit 30 for ID-53 N towards Athol.
2. Follow ID-53 N for approximately 62 miles.
3. Turn left onto ID-154 N towards Sandpoint.
4. Continue on ID-154 N for about 27 miles.
5. Turn right onto Forest Road 413 (marked as Pack River Road). The Pack River is accessible from various points along this road.

Land Type:

Most of the land along the Pack River is managed by the Kaniksu National Forest (https://www.fs.usda.gov/detail/ipnf/about-forest/offices/?cid=fsm9_019006), so it's public forest land.

Marlow's Idaho Rock Hounding Guide Book 2024

However, always double-check the specific area you plan to explore, as designations can vary.

County:

Bonner County, Idaho

GPS Location:

Pack River (general area): 48.3333° N, 116.3333° W (**Please note:** This is a general location for the Pack River. Specific rockhounding sites may have their own GPS coordinates.)

Best Season for Rockhounding:

Spring, summer, and early fall (typically July-September) offer the most favorable weather conditions for exploring the Pack River. Winter brings harsh conditions with significant snowfall, limiting accessibility.

Land Manager:

Kaniksu National Forest (https://www.fs.usda.gov/detail/ipnf/about-forest/offices/?cid=fsm9_019006)

Materials that can be Found:

- Agates (variety of colors)
- Jasper
- Garnets (less common)
- Petrified wood (occasionally)

Best Tools for Rockhounding:

- Rock hammer
- Rock pick (optional)

Marlow's Idaho Rock Hounding Guide Book 2024

- Chisel
- Safety glasses
- Knee pads (optional)
- Hand trowel (optional)
- Magnifying glass (optional)
- Sifting screen (optional)

Best Vehicles for Accessing and Traversing the Area:

A high-clearance vehicle (SUV, truck) is strongly recommended due to the often unpaved and potentially rough terrain leading to access points along the Pack River.

Accommodation Options:

Since the Pack River is a dispersed area, lodging options are limited. Here are some possibilities in nearby towns:

- **Sandpoint West Resort Hotel & Marina:** (208) 263-2201, 48.6904° N, 116.5928° W. Full-service lakeside resort in Sandpoint offering various room options.
- **Lakeside Lodge & Resort:** (208) 263-4999, 48.6889° N, 116.5903° W. Offers cabins, RV sites, and tent camping in Sandpoint.
- **Priest Lake KOA Campground:** (208) 443-2800, 48.7414° N, 116.7664° W. Offers RV sites, tent camping, and cabin rentals near Priest Lake.

Recommended Stops and Attractions:

- **Priest Lake:** (48.7333° N, 116.7000° W) This scenic lake offers stunning views and various recreational activities.
- **Roundhouse Mountain Visitor Center:** (48.7108° N, 116.6225° W) Scenic overlooks and interpretive exhibits about the area's natural history.

Directions to the Site:

The Pack River stretches for many miles, so pinpointing a specific site is difficult. However, Forest Road 413 provides access to various locations along the river. Once on Forest Road 413, consult a map or GPS to identify potential pull-offs or designated areas for exploring the riverbed.

Sun Exposure and Availability of Shade:

The Pack River area receives ample sunshine, especially during peak summer months. Sun protection is essential. Shade can be limited near the riverbed, so consider bringing a hat and breathable clothing.

Soil Type(s):

The soil types along the Pack River can vary depending on location. Generally, you might encounter:

- **Alluvial deposits:** These gravel and cobble deposits along the riverbed are prime areas for searching for agates, jasper, and other materials transported by water.
- **Talus slopes:** Steeper sections bordering the river might have slopes covered in large rock fragments, where some materials like agates or jasper might have accumulated after eroding from the riverbank.

Rock Type(s):

The bedrock underlying the Pack River area is a mix of sedimentary and metamorphic rocks. These can include basalt, quartzite, and schist. The target materials like agates and jasper are often found as pebbles or cobbles within the alluvial deposits, having originated from these various bedrock types.

Popularity of the Site:

The Pack River is a popular destination for fishing, kayaking, and other recreational activities. Rockhounding activity can vary depending on the specific location and accessibility. More accessible areas might see more traffic, while secluded spots further along Forest Road 413 might be less crowded.

Where to Buy Essential Supplies:

- **Sandpoint True Value Hardware:** (208) 263-3158, 48.6833° N, 116.5792° W. Offers tools, gloves, safety glasses, and other basic supplies.
- **Les Schwab Tire Center:** (208) 263-1252, 48.6833° N, 116.5861° W. Offers basic tools and supplies.

Car Parks:

Parking options depend on the specific location you choose to explore along Forest Road 413. Developed areas near campgrounds might have designated parking areas. For more dispersed locations along the river, park responsibly on the roadside shoulder, ensuring you don't block traffic or damage the environment.

RUBY CREEK

Ruby Creek, Washington, beckons rockhounds seeking agates, jasper, and quartz crystals. This guide equips you with the knowledge to navigate the area and potentially unearth hidden gems.

Detailed Route Description:

Reaching Ruby Creek requires navigating rural northwestern Washington. Here's a general route assuming you're coming from Seattle, WA:

1. Take I-5 N to Exit 226 for WA-530 E towards Arlington.
2. Follow WA-530 E for approximately 62 miles.
3. Turn right onto US-20 E towards Twisp.
4. Continue on US-20 E for about 22 miles.
5. Turn left onto Ruby Creek Road (Forest Road 2040). The road winds along Ruby Creek for several miles, with various potential pull-off points for rockhounding.

Land Type:

Most of the land around Ruby Creek is managed by the Okanogan-Wenatchee National Forest (https://www.fs.usda.gov/detail/okawen), so it's public forest land. Always double-check the specific area you plan to explore, as designations can vary.

County:

Whatcom County, Washington

GPS Location:

Ruby Creek (general area): 48.7167° N, 121.9000° W (**Please note:** This is a general location for Ruby Creek. Specific rockhounding sites may have their own GPS coordinates.)

Marlow's Idaho Rock Hounding Guide Book 2024

Best Season for Rockhounding:

Spring, summer, and early fall (typically July-September) offer the most favorable weather conditions for exploring Ruby Creek. Winter brings snowfall, limiting accessibility.

Land Manager:

Okanogan-Wenatchee National Forest (https://www.fs.usda.gov/detail/okawen)

Materials that can be Found:

- Agates (various colors and patterns)
- Jasper
- Quartz crystals (less common)

Best Tools for Rockhounding:

- Rock hammer
- Safety glasses
- Knee pads (optional)
- Hand trowel (optional)
- Rake (optional)
- Sifting screen (optional)

Best Vehicles for Accessing and Traversing the Area:

A high-clearance vehicle (SUV, truck) is recommended due to the often unpaved and potentially rough terrain along Ruby Creek Road.

Accommodation Options:

Since Ruby Creek is a remote location, lodging options are limited. Here are some possibilities in nearby towns:

- **Conconully Mountain Resort:** (509) 996-2131, 48.7222° N, 120.7278° W. Offers cabins and RV sites near Twisp.
- **Loup Loup Ski Bowl Resort:** (509) 996-2211, 48.7667° N, 120.7833° W. Offers cabins and RV sites near Twisp (may be closed during summer).
- **Methow Valley Inn:** (509) 996-2195, 48.7833° N, 120.6833° W. Offers motel-style accommodations in Mazama.

Recommended Stops and Attractions:

- **North Cascades National Park:** (48.7000° N, 121.2000° W) This stunning national park offers scenic views and various outdoor activities (a few hours' drive from Ruby Creek).
- **Sterling Ranch:** (509) 996-2388, 48.7333° N, 120.7833° W. Historical working ranch offering tours and horseback riding near Twisp.

Directions to the Site:

Ruby Creek stretches for several miles. Reaching specific rockhounding locations requires following Forest Road 2040 (Ruby Creek Road) and identifying potential pull-off points along the way. Consult a map or GPS to navigate and find suitable areas for exploring the creek bed.

Sun Exposure and Availability of Shade:

The area around Ruby Creek receives ample sunshine, especially during peak summer months. Sun protection is essential. Shade can be limited near the creek, so consider bringing a hat and breathable clothing.

Soil Type(s):

The soil types around Ruby Creek can vary depending on location. Generally, you might encounter:

- **Forest duff:** A layer of decomposing organic matter from trees and other vegetation.

- **Colluvium:** Loose rock and soil that has accumulated at the base of slopes due to gravity. This can obscure potential agate or jasper deposits, but you might find promising rock fragments within the colluvium that could warrant using a rock hammer to break them open, revealing hidden treasures (wear safety glasses!).
- **Alluvial deposits:** These gravel and cobble deposits along Ruby Creek are prime areas for searching for agates, jasper, and quartz crystals. Look for exposed areas during low water flow, especially around bends in the river where rocks might concentrate.

Rock Type(s):

The bedrock underlying the Ruby Creek area is a mix of volcanic and metamorphic rocks. These can include basalt, andesite, and schist. The target materials like agates and jasper are often found as pebbles or cobbles within the alluvial deposits, having originated from veins or pockets within these various bedrock types.

Popularity of the Site:

Ruby Creek is a popular destination for camping, fishing, and other outdoor activities. Rockhounding activity can vary depending on the specific location and accessibility. More accessible areas closer to the main road might see more traffic, while secluded spots further along Forest Road 2040 might be less crowded.

Where to Buy Essential Supplies:

- **Twisp True Value Hardware:** (509) 997-2233, 48.7833° N, 120.6833° W. Offers tools, gloves, safety glasses, and other basic supplies in Twisp.
- **Methow Valley Lumber & Hardware:** (509) 996-2121, 48.7833° N, 120.6833° W. Offers tools and basic supplies in Mazama.

MOYIE RIVER

The Moyie River, snaking through Idaho and British Columbia, offers a treasure hunt for rockhounds seeking unique finds. This guide equips you with the knowledge to navigate the area and potentially discover hidden gems.

Detailed Route Description:

Reaching the Moyie River requires navigating through scenic northern Idaho. Here's a general route assuming you're coming from Spokane, WA:

1. Take I-90 E to Exit 30 for ID-53 N towards Athol.
2. Follow ID-53 N for approximately 62 miles.
3. Turn left onto ID-154 N towards Sandpoint.
4. Continue on ID-154 N for about 27 miles.
5. Depending on your desired access point, various Forest Roads branch off from this highway to reach the Moyie River. Consult a map or GPS for specific routes.

Note: Some Forest Roads may require a high-clearance vehicle.

Marlow's Idaho Rock Hounding Guide Book 2024

Land Type:

Most of the land along the Moyie River is managed by the Colville National Forest (https://www.fs.usda.gov/colville), so it's public forest land. Always double-check the specific area you plan to explore, as designations can vary.

County:

Boundary County, Idaho

GPS Location:

Moyie River (general area): 48.8833° N, 116.2500° W (**Please note:** This is a general location for the Moyie River. Specific rockhounding sites may have their own GPS coordinates.)

Best Season for Rockhounding:

Spring, summer, and early fall (typically July-September) offer the most favorable weather conditions for exploring the Moyie River. Winter brings harsh conditions with significant snowfall, limiting accessibility.

Land Manager:

Colville National Forest (https://www.fs.usda.gov/colville)

Materials that can be Found:

- Quartz crystals (historically known, but the main digging area is closed)
- Jasper
- Agates (less common)
- Petrified wood (occasionally)

Best Tools for Rockhounding:

- Rock hammer (use with caution and proper safety gear)
- Safety glasses (essential)
- Knee pads (optional for comfort)
- Hand trowel (optional)
- Sifting screen (optional)
- Magnifying glass (optional for examining smaller finds)

Best Vehicles for Accessing and Traversing the Area:

A high-clearance vehicle (SUV, truck) is recommended due to unpaved and potentially rough terrain along some access roads and the possibility of uneven surfaces near the riverbed.

Accommodation Options:

- **Sandpoint West Resort Hotel & Marina:** (208) 263-2201, 48.6904° N, 116.5928° W. Full-service lakeside resort in Sandpoint offering various room options.
- **Lakeside Lodge & Resort:** (208) 263-4999, 48.6889° N, 116.5903° W. Offers cabins, RV sites, and tent camping in Sandpoint.
- **Priest Lake KOA Campground:** (208) 443-2800, 48.7414° N, 116.7664° W. Offers RV sites, tent camping, and cabin rentals near Priest Lake.

Recommended Stops and Attractions:

- **Priest Lake:** (48.7333° N, 116.7000° W) This scenic lake offers stunning views and various recreational activities.
- **Bonner County Historical Society Museum:** (208) 263-2163, 610 N, 1st Ave., Sandpoint (48.6889°

N, 116.5964° W). Learn about the region's history and culture. Look for the yellow brick building downtown.

Directions to the Site:

The Moyie River stretches for many miles, with access points at various locations along its course. Refer to a map or GPS to identify Forest Roads leading to the river. Once on a Forest Road, look for pull-offs or designated areas suitable for exploring the riverbed.

Sun Exposure and Availability of Shade:

The Moyie River area receives ample sunshine, especially during peak summer months. Sun protection is essential. Shade can be limited near the riverbed, so consider bringing a hat and breathable clothing.

Soil Type(s):

The soil types along the Moyie River can vary depending on location:

- **Forest duff:** A layer of decomposing organic matter from trees and other vegetation, most common along the banks.
- **Colluvium:** Loose rock and soil that has accumulated at the base of slopes due to gravity. This can obscure potential gemstone deposits, but you might find promising rock fragments within the colluvium.
- **Alluvial deposits:** Gravel and cobble deposits along the riverbed are prime areas for searching for materials like jasper and agates. Look for exposed areas during low water flow, especially around bends in the river or near rapids where rocks might have concentrated.

Rock Type(s):

The bedrock underlying the Moyie River area is a complex mix of metamorphic and sedimentary rocks. These can include schist, gneiss, quartzite, and limestone. The target materials like quartz crystals, jasper, and agates can be found within the alluvial deposits, having originated from veins or pockets within these various bedrock types.

Popularity of the Site:

The Moyie River is a popular destination for fishing, kayaking, and other recreational activities. Rockhounding activity can vary depending on the specific location and accessibility. More accessible areas closer to main roads might see more traffic, while secluded spots further along Forest Roads might be less crowded.

Important Note: The main historical digging area for quartz crystals is now closed.

Where to Buy Essential Supplies:

- **Sandpoint True Value Hardware:** (208) 263-3158, 48.6833° N, 116.5792° W. Offers tools, gloves, safety glasses, and other basic supplies in Sandpoint.
- **Les Schwab Tire Center:** (208) 263-1252, 48.6833° N, 116.5861° W. Offers basic tools and supplies in Sandpoint.

CLARK FORK

The Clark Fork, snaking through Montana, offers opportunities for rockhounds to unearth a variety of materials. This guide equips you with the knowledge to navigate the area and potentially discover hidden gems.

Marlow's Idaho Rock Hounding Guide Book 2024

Detailed Route Description:

Reaching the Clark Fork requires navigating western Montana. Here's a general route assuming you're coming from Missoula, MT:

1. Take I-90 W to Exit 133 for US-93 S towards Drummond.
2. Follow US-93 S for approximately 42 miles.
3. Depending on your desired access point, various roads branch off from US-93 to reach the Clark Fork. Consult a map or GPS for specific routes. **Note:** Some roads may require a high-clearance vehicle.

Land Type:

The land along the Clark Fork varies. Public lands managed by the Bureau of Land Management (BLM) (https://www.blm.gov/) and the Helena National Forest (https://www.fs.usda.gov/helena/) are common. Private property also borders the river in some areas. Always check land ownership before venturing off the road.

County:

Varies depending on the specific location along the Clark Fork. Counties it traverses include Missoula, Mineral, and Powell.

GPS Location:

Clark Fork (general area): 47.2833° N, 114.0833° W (**Please note:** This is a general location for the Clark Fork. Specific rockhounding sites may have their own GPS coordinates.)

Best Season for Rockhounding:

Spring, summer, and early fall (typically July-September) offer the most favorable weather conditions for exploring the Clark Fork. Winter brings snowfall, limiting accessibility. Spring runoff can also cause high water levels, so be mindful of water safety.

Land Manager:

Varies depending on location. Check with the BLM (https://www.blm.gov/) or Helena National Forest (https://www.fs.usda.gov/helena/) for specific areas.

Materials that can be Found:

- Agates (including plume jasper and moss agate)
- Jasper
- Petrified wood (occasionally)

Best Tools for Rockhounding:

- Rock hammer (use with caution and proper safety gear)
- Safety glasses (essential)
- Knee pads (optional for comfort)
- Hand trowel (optional)
- Sifting screen (optional)
- Magnifying glass (optional for examining smaller finds)

Best Vehicles for Accessing and Traversing the Area:

A high-clearance vehicle (SUV, truck) is recommended due to unpaved and potentially rough terrain along some access roads and the possibility of uneven surfaces near the riverbed.

Marlow's Idaho Rock Hounding Guide Book 2024

Accommodation Options:

- **Super 8 by Wyndham Missoula**: (406) 728-3600, 5630 N Reserve St., Missoula (46.8722° N, 114.0039° W). Budget-friendly hotel option in Missoula.
- **The Wilma Theatre Building**: (406) 728-9131, 131 W Main St., Missoula (46.8789° N, 114.0000° W). Upscale hotel in a historic building located downtown Missoula.
- **Gates of the Mountains Resort**: (406) 821-4000, 10200 US Highway 12 W, Helena (46.6000° N, 112.0333° W). Offers cabins, lodge rooms, and a campground near Helena (may require a drive to reach the Clark Fork).

Recommended Stops and Attractions:

- **Gates of the Mountains Wilderness Area** (46.3333° N, 111.8333° W): This stunning wilderness area offers hiking and backpacking opportunities (may require a drive from the Clark Fork). Look for the signs along US Highway 12 west of Helena.
- **Missoula Art Museum** (406) 728-3472, 33 S Higgins Ave., Missoula (46.8778° N, 114.0064° W). Located downtown Missoula, this museum features a variety of art exhibits.

Directions to the Site:

The Clark Fork stretches for many miles. Refer to a map or GPS to identify roads leading to the river. Once on an access road, look for pull-offs or designated areas suitable for exploring the riverbed. Public boat launches can also be access points, but be courteous to boaters.

Sun Exposure and Availability of Shade:

The Clark Fork area receives ample sunshine, especially during peak summer months. Sun protection is essential. Shade can be limited near the riverbed, so consider bringing a hat and breathable clothing.

Soil Type(s):

The soil types along the Clark Fork can vary depending on location:

- **Forest duff:** A layer of decomposing organic matter from trees and other vegetation, most common along the banks.
- **Alluvial deposits:** Gravel and cobble deposits along the riverbed are prime areas for searching for materials like agates, jasper, and petrified wood. Look for exposed areas during low water flow, especially around bends in the river or near rapids where rocks might have concentrated.
- **Talus slopes:** Steeper sections bordering the river might have slopes covered in large rock fragments, where some materials like agates or jasper might have accumulated after eroding from the riverbank.

Rock Type(s):

The bedrock underlying the Clark Fork area is a complex mix of sedimentary and igneous rocks. These can include limestone, sandstone, and volcanic rock. The target materials like agates, jasper, and petrified wood can be found within the alluvial deposits or talus slopes, having originated from veins or pockets within these various bedrock types.

Popularity of the Site:

The Clark Fork is a popular destination for fishing, kayaking, and other recreational activities. Rockhounding activity can vary depending on the specific location and accessibility. More accessible areas closer to towns might see more traffic, while secluded spots further along the river might be less crowded.

Where to Buy Essential Supplies:

- **Missoula Ace Hardware:** (406) 549-5100, 3225 N Reserve St., Missoula (46.8792° N, 114.0125° W). Offers tools, gloves, safety glasses, and other basic supplies in Missoula.
- **Helena Westgate Home Lumber & Hardware:** (406) 442-4466, 2700 Helena Ave., Helena (46.6033° N, 112.0256° W). Offers tools and basic supplies in Helena.

TALACHE

Talache, Idaho, beckons rockhounds seeking agates, jasper, and quartz crystals. This guide equips you with the knowledge to navigate the area and potentially discover hidden gems.

Detailed Route Description:

Reaching Talache requires navigating rural northern Idaho. Here's a general route assuming you're coming from Spokane, WA:

1. Take I-90 E to Exit 30 for ID-53 N towards Athol.
2. Follow ID-53 N for approximately 62 miles.
3. Turn left onto ID-154 N towards Sandpoint.
4. Continue on ID-154 N for about 27 miles.

5. Turn right onto Talache Beach Road (Forest Road 2720). Follow this road for several miles until you reach your desired pull-off point along the lakeshore or riverbed.

Land Type:

Most of the land around Talache is managed by the Idaho Panhandle National Forests (https://www.fs.usda.gov/ipnf), so it's public forest land. Always double-check the specific area you plan to explore, as designations can vary.

County:

Bonner County, Idaho

GPS Location:

Talache, Idaho (general area): 48.7333° N, 116.9000° W (**Please note:** This is a general location. Specific rockhounding sites may have their own GPS coordinates.)

Best Season for Rockhounding:

Spring, summer, and early fall (typically July-September) offer the most favorable weather conditions for exploring Talache. Winter brings snowfall, limiting accessibility. Spring runoff can cause high water levels near the lake and river, so be mindful of water safety.

Land Manager:

Idaho Panhandle National Forests (https://www.fs.usda.gov/ipnf)

Materials that can be Found:

- Agates (various colors and patterns)
- Jasper
- Quartz crystals (less common)

Best Tools for Rockhounding:

- Rock hammer (use with caution and proper safety gear)
- Safety glasses (essential)
- Knee pads (optional for comfort)
- Hand trowel (optional)
- Sifting screen (optional)
- Magnifying glass (optional for examining smaller finds)

Best Vehicles for Accessing and Traversing the Area:

A high-clearance vehicle (SUV, truck) is recommended due to the unpaved Talache Beach Road and potentially uneven terrain near the lakeshore and riverbed.

Accommodation Options:

- **Sandpoint West Resort Hotel & Marina:** (208) 263-2201, 48.6904° N, 116.5928° W. Full-service lakeside resort in Sandpoint offering various room options.
- **Lakeside Lodge & Resort:** (208) 263-4999, 48.6889° N, 116.5903° W. Offers cabins, RV sites, and tent camping in Sandpoint.
- **Priest Lake KOA Campground:** (208) 443-2800, 48.7414° N, 116.7664° W. Offers RV sites, tent camping, and cabin rentals near Priest Lake (may require a drive from Talache).

Recommended Stops and Attractions:

- **Priest Lake:** (48.7333° N, 116.7000° W) This scenic lake offers stunning views and various recreational activities (a short drive from Talache).
- **Sandpoint:** (48.6833° N, 116.5792° W) This charming lakeside town offers restaurants, shops, and cultural attractions (a drive from Talache). Look for the town center with a variety of shops and restaurants lining the main streets.

Directions to the Site:

Talache Beach stretches for several miles along the shore of Lake Pend Oreille. Follow Talache Beach Road (Forest Road 2720) until you find a suitable pull-off point with access to the lakeshore or the nearby Clark Fork River. Look for signs or consult a map for designated parking areas.

Sun Exposure and Availability of Shade:

The Talache area receives ample sunshine, especially during peak summer months. Sun protection is essential. Shade can be limited near the lakeshore and riverbed, so consider bringing a hat and breathable clothing.

Soil Type(s):

The soil types around Talache vary depending on location:

- **Forest duff:** A layer of decomposing organic matter from trees and other vegetation, most common along the edges of the lakeshore and riverbank.
- **Colluvium:** Loose rock and soil that has accumulated at the base of slopes due to gravity. This can obscure potential agate or jasper deposits, but you might find promising rock fragments within the colluvium that

could warrant using a rock hammer to break them open (wear safety glasses!).
- **Alluvial deposits:** Gravel and cobble deposits along the lakeshore and riverbed are prime areas for searching for agates, jasper, and quartz crystals. Look for exposed areas during low water flow, especially around bends or inlets where water flow might have concentrated rocks.

Rock Type(s):

The bedrock underlying the Talache area is a complex mix of volcanic and metamorphic rocks. These can include basalt, andesite, and schist. The target materials like agates, jasper, and quartz crystals can be found within the alluvial deposits, having originated from veins or pockets within these various bedrock types. **Important Note:** The historical digging area for quartz crystals in the Talache Mine is now closed.

Popularity of the Site:

Talache Beach is a popular destination for camping, fishing, boating, and other recreational activities. Rockhounding activity can vary depending on the specific location and accessibility. Areas closer to the main road might see more traffic, while secluded spots further along Talache Beach Road might be less crowded.

Where to Buy Essential Supplies:

- **Sandpoint True Value Hardware:** (208) 263-3158, 48.6833° N, 116.5792° W. Offers tools, gloves, safety glasses, and other basic supplies in Sandpoint.
- **Les Schwab Tire Center:** (208) 263-1252, 48.6833° N, 116.5861° W. Offers basic tools and supplies in Sandpoint.

VULCAN MINE

The Vulcan Mine, located near Wallace, Idaho, holds a rich history in the state's mining industry. However, due to safety hazards and environmental concerns, the mine itself is now closed to the public. This guide focuses on exploring Wallace and the surrounding area, while respecting the closure of the Vulcan Mine.

Important Note: Entering the Vulcan Mine is strictly prohibited. Abandoned mines can be dangerous due to potential cave-ins, unstable structures, and hazardous materials.

Detailed Route Description:

Reaching Wallace, Idaho, requires navigating through scenic northern Idaho. Here's a general route assuming you're coming from Spokane, WA:

1. Take I-90 E to Exit 30 for ID-53 N towards Athol.
2. Follow ID-53 N for approximately 67 miles.
3. Turn left onto US-95 N towards Wallace.
4. Continue on US-95 N for about 11 miles until you reach Wallace.

Land Type:

The area surrounding Wallace is a mix of public and private land. The mountains surrounding the town are within the Coeur d'Alene National Forest (https://www.fs.usda.gov/organization/Idaho%20Panhandle%20National%20Forests), while the town itself is private property.

County:

Shoshone County, Idaho

GPS Location:

Wallace, Idaho (general area): 47.4333° N, 115.9333° W **(Please note:** This is a general location for Wallace. The specific location of the Vulcan Mine is not provided due to the closure)

Best Season to Visit:

Summer (June-August) offers pleasant weather for exploring Wallace. Spring (April-May) and fall (September-October) can also be enjoyable, but be prepared for potential rain or cooler temperatures. Winter brings snowfall, limiting accessibility.

Land Manager (for surrounding areas):

Coeur d'Alene National Forest (https://www.fs.usda.gov/organization/Idaho%20Panhandle%20National%20Forests)

Materials you WON'T find at the Vulcan Mine (due to closure):

- The Vulcan Mine was historically known for copper, but public access is prohibited.

Focus on Responsible Exploration:

The Wallace area offers opportunities for outdoor recreation and historical exploration. Here are some ideas:

- **Visit the Wallace Mining Museum:** (208) 752-2112, 702 Main St., Wallace, ID 83873 (47.4322° N, 115.9322° W). Learn about the region's mining history through exhibits and artifacts.
- **Hike Sierra Star Mine Loop:** This 2.2-mile loop trail offers scenic views and historical remnants of past mining activity. **Note:** This trail does not lead to the Vulcan Mine.
- **Explore Downtown Wallace:** Wallace boasts historic buildings and a charming atmosphere. Enjoy local shops, restaurants, and art galleries.

Best Tools for Exploring Wallace:

- Comfortable walking shoes
- Camera
- National Forest map (if planning outdoor adventures)

Best Vehicles for Accessing Wallace:

Any vehicle type can navigate the roads to Wallace.

Accommodation Options in Wallace:

- **The Wallace Inn:** (208) 752-2100, 1005 Bank St., Wallace, ID 83873 (47.4317° N, 115.9342° W). Historic hotel located in downtown Wallace.
- **The Wallace Sho Lodge:** (208) 744-0521, 770 Bank St., Wallace, ID 83873 (47.4314° N, 115.9347° W). Offers budget-friendly motel rooms.
- **Nine Mile Recreation Area:** (208) 744-0400, Wallace, ID 83873 (camping available outside of town, specific GPS coordinates depend on chosen campsite). Offers campsites near the Coeur d'Alene River.

Sun Exposure and Availability of Shade:

Wallace receives ample sunshine, especially during summer months. Sun protection is recommended. Sidewalks and some streets offer shade, and many shops and restaurants have awnings.

Soil Type(s) in the Surrounding Area:

The soil types around Wallace vary depending on location, but can include:

- **Forest duff:** A layer of decomposing organic matter from trees and other vegetation, common on hillsides.
- **Spodic soils:** Ash-influenced soils with a reddish layer due to iron oxides, found in some forested areas.

Rock Type(s) in the Surrounding Area:

The mountains surrounding Wallace are composed of a complex mix of rock types, including:

- **Metamorphic rocks:** Such as schist, gneiss, and quartzite, formed from the alteration of older rock types through heat and pressure.
- **Sedimentary rocks:** Including limestone and sandstone, formed from the deposition and consolidation of sediments.

Popularity of the Vulcan Mine (as a destination):

While the Vulcan Mine itself is closed, Wallace attracts visitors interested in the region's mining history. The town offers historical sites, museums, and a chance to experience the atmosphere of an old mining community.

Where to Buy Essential Supplies in Wallace:

- **Wallace Ace Hardware:** (208) 752-1212, 501 Main St., Wallace, ID 83873 (47.4333° N, 115.9347° W). Offers basic supplies, snacks, and beverages.

CRYSTAL GOLD MINE

The Crystal Gold Mine, located near Kellogg, Idaho, offers a unique opportunity to combine rockhounding with a historical adventure. This guide equips you with the knowledge to navigate the area, explore an old mine, and potentially discover hidden gems.

Detailed Route Description:

Reaching the Crystal Gold Mine requires a scenic drive through northern Idaho. Here's how to get there:

1. Take I-90 E to Exit 54 for the Miner's Memorial (located on the north side of the freeway).
2. Turn left (west) onto Silver Valley Road.
3. Continue on Silver Valley Road for approximately 2 miles.
4. The Crystal Gold Mine will be on your right side. Look for signage.

Land Type:

The Crystal Gold Mine sits on private land. The surrounding area is a mix of public and private lands managed by the Shoshone National Forest (https://www.fs.usda.gov/shoshone) and private owners.

County:

Shoshone County, Idaho

GPS Location:

Crystal Gold Mine, Kellogg, Idaho: 47.6122° N, 116.6200° W

Best Season for Rockhounding:

The Crystal Gold Mine offers paid tours year-round. However, for exploring the surrounding public lands for rockhounding, spring, summer, and early fall (typically July-September) offer the most favorable weather conditions. Winter brings snowfall, limiting accessibility. Spring runoff can cause high water levels near streams, so be mindful of water safety.

Land Manager (for surrounding public lands):

Shoshone National Forest (https://www.fs.usda.gov/shoshone)

Materials that can be Found:

- At the Crystal Gold Mine (through their tours): Visitors can see gold and wire silver in the quartz vein.
- In the surrounding public lands (depending on location): Rockhounding opportunities may reveal agates, jasper, and petrified wood depending on the specific geology of the area.

Important Note: Always check regulations and respect private property boundaries when exploring public lands around the Crystal Gold Mine.

Marlow's Idaho Rock Hounding Guide Book 2024

Best Tools for Rockhounding (for surrounding public lands):

- Rock hammer (use with caution and proper safety gear)
- Safety glasses (essential)
- Knee pads (optional for comfort)
- Hand trowel (optional)
- Sifting screen (optional)
- Magnifying glass (optional for examining smaller finds)

Best Vehicles for Accessing and Traversing the Area:

- For reaching the Crystal Gold Mine: Any vehicle type can navigate the paved roads.
- For exploring surrounding public lands: A high-clearance vehicle (SUV, truck) may be helpful for navigating unpaved Forest Roads or uneven terrain near streams.

Accommodation Options:

- **Super 8 Kellogg:** (208) 784-1000, 100 S Main St, Kellogg, ID 83843 (47.6103° N, 116.6192° W). Budget-friendly hotel option near the Crystal Gold Mine.
- **The Wallace Inn:** (208) 752-2100, 1005 Bank St., Wallace, ID 83873 (47.4317° N, 115.9342° W). Historic hotel located in a nearby town (Wallace) with a charming atmosphere (approximately a 30-minute drive from the Crystal Gold Mine).
- Camping options are also available within the Shoshone National Forest. Search on the Forest Service website like Recreation.gov

Marlow's Idaho Rock Hounding Guide Book 2024

Recommended Stops and Attractions:

- **Crystal Gold Mine Tour:** Take a guided tour through the historic mine and learn about its past.
- **Sierra Silver Mine Tour:** (208) 784-3399, 412 Bunker Ave, Kellogg, ID 83843 (47.6139° N, 116.6167° W). Explore another historic mine in the area (separate operation from Crystal Gold Mine).
- **National Wallace Mining Museum:** (208) 752-2112, 702 Main St., Wallace, ID 83873 (47.4322° N, 115.9322° W). Learn about the rich mining history of the region (located in Wallace, a 30-minute drive from the Crystal Gold Mine).

Directions to the Site (surrounding public lands):

Exploring public lands for rockhounding requires more specific information on the location you choose. Consult the Shoshone National Forest website or maps to identify trails or access points near streams or areas with exposed geology that might be promising for rockhounding.

Sun Exposure and Availability of Shade:

The Crystal Gold Mine itself is located underground. The surrounding areas can vary depending on the specific public land you explore. In general, expect ample sunshine during summer months. Sun protection is recommended. Wooded areas can offer shade, and some trails might have limited overhead cover.

Soil Type(s) (surrounding public lands):

The soil types around the Crystal Gold Mine can vary depending on location:

- **Forest duff:** A layer of decomposing organic matter from trees and other vegetation, most common along hillsides or streambanks.
- **Colluvium:** Loose rock and soil that has accumulated at the base of slopes due to gravity. This can obscure potential agate or jasper deposits, but you might find promising rock fragments within the colluvium that could warrant using a rock hammer (wear safety glasses!).
- **Alluvial deposits:** Gravel and cobble deposits along streams are prime areas for searching for agates, jasper, and petrified wood. Look for exposed areas during low water flow, especially around bends or inlets where water flow might have concentrated rocks.

Rock Type(s) (surrounding public lands):

The bedrock underlying the area is likely a complex mix of volcanic and metamorphic rocks, similar to those found near Talache Beach. These can include basalt, andesite, and schist. The target materials for rockhounding (agates, jasper, petrified wood) may originate from veins or pockets within these various bedrock types, having been transported by water erosion to their current locations in streambeds.

Popularity of the Site:

The Crystal Gold Mine itself is a popular tourist destination, especially during summer months. Public lands around the mine can also see traffic from hikers, campers, and rockhounds. Popularity can vary depending on the specific location and accessibility.

Where to Buy Essential Supplies:

- **Kellogg True Value Hardware:** (208) 784-1261, 112 Main St, Kellogg, ID 83843 (47.6108° N, 116.6183°

W). Offers tools, gloves, safety glasses, and other basic supplies in Kellogg.

SIERRA SILVER MINE TOUR

The Sierra Silver Mine Tour, located in Wallace, Idaho, offers a unique opportunity to delve into the region's rich mining history. This guide equips you with the knowledge to navigate to the mine, embark on a fascinating tour, and gain insights into the area's geology.

Detailed Route Description:

Reaching the Sierra Silver Mine Tour requires a scenic drive through northern Idaho:

1. Take I-90 E to Exit 30 for ID-53 N towards Athol.
2. Follow ID-53 N for approximately 67 miles.
3. Turn left onto US-95 N towards Wallace.
4. Continue on US-95 N for about 11 miles until you reach Wallace.
5. The Sierra Silver Mine Tour ticket office is located at 412 Bunker Ave, Kellogg, ID 83843 (47.6139° N, 116.6167° W). Look for signage for the mine tour.

Land Type:

The Sierra Silver Mine Tour operates on private land. The surrounding area is a mix of public and private lands managed by the Shoshone National Forest (https://www.fs.usda.gov/shoshone) and private owners.

County:

Shoshone County, Idaho

Marlow's Idaho Rock Hounding Guide Book 2024

GPS Location:

Sierra Silver Mine Tour, Wallace, Idaho: 47.6139° N, 116.6167° W

Best Season for Rockhounding:

While the Sierra Silver Mine Tour itself doesn't involve rockhounding, the surrounding public lands offer opportunities for exploration. Spring, summer, and early fall (typically July-September) offer the most favorable weather conditions. Winter brings snowfall, limiting accessibility. Spring runoff can cause high water levels near streams, so be mindful of water safety.

Land Manager (for surrounding public lands):

Shoshone National Forest (https://www.fs.usda.gov/shoshone)

Materials You Won't Find at the Mine (but Might Find Nearby):

The Sierra Silver Mine Tour focuses on the historical aspects of mining. However, exploring public lands in the vicinity might reveal agates, jasper, and petrified wood, depending on the specific location and geology.

Focus on the Tour:

The Sierra Silver Mine Tour offers a guided experience through a retired mine. Enjoy learning about the history, mining techniques, and the lives of miners.

Best Tools (for exploring surrounding public lands):

- Comfortable walking shoes (for the mine tour)

Marlow's Idaho Rock Hounding Guide Book 2024

- Camera (to capture the mine tour experience)
- National Forest map and compass (if planning adventures on public lands)
- Rock hammer (use with caution and proper safety gear) for exploring public lands (optional)
- Safety glasses (essential for using a rock hammer)
- Hand trowel (optional, for exploring public lands)
- Sifting screen (optional, for exploring public lands)
- Magnifying glass (optional, for examining smaller finds on public lands)

Best Vehicles for Accessing the Area:

- Any vehicle type can navigate the paved roads to the Sierra Silver Mine Tour.
- A high-clearance vehicle (SUV, truck) may be helpful for exploring unpaved Forest Roads or uneven terrain on public lands.

Accommodation Options:

- **Super 8 Kellogg:** (208) 784-1000, 100 S Main St, Kellogg, ID 83843 (47.6103° N, 116.6192° W). Budget-friendly hotel option near the mine tour.
- **The Wallace Inn:** (208) 752-2100, 1005 Bank St., Wallace, ID 83873 (47.4317° N, 115.9342° W). Historic hotel located in a charming nearby town (Wallace) - a 30-minute drive from the mine tour.
- Camping options are also available within the Shoshone National Forest. Search on the Forest Service website or apps like Recreation.gov.

Recommended Stops and Attractions:

- **National Wallace Mining Museum:** (208) 752-2112, 702 Main St., Wallace, ID 83873 (47.4322° N, 115.9322° W). Learn more about the region's mining past after your tour (located in Wallace, a 30-minute drive).

- **Crystal Gold Mine Tour:** (208) 784-3399, 412 Bunker Ave, Kellogg, ID 83843 (47.6139° N, 116.6167° W). Explore another historic mine in the area (located right next to the Sierra Silver Mine Tour).
- **Hike Sierra Star Mine Loop:** This 2.2-mile loop trail, accessible from the Wallace area, offers scenic views and remnants of past mining activity.

Directions to Explore Public Lands for Rockhounding:

Exploring public lands for rockhounding requires more specific information on your chosen location. Consult the Shoshone National Forest website or maps to identify trails or access points near streams or areas with exposed geology that might be promising for finding agates, jasper, or petrified wood.

Sun Exposure and Availability of Shade:

The Sierra Silver Mine Tour takes place underground. The surrounding public lands can vary in sun exposure. In general, expect ample sunshine during summer months. Sun protection is recommended for exploring public lands. Wooded areas can offer shade, and some trails might have limited overhead cover.

Soil Type(s) (surrounding public lands):

The soil types around the Sierra Silver Mine Tour can vary depending on location:

- **Forest duff:** A layer of decomposing organic matter from trees and other vegetation, most common along hillsides or streambanks.
- **Colluvium:** Loose rock and soil that has accumulated at the base of slopes due to gravity. This can obscure potential agate or jasper deposits, but you might find promising rock fragments within the colluvium that could warrant using a rock hammer (wear safety glasses!).
- **Alluvial deposits:** Gravel and cobble deposits along streams are prime areas for searching for agates, jasper, and petrified wood. Look for exposed areas during low water flow, especially around bends or inlets where water flow might have concentrated rocks.

Rock Type(s) (surrounding public lands):

The bedrock underlying the area is likely a complex mix of volcanic and metamorphic rocks, similar to those found near Talache Beach. These can include basalt, andesite, and schist. The target materials for rockhounding (agates, jasper, petrified wood) may originate from veins or pockets within these various bedrock types, having been transported by water erosion to their current locations in streambeds.

Popularity of the Site:

The Sierra Silver Mine Tour is a popular tourist attraction, especially during summer months. Public lands around the area can also see traffic from hikers, campers, and rockhounds. Popularity can vary depending on the specific location and accessibility.

Where to Buy Essential Supplies:

- **Kellogg True Value Hardware:** (208) 784-1261, 112 Main St, Kellogg, ID 83843 (47.6108° N, 116.6183°

W). Offers tools, gloves, safety glasses, and other basic supplies in Kellogg.

ST. JOE RIVER

The St. Joe River, Idaho, winds through a scenic wilderness known for its abundant wildlife, breathtaking landscapes, and hidden treasures for rockhounds. This guide equips you with the knowledge to navigate the area, responsibly explore the riverbanks, and potentially discover gems and unique geological wonders.

Detailed Route Description:

Reaching the St. Joe River requires a scenic drive through northern Idaho. The specific route depends on your chosen access point. Here's a general example:

1. Identify your target access point along the St. Joe River. Popular locations include public boat launches or campgrounds managed by the Forest Service.
2. Look up driving directions to the chosen access point using online maps or the National Forest Service website (https://www.fs.usda.gov/node/232695).

Land Type:

The St. Joe River flows primarily through public lands managed by the Idaho Panhandle National Forests (https://www.fs.usda.gov/ipnf), specifically the St. Joe Ranger District. Private property exists along some stretches, so be mindful of boundaries.

County:

Shoshone County (primarily), with some sections flowing through Clearwater and Latah Counties, Idaho.

GPS Location (general area):

St. Joe River, Idaho (due to its length, specific coordinates aren't provided): 47°22′ N, 115°48′ W (approximate center point)

Best Season for Rockhounding:

Spring, summer, and early fall (typically July-September) offer the most favorable weather conditions. Winter brings snowfall, limiting access. Spring runoff can cause high water levels, so be cautious near the riverbank.

Land Manager:

Idaho Panhandle National Forests (https://www.fs.usda.gov/ipnf), St. Joe Ranger District

Treasures to Unearth (Rockhounding):

The St. Joe River is known for its abundance of garnets, particularly red garnets. With careful searching, you might also uncover jasper, agates, and other interesting rock specimens exposed along the riverbanks.

Remember:

- Always check regulations and adhere to limitations on rock collection within the specific National Forest area you visit.
- Focus on responsible rockhounding practices: take only what you need and leave no trace.

Best Tools for Rockhounding:

- Sturdy boots with good ankle support
- Safety glasses (essential for using a rock hammer)
- Rock hammer (use with caution)
- Hand trowel (optional)
- Sifting screen (optional, for sifting through gravel deposits)
- Magnifying glass (optional, for examining smaller finds)

Best Vehicles for Accessing the Area:

A high-clearance vehicle (SUV, truck) is recommended, especially for navigating unpaved Forest Service roads leading to access points. Some areas might be accessible with a car during dry conditions.

Accommodation Options:

- Camping options are plentiful within the Idaho Panhandle National Forests. Search for campgrounds near your chosen access point on the Forest Service website (https://www.fs.usda.gov/node/232695) or apps like Recreation.gov.
- Private cabins or lodges might also be available near the river. Research online or inquire with local chambers of commerce.

Recommended Stops and Attractions:

- **Scenic Overlooks:** Numerous scenic overlooks along the St. Joe River offer breathtaking views of the surrounding wilderness. Consult Forest Service maps or inquire at ranger stations for their locations.
- **Hiking Trails:** The St. Joe River area boasts a network of hiking trails catering to various difficulty

levels. Explore the diverse landscapes and immerse yourself in nature.
- **Wildlife Viewing:** Keep an eye out for deer, elk, moose, bald eagles, and other wildlife species inhabiting the area.

Directions to the Site (Specific Access Point):

As mentioned, the St. Joe River stretches for many miles. Identify your chosen access point (boat launch, campground) and utilize online maps or the Forest Service website to find driving directions. Look for signage upon arrival to navigate the specific area.

Sun Exposure and Availability of Shade:

Sun exposure can vary depending on the time of day and specific location along the river. Open areas near the riverbank receive full sun, while forested sections offer more shade. Sun protection, such as a hat and sunscreen, is recommended.

Soil Type(s):

The soil types along the St. Joe River can vary depending on location:

- **Forest duff:** A layer of decomposing organic matter from trees and other vegetation, most common along hillsides or riverbanks.

- **Alluvial deposits:** Gravel and cobble deposits near the riverbank are prime areas for rockhounding. Look for exposed areas during low water flow, especially around bends or inlets where water flow might have concentrated rocks containing garnets and other minerals.

Rock Type(s):

The underlying bedrock in the St. Joe River watershed is a complex mix of metamorphic and igneous rocks. Here are some common types:

- **Metamorphic rocks:** Such as schist and gneiss, formed from the alteration of older rock types through heat and pressure. These rocks may contain mineral veins where garnets and other crystals have formed.
- **Igneous rocks:** Like granite and diorite, formed from the cooling and solidification of magma or lava. These rocks may not be directly exposed along the riverbank but can contribute to the gravel deposits containing interesting minerals.

Popularity of the Site:

The St. Joe River is a popular destination for outdoor recreation, including camping, fishing, boating, and hiking. Popularity can vary depending on the specific access point and time of year. Expect more crowds during summer weekends and holidays.

Where to Buy Essential Supplies:

- Look for outfitters or sporting goods stores in the nearest town (e.g., St. Maries, Avery, Missoula) based on your chosen access point. These stores can provide:
  - Basic supplies like sunscreen, insect repellent, snacks, and first-aid kits.
  - Sturdy boots and appropriate clothing for the weather conditions.
  - Fishing licenses (if planning to fish).
- Ranger stations within the Idaho Panhandle National Forests might also sell basic supplies and maps.

BIG CARPENTER CREEK

Big Carpenter Creek, snaking through Shoshone County, Idaho, offers opportunities for outdoor enthusiasts and rockhounds alike. This guide equips you with the knowledge to navigate the area, explore the creek responsibly, and potentially discover hidden gems.

Detailed Route Description:

Reaching Big Carpenter Creek requires a scenic drive through northern Idaho:

1. **Identify your access point:** Big Carpenter Creek stretches for several miles. Popular access points include the public boat launch near Fernwood (maintained by Idaho Department of Fish and Game) or dispersed camping areas along the creek managed by the Forest Service.
2. **Look up driving directions:** Utilize online maps or the Idaho Department of Fish and Game website (https://idfg.idaho.gov/) to find directions to your chosen access point.

Land Type:

The land surrounding Big Carpenter Creek is a mix of public and private property. Public lands are managed by the Shoshone National Forest (https://www.fs.usda.gov/shoshone) while private lands are clearly marked with signage.

County:

Shoshone County, Idaho

Marlow's Idaho Rock Hounding Guide Book 2024

GPS Location (general area):

Big Carpenter Creek, Idaho (due to its length, specific coordinates aren't provided): 47°31′ N, 116°18′ W (approximate center point)

Best Season for Rockhounding:

Spring, summer, and early fall (typically July-September) offer the most favorable conditions. Winter brings snowfall, limiting access. Spring runoff can cause high water levels, so be cautious near the creek bed.

Land Manager (for Public Lands):

Shoshone National Forest (https://www.fs.usda.gov/shoshone)

Rockhounding Potential:

Big Carpenter Creek is known for its deposits of staurolite, a dark-colored metamorphic rock with a unique cross-shaped crystal pattern. You might also find jasper and agate along the creek banks, especially in exposed gravel areas.

Remember:

- Always check regulations and adhere to limitations on rock collection within the specific National Forest area you visit.
- Focus on responsible rockhounding practices: take only what you need and leave no trace.

Best Tools for Rockhounding:

- Sturdy boots with good ankle support
- Safety glasses (essential for using a rock hammer)

- Rock hammer (use with caution)
- Hand trowel (optional)
- Sifting screen (optional, for sifting through gravel deposits)
- Magnifying glass (optional, for examining smaller finds)

Best Vehicles for Accessing the Area:

A high-clearance vehicle (SUV, truck) is recommended, especially for navigating unpaved Forest Service roads leading to access points. Some areas might be accessible with a car during dry conditions. 4x4 might be necessary on some trails leading closer to the creek bed.

Accommodation Options:

- **Camping:** Several dispersed camping opportunities exist along Big Carpenter Creek managed by the Forest Service. Check the Forest Service website (https://www.fs.usda.gov/shoshone) for availability and regulations.
- **Lodging:** Limited lodging options are available near Big Carpenter Creek. Consider nearby towns like Kellogg or Wallace for hotels or motels.

Recommended Stops and Attractions:

- **Crystal Gold Mine Tour:** (208) 784-3399, 412 Bunker Ave, Kellogg, ID 83843 (47.6139° N, 116.6167° W). Explore a historic mine and learn about the region's mining past.
- **Hike to Emerald Mountain Lookout:** This moderate hike offers panoramic views of the surrounding mountains and forests. Consult Forest Service maps for trail details.

Marlow's Idaho Rock Hounding Guide Book 2024

Directions to the Site (Specific Access Point):

As mentioned, specific directions depend on your chosen access point. Utilize online maps or Forest Service resources to find driving directions. Look for signage upon arrival to navigate the specific area.

Sun Exposure and Availability of Shade:

Sun exposure can vary depending on the time of day and location along the creek. Open areas near the creekbank receive full sun, while forested sections offer more shade. Sun protection is recommended.

Soil Type(s):

The soil types around Big Carpenter Creek can vary depending on location:

- **Forest duff:** A layer of decomposing organic matter from trees and other vegetation, most common along hillsides or streambanks.

- **Alluvial deposits:** Gravel and cobble deposits near the creekbank are prime areas for rockhounding. Look for exposed areas during low water flow, especially around bends or inlets where water flow might have concentrated rocks containing staurolite, jasper, and agate.

Rock Type(s):

The underlying bedrock in the Big Carpenter Creek watershed is a complex mix of metamorphic and igneous rocks. Here are some common types:

- **Metamorphic rocks:** These include schist, gneiss, and mica schist, formed from the alteration of older rock types through heat and pressure. Staurolite typically occurs within these metamorphic rocks.
- **Igneous rocks:** Like granite and diorite, formed from the cooling and solidification of magma or lava. These rocks may not be directly exposed along the creekbed but can contribute to the gravel deposits containing interesting minerals.

Popularity of the Site:

The popularity of Big Carpenter Creek can vary depending on the location and time of year. Areas near the boat launch might see more traffic, while dispersed camping areas further upstream might be less crowded. Expect more visitors during summer weekends and holidays.

Where to Buy Essential Supplies:

- **Kellogg True Value Hardware:** (208) 784-1261, 112 Main St, Kellogg, ID 83843 (47.6108° N, 116.6183° W). Offers tools, gloves, safety glasses, and other basic supplies.
- **Wallace Ace Hardware:** (208) 752-1222, 701 Main St, Wallace, ID 83873 (47.6422° N, 115.9400° W). Provides similar supplies as Kellogg True Value Hardware.

EMERALD CREEK

Emerald Creek, winding through Shoshone County, Idaho, holds historical significance and ecological value. However, due to past mining activities and environmental concerns, rockhounding is not recommended. This guide focuses on exploring the area responsibly and appreciating its unique character.

Detailed Route Description:

Reaching Emerald Creek requires navigating through scenic northern Idaho. A specific route depends on the town nearest your target access point along Emerald Creek. Here's a general example:

1. Identify the closest major city (e.g., Coeur d'Alene, Boise).
2. Look up driving directions to a National Forest encompassing Emerald Creek (e.g., Coeur d'Alene National Forest, Kaniksu National Forest).
3. Utilize Forest Service maps or a GPS to locate Forest Roads leading to access points along Emerald Creek.
4. Be aware that some Forest Roads may require a high-clearance vehicle.

Land Type:

Public lands managed by the National Forest Service (https://www.fs.usda.gov/node/232695) are common along Emerald Creek. Always check land ownership before venturing off designated roads.

County:

Shoshone County, Idaho

GPS Location (general area):

Emerald Creek, Idaho (due to multiple locations, specific GPS coordinates aren't provided)

Best Season to Visit:

Spring, summer, and early fall (typically July-September) offer the most favorable weather conditions for exploring Emerald Creek. Winter brings snowfall, limiting accessibility. Spring runoff can cause high water levels, so be mindful of water safety.

Land Manager:

National Forest Service (https://www.fs.usda.gov/node/232695)

Materials You Won't Find Here (Due to Conservation):

Rockhounding is not recommended on Emerald Creek due to past mining activities and ongoing restoration efforts. The focus should be on appreciating the restored habitat and ecological value of the creek.

Focus on Responsible Exploration:

Enjoy hiking, wildlife viewing, and photography while respecting the fragile environment.

Best Tools for Responsible Exploration:

- Comfortable walking shoes or hiking boots
- Camera
- National Forest map and compass (for navigation)
- Binoculars (optional, for wildlife viewing)

Marlow's Idaho Rock Hounding Guide Book 2024

Best Vehicles for Accessing and Traversing the Area:

A high-clearance vehicle (SUV, truck) is recommended due to unpaved Forest Roads and potentially uneven terrain near the creek bed.

Accommodation Options (assuming near a National Forest):

- Look for campgrounds or cabin rentals managed by the National Forest Service near your target Emerald Creek location. Search on the Forest Service website or apps like Recreation.gov.
- Private campgrounds or lodging options may also be available near National Forests. Research online or inquire with local chambers of commerce.

Recommended Stops and Attractions (assuming near a National Forest):

- Visitor centers managed by the National Forest Service can offer valuable information on the surrounding area, including restored areas along Emerald Creek.
- Scenic overlooks, hiking trails, and wildlife viewing areas may be present within the National Forest. Consult Forest Service maps or inquire at visitor centers.

Directions to the Site:

The specific directions depend on the location of your target access point along Emerald Creek. Refer to Forest Service maps or a GPS to identify roads leading to the creek. Once on an access road, look for pull-offs or designated areas suitable for exploring the creek bed. Public boat launches can also be access points, but be courteous to boaters.

Sun Exposure and Availability of Shade:

The Emerald Creek area likely receives ample sunshine, especially during peak summer months. Sun protection is essential. Shade can be limited near the creek bed, so consider bringing a hat and breathable clothing.

Soil Type(s):

The soil types along Emerald Creek can vary depending on location:

- **Forest duff:** A layer of decomposing organic matter from trees and other vegetation, most common along the banks.
- **Alluvial deposits:** Gravel and cobble deposits along the creek bed may contain remnants of past mining activity, but collecting these is not permitted. Observe and appreciate from a distance.
- **Restored areas:** Look for areas where native vegetation has been replanted as part of ongoing restoration efforts.

Rock Type(s):

The mountains surrounding Emerald Creek are composed of a complex mix of rock types, including:

- **Metamorphic rocks:** Such as schist, gneiss, and quartzite, formed from the alteration of older rock types through heat and pressure.
- **Sedimentary rocks:** Including limestone and sandstone, formed from the deposition and consolidation of sediments.

Popularity of the Site:

The popularity of access points along Emerald Creek can vary. Some areas might receive moderate traffic from hikers, campers, and anglers. Choose locations suitable for your interests, considering tranquility or opportunities for wildlife viewing.

Where to Buy Essential Supplies (general recommendations):

- Look for outfitters or sporting goods stores in the nearest town (e.g., Coeur d'Alene, Wallace) based on your chosen access point. These stores can provide:
  - Basic supplies like sunscreen, insect repellent, and snacks.
  - Hiking gear recommendations or rentals.
  - Local fishing licenses (if planning to fish).

CHAPTER 4
CENTRAL IDAHO

BETCHEL MOUNTAIN

Betchel Mountain, rising majestically in the Medicine Bow Range of southeastern Wyoming, offers breathtaking vistas and opportunities for outdoor enthusiasts. However, due to its ecological importance and designated wilderness status, rockhounding is not permitted. This guide focuses on exploring the area responsibly and appreciating its scenic beauty.

Detailed Route Description:

Reaching Betchel Mountain requires navigating along scenic highways and potentially unpaved roads. Here's a general approach:

1. Identify your starting point: Depending on your preference, you can choose Laramie, WY, or Saratoga, WY, as your base town.
2. Look up driving directions: Utilize online maps or GPS navigation to find the route to the trailhead you plan to use for accessing Betchel Mountain. Popular options include the Libby Flats Trail or the Sheep Mountain Trail.
3. Trailhead access: Some trailheads might be accessible via paved roads, while others might require a high-clearance vehicle due to unpaved or rough road conditions.

Land Type:

Betchel Mountain lies within the Medicine Bow National Forest (https://www.fs.usda.gov/organization/Medicine%20Bow-Routt%20National%20Forests%20and%20Thunder%20Basin%20National%20Grassland), designated as a wilderness area. Wilderness areas have the highest level of protection for lands managed by the Forest Service.

County:

Albany County, Wyoming

GPS Location (general area):

Betchel Mountain, Medicine Bow National Forest, WY (41.3233° N, 106.0522° W) - This is a general area indicator due to the mountain's vastness.

Best Season to Visit:

Summer (typically July-August) offers the most favorable weather conditions for hiking and exploring Betchel Mountain. Spring and fall can be beautiful but may have lingering snow or unpredictable weather. Winters are harsh and not recommended for casual exploration.

Land Manager:

Medicine Bow National Forest (https://www.fs.usda.gov/organization/Medicine%20Bow-Routt%20National%20Forests%20and%20Thunder%20Basin%20National%20Grassland)

Marlow's Idaho Rock Hounding Guide Book 2024

Materials You Won't Find Here (Due to Conservation):

Rockhounding is strictly prohibited within the Medicine Bow National Forest Wilderness Area. The focus should be on enjoying the scenery, wildlife, and unique ecosystem.

Focus on Responsible Exploration:

- Hike designated trails, staying on the path to minimize environmental impact.
- Leave No Trace principles apply: Pack out all trash, avoid disturbing vegetation, and practice responsible toileting habits.
- Be mindful of wildlife: Maintain a safe distance and avoid altering their natural behavior.

Best Tools for Responsible Exploration:

- Sturdy hiking boots with good ankle support
- Backpack with sufficient water and food for your planned hike
- Weather-appropriate clothing (including layers for changing conditions)
- Map and compass (or GPS device) for navigation
- First-aid kit
- Sunscreen, insect repellent, and sunglasses (optional)

Best Vehicles for Accessing and Traversing the Area:

A high-clearance vehicle (SUV, truck) is recommended, especially for navigating unpaved roads leading to some trailheads. Double-check road conditions before your trip, especially if planning to visit after spring snowmelt.

Accommodation Options (near the Medicine Bow National Forest):

- Camping: Numerous campgrounds are scattered throughout the Medicine Bow National Forest. Search options and availability on the Forest Service website (https://www.fs.usda.gov/organization/Medicine%20Bow-Routt%20National%20Forests%20and%20Thunder%20Basin%20National%20Grassland) or apps like Recreation.gov.
- Lodging: Hotels, motels, and cabins can be found in nearby towns like Laramie or Saratoga. Research online or contact local chambers of commerce for options.

Recommended Stops and Attractions (within Medicine Bow National Forest):

- Visitors Centers: Several visitor centers operated by the Forest Service provide valuable information on hiking trails, wilderness regulations, and the surrounding area.
- Scenic Overlooks: Breathtaking vistas abound throughout the Medicine Bow National Forest. Consult Forest Service maps or inquire at visitor centers for specific locations.
- Other Hiking Trails: The Medicine Bow National Forest offers a network of trails catering to various difficulty levels. Explore meadows, forests, and alpine lakes.

Sun Exposure and Availability of Shade:

Expect significant sun exposure on Betchel Mountain, especially during peak summer months. Sun protection, including sunscreen, sunglasses, and a hat, is essential. Shade availability can be limited, especially above the tree line. Bring appropriate clothing for sun protection and potential wind exposure.

Soil Types:

The soil types on Betchel Mountain vary depending on elevation:

- **Forest duff:** A layer of decomposing organic matter from trees and other vegetation, most common in lower elevation forests.
- **Alpine soils:** Thin, rocky soils with low organic content, dominant at higher elevations.

Rock Types:

Betchel Mountain is composed primarily of igneous rocks, formed from the cooling and solidification of magma or lava. Common rock types include:

- **Granite:** A light-colored, coarse-grained igneous rock composed of quartz, feldspar, and mica.
- **Gneiss:** A metamorphic rock formed from the transformation of granite under intense heat and pressure. It often has a banded appearance.

Popularity of the Site:

The popularity of Betchel Mountain can vary depending on the season and specific trailhead. Summer weekends are likely to see the most visitors. Weekdays and trails with a more challenging rating might be less crowded.

Marlow's Idaho Rock Hounding Guide Book 2024

Where to Buy Essential Supplies (general recommendations):

- Look for outfitters or sporting goods stores in nearby towns like Laramie or Saratoga. These stores can provide:
    - Hiking gear rentals or purchases (boots, backpacks, etc.).
    - Maps, compasses, and GPS devices.
    - Clothing and footwear suitable for hiking.
    - Food and camping supplies (if planning to camp).

FOSSIL BOWL

The Fossil Bowl, nestled within the Clarkia Valley of northern Idaho, is a haven for paleontology enthusiasts and rockhounds alike. This guide equips you with the knowledge to explore the area responsibly, unearth hidden treasures, and delve into its geological history.

Detailed Route Description:

Reaching the Fossil Bowl requires a scenic drive through Idaho:

1. **Identify your access point:** The Fossil Bowl encompasses a large area. Popular access points include the public boat launch managed by Idaho Department of Fish and Game near Clarkia, or dispersed camping areas along the river managed by the Forest Service.
2. **Look up driving directions:** Utilize online maps or the Idaho Department of Fish and Game website (https://idfg.idaho.gov/) to find directions to your chosen access point.

Marlow's Idaho Rock Hounding Guide Book 2024

Land Type:

A mix of public and private property exists within the Clarkia Valley. Public lands are managed by the Clearwater National Forest while private lands are clearly marked with signage.

County:

Idaho County, Idaho

GPS Location (general area):

Fossil Bowl, Clarkia Valley, Idaho (46°31′ N, 116°38′ W) - This is a general area indicator due to the vastness of the Fossil Bowl.

Best Season for Rockhounding:

Spring, summer, and early fall (typically July-September) offer the most favorable conditions. Winter brings snowfall, limiting access. Spring runoff can cause high water levels, so be cautious near the riverbank.

Land Manager (for Public Lands):

Clearwater National Forest (https://www.fs.usda.gov/nezperceclearwater)

Rockhounding Potential:

The Fossil Bowl is renowned for its abundance of Miocene-era fossils, particularly fossilized marine creatures like:

- Ammonites (coiled cephalopods)
- Orthoceras (straight cephalopods)
- Other marine invertebrates

Remember: Always check regulations and adhere to limitations on fossil collection within the specific National Forest area you visit. Focus on responsible rockhounding practices: take only what you need and leave no trace.

Best Tools for Rockhounding:

- Sturdy boots with good ankle support
- Safety glasses (essential for using a rock hammer)
- Rock hammer (use with caution)
- Hand trowel (optional)
- Sifting screen (optional, for sifting through gravel deposits)
- Magnifying glass (optional, for examining smaller fossils)

Best Vehicles for Accessing and Traversing the Area:

A high-clearance vehicle (SUV, truck) is recommended, especially for navigating unpaved Forest Service roads leading to some access points. Some areas might be accessible with a car during dry conditions.

Accommodation Options:

- **Camping:** Dispersed camping opportunities are available along the river managed by the Forest Service. Check the Forest Service website for availability and regulations.
- **Lodging:** Limited lodging options are available near the Fossil Bowl. Consider nearby towns like Lewiston or Grangeville for hotels or motels.

Recommended Stops and Attractions:

- **Hells Canyon National Recreation Area:** (509) 751-4531, located further along the Snake River. Offers

stunning scenery, whitewater rafting opportunities, and a visitor center with geological exhibits. Look for signs along the main highway (US-95) for access points.
- **Nez Perce National Historical Park:** (208) 843-7700, scattered locations throughout the Nez Perce homeland. Offers historical sites and cultural centers commemorating the Nez Perce people. (https://www.nps.gov/Nezperce/index.htm) Consult park websites or maps for locations.

Directions to the Site (Specific Access Point):

As mentioned, specific directions depend on your chosen access point. Utilize online maps or Forest Service resources to find driving directions. Look for signage upon arrival to navigate the specific area.

Sun Exposure and Availability of Shade:

Sun exposure can vary depending on the time of day and location within the Fossil Bowl. Open areas near the riverbank receive full sun, while forested sections offer more shade. Sun protection is recommended.

Soil Type(s):

The soil types in the Fossil Bowl can be categorized as follows:

- **Alluvial deposits:** This is the primary target area for rockhounding. These are loose deposits of gravel, cobbles, and sand left behind by the ancestral Snake River. Fossils are often concentrated within these deposits, exposed through erosion.

- **Hillslope soils:** Steeper areas have well-drained soils with a higher clay content and less rock exposure. Look for exposed bedrock on hillsides for potential fossil-bearing rock formations.

Rock Types:

The underlying bedrock in the Fossil Bowl area consists mainly of sedimentary rocks:

- **Calcareous siltstone and mudstone:** Fine-grained sedimentary rocks rich in calcium carbonate, ideal for fossilization due to their ability to preserve hard body parts of marine organisms.
- **Basalt:** Volcanic rock flows may be present in some areas, but these are not typically targeted for fossil hunting.

Popularity of the Site:

The popularity of the Fossil Bowl can vary depending on the season and specific access point. Summer weekends are likely to see the most visitors, particularly rockhounds and kayakers. Weekdays and areas requiring a longer hike might be less crowded.

Where to Buy Essential Supplies (general recommendations):

- **Lewiston** (closest major city):
  - **Clarkston Valley Hardware:** (208) 743-5521, 731 Fairway Dr, Lewiston, ID 83501 (46°27'22.3"N, 117°1'42.9"W). Offers tools, safety equipment, and basic supplies.
  - **Walmart:** (208) 743-1500, 1645 vek rd, Lewiston, ID 83501 (46°25'33.2"N,

117°0′48.2″W). Provides a wider selection of supplies, including camping gear and snacks.

MICA MOUNTAIN

Mica Mountain, a prominent peak within Saguaro National Park in Arizona, offers breathtaking vistas and diverse desert ecosystems. However, due to its protected status and ecological value, rockhounding is not permitted. This guide focuses on exploring the area responsibly and appreciating its natural beauty.

Detailed Route Description:

Reaching Mica Mountain requires navigating through scenic southern Arizona. Here's a general approach:

1. **Identify your starting point:** Popular access points include the Douglas Spring Trailhead or the Manning Camp Trailhead, both located near Tucson.
2. **Look up driving directions:** Utilize online maps or a GPS to find directions to your chosen trailhead. Saguaro National Park charges an entrance fee (https://www.nps.gov/sagu/planyourvisit/fees.htm).
3. **Trail access:** Both trailheads are accessible via paved roads. Parking availability can be limited, especially during peak season.

Land Type:

Mica Mountain lies entirely within Saguaro National Park, managed by the National Park Service (https://www.nps.gov/).

Marlow's Idaho Rock Hounding Guide Book 2024

County:

Pima County, Arizona

GPS Location (general area):

Mica Mountain, Saguaro National Park, AZ (31°43′32″N, 110°32′11″W) - This is a general area indicator due to the mountain's size.

Best Season to Visit:

Fall (typically October-November) and spring (March-April) offer the most pleasant hiking conditions with moderate temperatures. Summers are scorching and winters can be unpredictable.

Land Manager:

National Park Service (https://www.nps.gov/)

Materials You Won't Find Here (Due to Conservation):

Rockhounding is strictly prohibited within Saguaro National Park. The focus should be on enjoying the scenery, wildlife, and unique desert flora.

Explore Responsibly:

- **Stay on designated trails:** Minimize your impact on the park's ecosystem by staying on marked paths.
- **Leave No Trace:** Pack out all trash and avoid disturbing vegetation or wildlife.
- **Respect wildlife:** Maintain a safe distance from animals and avoid altering their natural behavior.

- **Hydration is key:** Carry sufficient water, especially during warm weather hikes.

Best Tools for Responsible Exploration:

- Sturdy hiking boots with good ankle support
- Backpack with enough water and food for your planned hike
- Sunscreen, hat, and sunglasses (sun protection is essential)
- Camera (optional)
- Map and compass (or GPS device) for navigation (optional, but recommended)

Best Vehicles for Accessing the Area:

Any standard vehicle can access the trailheads leading to Mica Mountain. However, during heavy rains, high-clearance vehicles might be beneficial due to potential muddy conditions near parking areas.

Accommodation Options (near Saguaro National Park):

- **Campgrounds:** Several campgrounds are available within Saguaro National Park (https://www.recreation.gov/camping/campgrounds/10028678). Make reservations in advance, especially during peak season.
- **Lodging:** Hotels, motels, and vacation rentals can be found in nearby Tucson (https://www.hotels.com/de1470658/hotels-tucson-arizona/).

Recommended Stops and Attractions (within Saguaro National Park):

- **Visitor Centers:** Saguaro National Park Visitor Centers offer valuable information on hiking trails, park regulations, and the desert ecosystem (https://www.nps.gov/sagu/).
- **Rincon Mountain District:** Explore the west side of the Rincon Mountains, offering scenic drives and additional hiking trails.
- **Desert Ecology Exhibits:** Learn about the unique plants and animals that thrive in the Sonoran Desert.

Directions to the Trailhead:

As mentioned earlier, specific directions depend on your chosen trailhead. Utilize online maps or National Park Service resources (https://www.nps.gov/sagu/) to find driving directions to your starting point. Look for signage upon arrival for further guidance.

Sun Exposure and Availability of Shade:

Expect significant sun exposure on Mica Mountain, especially during peak hiking seasons. Shade availability is limited, particularly in higher elevations. Bring sun protection gear and wear breathable clothing.

Soil Type(s):

The soil types on Mica Mountain vary depending on elevation:

- **Aridisols:** These are dry, desert soils with low organic content, dominant throughout the park.
- **Lithic soils:** Shallow soils with high rock content, often found on steeper slopes.

Rock Type(s):

Mica Mountain is composed primarily of metamorphic and igneous rocks:

- **Metamorphic rocks:** Gneiss, a banded rock formed from the transformation of granite under intense heat and pressure, is a common rock type on Mica Mountain.
- **Igneous rocks:** Granite, a light-colored, coarse-grained igneous rock, may also be present in some areas.

Popularity of the Site:

Mica Mountain can be moderately popular, especially during peak hiking seasons (spring and fall). Weekdays and less popular trails within Saguaro National Park might see fewer visitors.

Where to Buy Essential Supplies (near Tucson):

- **Tucson Outfitters:** (520) 299-4496, 6401 E Broadway Blvd, Tucson, AZ 85710 (32°13′23.2″N, 110°56′42.9″W). Offers a wide selection of hiking gear, apparel, and footwear.
- **Walmart:** Multiple locations throughout Tucson. Provides a variety of supplies, including snacks, water, and basic camping gear (if planning to camp).

FREEZEOUT RIDGE

Freezeout Ridge offers a captivating experience for outdoor enthusiasts. Whether you seek hidden treasures or panoramic views, this guide equips you for a fulfilling adventure.

Marlow's Idaho Rock Hounding Guide Book 2024

Detailed Route Description:

Reaching Freezeout Ridge requires navigating scenic routes:

1. **Identify your Starting Point:** Popular access points include the trailhead near Rainy Pass or the west end of Freezeout Ridge Road (Forest Service Road 345).
2. **Look Up Driving Directions:** Utilize online maps or Forest Service resources (https://www.fs.usda.gov/colville) to find directions to your chosen access point.
3. **Trail Access:** The trailhead near Rainy Pass might require a high-clearance vehicle, especially after spring runoff. Freezeout Ridge Road is generally accessible by car during dry conditions.

Land Type:

Freezeout Ridge lies within the Colville National Forest, managed by the US Forest Service (https://www.fs.usda.gov/colville).

County:

Okanogan County, Washington

GPS Location (general area):

Freezeout Ridge, Colville National Forest, WA (48.7238° N, 119.2322° W) - This is a general area indicator due to the ridge's extent.

Best Season for Rockhounding:

Summer (typically July-August) offers the most favorable weather conditions for exploring and rockhounding. Spring can be beautiful but may have lingering snow. Winters are harsh and not recommended for casual exploration.

Land Manager:

US Forest Service (https://www.fs.usda.gov/colville)

Rockhounding Potential:

Freezeout Ridge is known for its deposits of Kyanite, a blue-colored metamorphic rock prized for its hardness and beauty. However, always check current regulations and obtain any permits required by the Forest Service for rockhounding in specific areas. Responsible collection practices are crucial: take only what you need and leave no trace.

Best Tools for Rockhounding:

- Sturdy hiking boots with good ankle support
- Safety glasses (essential for using a rock hammer)
- Rock hammer (use with caution and consider local regulations)
- Hand trowel (optional)
- Sifting screen (optional, for sifting through loose material)
- Magnifying glass (optional, for examining smaller specimens)
- GPS device or map and compass (recommended for navigation)

Best Vehicles for Accessing and Traversing the Area:

A high-clearance vehicle (SUV, truck) is recommended, particularly for navigating the trailhead near Rainy Pass or unpaved sections of Freezeout Ridge Road.

Marlow's Idaho Rock Hounding Guide Book 2024

Accommodation Options (near Colville National Forest):

- **Camping:** Developed campgrounds are scattered throughout the Colville National Forest. Search options and availability on the Forest Service website (https://www.fs.usda.gov/colville) or apps like Recreation.gov.
- **Lodging:** Hotels, motels, and cabins can be found in nearby towns like Omak or Winthrop. Research online or contact local chambers of commerce for options.

Recommended Stops and Attractions (within Colville National Forest):

- **Lake Roosevelt National Recreation Area:** (509) 754-0028, offers stunning scenery, boating opportunities, and historical sites. Look for signs along highways for access points (https://www.nps.gov/laro/).
- **Fort Okanogan State Park:** (509) 468-1508, a historic fort showcasing the fur trade era. Look for signs along highways for access (https://parks.wa.gov/passes-permits/reservations).

Directions to the Site (Specific Access Point):

As mentioned earlier, specific directions depend on your chosen access point. Utilize online maps or Forest Service resources to find driving directions. Look for signage upon arrival for further guidance.

Sun Exposure and Availability of Shade:

Expect significant sun exposure on exposed sections of Freezeout Ridge. The trail might have pockets of shade offered by trees, especially in lower areas. Sun protection gear is essential.

Soil Types:

The soil types on Freezeout Ridge can be categorized as follows:

- **Subalpine forest soils:** These are well-drained soils with a mix of organic matter and mineral components, found in areas with tree cover.
- **Lithic soils:** Shallow soils with high rock content, prevalent on steeper slopes and rocky outcrops.

Rock Types:

The underlying bedrock on Freezeout Ridge is primarily composed of:

- **Metamorphic Rocks:** Gneiss, a banded rock formed from the transformation of granite under intense heat and pressure, is the dominant rock type on Freezeout Ridge.
- **Schist:** Another metamorphic rock with a layered structure, may also be present in some areas. These rocks often contain Kyanite crystals.

Popularity of the Site:

The popularity of Freezeout Ridge can vary depending on the season and specific access point. Summer weekends are likely to see the most visitors, particularly rockhounds and hikers. Weekdays and areas requiring a longer hike might be less crowded.

Marlow's Idaho Rock Hounding Guide Book 2024

Where to Buy Essential Supplies (near Colville National Forest):

- **Omak** (closest major town):
    - **Omak Valley Hardware:** (509) 826-1121, 1025 S Elm St, Omak, WA 98841 (48.4502° N, 119.7702° W). Offers tools, safety equipment, and basic supplies.
    - **Walmart:** (509) 826-1241, 1801 S Cloverdale St, Omak, WA 98841 (48.4377° N, 119.7622° W). Provides a wider selection of supplies, including camping gear, snacks, and water.

CRATER PEAK

Crater Peak, nestled within the mountains of Idaho, beckons rockhounds and outdoor enthusiasts alike. This guide equips you with the knowledge to navigate the area responsibly, discover hidden treasures, and delve into its geological history.

Detailed Route Description:

Reaching Crater Peak requires traversing scenic Idaho landscapes:

1. **Identify your access point:** Crater Peak is a vast area. Popular access points include:
    - **BLM Road 301:** This route is accessible by high-clearance vehicles only. Look for signs along State Highway 3 near Clarkia, Idaho.
    - **Forest Service roads and trails:** Several trails lead to the peak from surrounding forests. Utilize Forest Service resources (https://www.fs.usda.gov/main/ipnf/home) for specific trailhead information.

2. **Look up driving directions:** Utilize online maps or apps to find directions to your chosen access point. Be prepared for unpaved roads and potential switchbacks.

Land Type:

The area around Crater Peak encompasses a mix of public and private lands:

- **Public Lands:** Managed by the Bureau of Land Management (BLM) (https://www.blm.gov/idaho) and the Forest Service (https://www.fs.usda.gov/main/ipnf/home).
- **Private Lands:** Clearly marked with signage. Respect private property boundaries.

County:

Idaho County, Idaho

GPS Location (general area):

Crater Peak, Idaho County, ID (47.0442° N, 115.9461° W) - This is a general area indicator due to the size of Crater Peak.

Best Season for Rockhounding:

Spring (typically May-June) and fall (September-October) offer pleasant weather conditions. Summer can be hot and dry, while winter brings snow and limited access.

Land Manager (for Public Lands):

- **Bureau of Land Management (BLM) for some areas:** (https://www.blm.gov/idaho)
- **Forest Service for other areas:** (https://www.fs.usda.gov/main/ipnf/home)

Rockhounding Potential:

Crater Peak is known for a variety of collectible rocks and minerals, including:

- **Jasper:** A hard, multicolored variety of quartz prized for its beauty and durability.
- **Agate:** A banded variety of chalcedony with a glassy luster, often found in colorful forms.
- **Petrified wood:** Fossilized trees that have been replaced by minerals, preserving their natural textures.
- **Opals:** These can be rare but can be found in some areas, known for their play-of-color iridescence.

Always check current regulations and obtain any permits required by the land manager for rockhounding in specific locations. Responsible collection practices are crucial: take only what you need and leave no trace.

Best Tools for Rockhounding:

- Sturdy hiking boots with good ankle support
- Safety glasses (essential for using a rock hammer)
- Rock hammer (use with caution and consider local regulations)
- Hand trowel (optional)
- Sifting screen (optional, for sifting through loose material)
- Magnifying glass (optional, for examining smaller specimens)
- GPS device or map and compass (recommended for navigation)

Marlow's Idaho Rock Hounding Guide Book 2024

Best Vehicles for Accessing and Traversing the Area:

A high-clearance vehicle (SUV, truck) is strongly recommended due to rough and unpaved roads, especially for accessing BLM Road 301.

Accommodation Options (near Idaho County):

- **Camping:** Several campgrounds are scattered across public lands. Check with the BLM or Forest Service for availability and regulations.
- **Lodging:** Limited lodging options are available near Crater Peak. Consider nearby towns like Grangeville or Salmon for hotels or motels.

Recommended Stops and Attractions (within Idaho County):

- **Nez Perce National Historical Park:** (208) 843-7700, scattered locations throughout the Nez Perce homeland. Offers historical sites and cultural centers commemorating the Nez Perce people. Consult park websites or maps for locations (https://www.nps.gov/Nezperce/index.htm).
- **Salmon River:** Renowned for whitewater rafting adventures. Look for outfitters in nearby towns like Grangeville or Salmon.

Directions to the Site (Specific Access Point):

As mentioned earlier, specific directions depend on your chosen access point. Utilize online maps, Forest Service resources, or BLM websites to find driving directions. Look for signage upon arrival.

Directions to the Site (Specific Access Point):

- Look for signage upon arrival to navigate further within the area. Be prepared for limited cellphone service in remote locations. Download maps for offline use if necessary.

Sun Exposure and Availability of Shade:

Sun exposure can vary depending on the specific location around Crater Peak. Open areas near ridges and slopes receive full sun. Denser forested areas might offer more shade. Sun protection gear (hat, sunscreen) is recommended.

Soil Types:

The soil types around Crater Peak can be categorized as follows:

- **Mountain soils:** Well-drained soils with a mix of mineral components and decomposed organic matter, typical on forested slopes.
- **Alluvial deposits:** Loose deposits of gravel, cobbles, and sand left behind by streams, potentially containing fossils or gemstones.

Rock Types:

The underlying bedrock in the Crater Peak area consists mainly of igneous rocks:

- **Basalt:** A dark-colored volcanic rock, most common in the region.
- **Granite:** A lighter-colored, coarse-grained intrusive igneous rock, may be present in some areas.

Marlow's Idaho Rock Hounding Guide Book 2024

Popularity of the Site:

The popularity of Crater Peak can vary depending on the season and specific access point. Summer weekends might see more visitors, particularly rockhounds and hikers. Weekdays and areas requiring a longer trek are likely less crowded.

Where to Buy Essential Supplies (near Idaho County):

- **Grangeville** (closest major town):
    - **Grangeville Hardware and Supply:** (208) 983-2411, 104 S Main St, Grangeville, ID 83539 (45.9233° N, 116.0122° W). Offers tools, safety equipment, and basic supplies.
    - **Walmart:** (208) 983-1110, 1400 W Main St, Grangeville, ID 83539 (45.9233° N, 116.0300° W). Provides a wider selection of supplies, including camping gear, snacks, and water.

OROFINO CREEK

Pierce, Idaho, nestled in Clearwater County, offers a glimpse into Idaho's rich past and a gateway to outdoor adventures. This guide focuses on exploring Pierce responsibly and appreciating its unique character.

Detailed Route Description:

Reaching Pierce is straightforward:

1. **Identify Your Route:** Pierce is conveniently located near US Highway 11, designated as the Gold Rush Historic Byway. Utilize online maps or GPS for directions from your starting point.

2. **Entering Pierce:** The town itself is relatively small. Look for signage upon arrival, and designated parking areas might be available near points of interest.

Land Type:

Pierce is situated within Clearwater County. The surrounding land can be categorized as:

- Private Property (within the town limits)
- Public Land (managed by the Forest Service or Bureau of Land Management in surrounding areas)

County:

Clearwater County, Idaho

GPS Location (town center):

46.6833° N, 115.4667° W (This is a general indicator due to the town's extent)

Best Season to Visit:

- **Spring (April-May):** Enjoy pleasant weather for exploring and outdoor activities.
- **Fall (September-October):** Experience vibrant fall foliage and comfortable temperatures.
- **Summer (June-August):** While warm, summer offers opportunities for festivals and events (check for specific dates). Winter can bring snowfall, limiting accessibility.

Land Manager (for Public Lands surrounding Pierce):

- Forest Service (FS) (https://www.fs.usda.gov/)

- Bureau of Land Management (BLM) (https://www.blm.gov/) (depending on the specific area)

Materials NOT Found While Rockhounding (within Town Limits):

Rockhounding is not permitted within the town limits of Pierce.

Best Tools for Exploring Pierce:

- Comfortable walking shoes
- Camera (to capture the historic charm)
- Light backpack with water and snacks (optional)
- Local history guide or brochure (available from the Pierce Area Chamber of Commerce or visitor center)

Best Vehicle for Accessing Pierce:

A standard vehicle suffices to reach Pierce via US Highway 11.

Accommodation Options (near Pierce):

- Lodging options are limited within Pierce itself. Consider nearby towns like Orofino or Grangeville:
    - Hotels: Search online booking platforms for hotels in Orofino or Grangeville.
    - Motels: Motels offer a convenient option near Pierce.
    - Camping: Campgrounds are available in the surrounding Clearwater National Forest. Contact the Forest Service for details.

Recommended Stops and Attractions (within Pierce):

- **Pierce Courthouse:** (402 S Main St, Pierce, ID 83547) - Idaho's oldest public building, steeped in history and a designated landmark.
- **Pierce Free Public Library:** (408 S Main St, Pierce, ID 83547) - A treasure trove of local history and a resource for exploring the area further.
- **Gold Rush Interpretive Kiosk:** Located along the main street, this kiosk showcases the town's rich gold mining past through artwork and historical information.

Directions to the Site (Specific Location):

Specific directions depend on your chosen starting point. Utilize online maps or GPS with "Pierce, Idaho" as your destination. Look for signage upon arrival, especially if visiting the Pierce Courthouse or Free Public Library.

Sun Exposure and Availability of Shade:

- Within the town limits, expect varying sun exposure depending on the street layout and presence of trees.
- Surrounding public lands might offer more shade, especially in forested areas.

Soil Types (surrounding areas):

The soil types surrounding Pierce can vary depending on the specific location but generally include:

- Mollisols (fertile soils with a dark-colored upper layer) in some areas with good vegetation cover.
- Alfisols (well-developed soils with a reddish brown upper layer) in drier areas with some vegetation.

Rock Types (surrounding areas):

The dominant rock type in the Pierce area is granite, forming the core of the surrounding mountains.

Popularity of the Site:

Pierce is a relatively small town with a loyal local community. Tourist traffic can pick up during peak seasons (spring and fall) due to its historical significance and location along the Gold Rush Historic Byway.

MUSSELSHELL

Musselshell, Idaho, isn't a town itself, but a location encompassing historical significance and scenic landscapes. Here's a guide to navigate this area responsibly and appreciate its unique offerings.

Detailed Route Description:

Reaching Musselshell depends on what aspect interests you most:

- **Musselshell Meadow (historical and recreational site):**
    1. **Identify Your Starting Point:** Musselshell Meadow is located approximately 30 minutes southeast of Pierce, Idaho. Utilize online maps or GPS for directions from your starting point.
    2. **Follow Signs:** Look for signs along North Main Street in Pierce directing you towards Pierce Street East. This road becomes Musselshell Road, which leads to the Musselshell Meadow parking area.

Land Type:

The land type around Musselshell, Idaho, varies:

- **Public Land (managed by the Nez Perce National Historical Park or Clearwater National Forest):** Musselshell Meadow falls under this category.
- **Private Property:** Be aware of private land ownership, especially in surrounding areas.

County:

The county depends on the specific location:

- **Clearwater County:** If visiting Musselshell Meadow, this is the most likely county.

GPS Location:

46°22′14″N, 114°52′23″W (This is a general indicator due to the meadow's extent)

Best Season for Rockhounding:

Rockhounding regulations can vary depending on the specific land manager. Generally, it's not a permitted activity at Musselshell Meadow due to its historical significance. The focus here is on appreciating the cultural and natural heritage.

Land Manager:

- Nez Perce National Historical Park (https://www.nps.gov/nepe/) or Clearwater National Forest (https://www.fs.usda.gov/nezperceclearwater) (depending on the specific location)

Marlow's Idaho Rock Hounding Guide Book 2024

Materials NOT Found While Rockhounding:

Rockhounding is not permitted at Musselshell Meadow. Respect the cultural and historical significance of the area.

Best Tools for Exploring the Area:

- Sturdy hiking boots with good ankle support
- Daypack with water, sunscreen, hat, and insect repellent
- Camera
- Map and compass or GPS device (recommended for navigation)

Best Vehicles for Accessing and Traversing the Area:

- **Musselshell Meadow:** A high-clearance vehicle might be helpful, especially after heavy rain, due to potential unpaved sections on the access road.

Accommodation Options (near Musselshell Meadow):

- Lodging options are limited near Musselshell Meadow itself. Consider nearby towns like Pierce, Orofino, or Grangeville:
    - Hotels: Search online booking platforms for hotels in these towns.
    - Motels: Motels offer a convenient option near Musselshell Meadow.
    - Camping: Campgrounds are available in the surrounding Clearwater National Forest. Contact the Forest Service (https://www.fs.usda.gov/ipnf) for details.

Recommended Stops and Attractions (on the Way or Nearby):

- **Nez Perce National Historical Park Visitor Center (Lapwai, ID):** (46.2900° N, 117.0122° W) Learn about the rich history and culture of the Nez Perce people. Features exhibits, films, and a bookstore. Identify the visitor center by signage depicting the park logo.
- **Lewiston (ID):** (46.4350° N, 117.0186° W) Explore Lewis and Clark State Park, with its reconstructed Fort Nez Perce, or delve into Nez Perce culture at the Nez Perce National Historical Park Spalding Unit (further north). Identify these locations by signage or consult online resources for descriptions.

Directions to the Site:

Follow the detailed route description provided earlier. Look for signs along the way, especially after turning onto Musselshell Road from Pierce.

Sun Exposure and Availability of Shade:

- Expect some sun exposure in open meadow areas.
- Denser forested areas bordering the meadow can offer shade.

Soil Types:

The soil type at Musselshell Meadow is likely an Alfisol, a well-developed soil with a reddish-brown upper layer, suitable for supporting some vegetation.

Rock Types:

Musselshell Meadow enjoys moderate popularity. It's a significant cultural site for the Nez Perce Tribe and attracts visitors interested in history and outdoor recreation.

However, it doesn't experience the same level of crowds as some national parks.

Where to Buy Essential Supplies:

- **Limited options near Musselshell Meadow:** Due to its remote location, essential supplies might be scarce nearby.
- **Pierce, Idaho (approximately 30 minutes northwest):**
    - Pierce General Store (404 S Main St, Pierce, ID 83547) - Offers a limited selection of groceries, camping essentials, and outdoor gear. Identify the store by its signage.

LOLO PASS

Lolo Pass, Idaho, nestled within the Lewis Range, offers breathtaking mountain scenery and a significant chapter in Pacific Northwest history. This guide equips you for a responsible and enriching visit.

Detailed Route Description:

Reaching Lolo Pass depends on your starting point:

1. **Identify Your Access Point:** There are two primary access points:
    - **Western Approach (from Missoula, Montana):** Take I-90 west for approximately 25 miles to exit 130. Follow signs for US-12 W/Lewis and Clark Highway for about 30 miles to reach Lolo Pass Visitor Center.
    - **Eastern Approach (from Grangeville, Idaho):** Take US-95 S for about 37 miles to Grangeville. Follow signs for US-12 E towards

Lolo for approximately 42 miles until reaching Lolo Pass Visitor Center.
2. **Look Up Driving Directions:** Utilize online maps or GPS for specific directions based on your chosen access point. Be aware that winter weather can sometimes close the pass.

Land Type:

- Public Land (managed by the Nez Perce-Clearwater National Forests)

County:

- Idaho County, Idaho (although the pass itself straddles the Montana-Idaho border)

GPS Location (Lolo Pass Visitor Center):

46°23′31″N, 114°40′12″W (This is a general indicator due to the extent of the pass)

Best Season to Visit:

- **Summer (June-August):** Enjoy warm weather for hiking, scenic drives, and exploring historical sites. However, expect more crowds.
- **Fall (September-October):** Witness vibrant fall foliage with comfortable temperatures and potentially fewer crowds.
- **Spring (April-May):** Offers opportunities for wildflower viewing and pleasant weather, but be aware of lingering snow at higher elevations. Winter brings snowfall, making the pass inaccessible by vehicle.

Land Manager:

- Nez Perce-Clearwater National Forests (https://www.fs.usda.gov/nezperceclearwater)

Materials NOT Found While Rockhounding:

Rockhounding is not permitted within the immediate vicinity of Lolo Pass due to its ecological and historical significance. The focus here is on appreciating the natural beauty and cultural heritage.

Best Tools for Exploring the Area:

- Sturdy hiking boots with good ankle support
- Daypack with water, sunscreen, hat, insect repellent, and snacks
- Camera
- Map and compass or GPS device (recommended for navigation, especially on trails)
- Nez Perce National Historical Park brochures or guide (available at visitor centers)

Best Vehicles for Accessing and Traversing the Area:

- A standard vehicle is sufficient during the summer months.
- During spring or fall, a high-clearance vehicle might be advisable due to potential lingering snow or muddy conditions.
- Winter access is not recommended due to snowfall road closures.

Accommodation Options (near Lolo Pass):

- **Western Approach (Missoula, Montana):** Offers a wider variety of options:

- - Hotels: Search online booking platforms for hotels in Missoula.
  - Motels: Motels provide a convenient option near I-90.
  - Camping: Campgrounds are available within the Lolo National Forest. Contact the Forest Service for details (https://www.fs.usda.gov/lolo).
- **Eastern Approach (Grangeville, Idaho):** Lodging options are limited:
  - Hotels: A few hotels are available in Grangeville.
  - Camping: Campgrounds are also available near Grangeville. Explore options online or contact the Idaho Department of Parks and Recreation (https://parksandrecreation.idaho.gov/).

Recommended Stops and Attractions (on the Way or Nearby):

- **Lolo Pass Visitor Center (Idaho):** Learn about the Lewis and Clark Expedition's passage through the area and the Nez Perce Tribe's history. Identify the center by signage depicting the Nez Perce-Clearwater National Forests logo.
- **National Historic Trail Interpretative Center (Montana):** (46°24′11″N, 114°39′21″W) Explore interactive exhibits showcasing the Lewis and Clark Trail. Look for signage with the Lewis and Clark Trail logo.
- **The Smokestack Restaurant (Idaho):** (46°23′21″N, 114°40′07″W) Enjoy a historic dining experience in a restored 1930s lodge (check for seasonal hours). Identify the restaurant by its distinctive signage.

Directions to the Site (Lolo Pass Visitor Center):

- **Western Approach (from Missoula, Montana):**
  1. Follow the detailed route description provided earlier, taking I-90 west and then US-12 W/Lewis and Clark Highway.
  2. Look for signs for the Lolo Pass Visitor Center as you approach the summit of the pass. The center will be on the right side of the road.
- **Eastern Approach (from Grangeville, Idaho):**
  1. Follow the route description provided earlier, taking US-95 S and then US-12 E towards Lolo.
  2. As you near the summit of the pass, watch for signs for the Lolo Pass Visitor Center on the left side of the road.

Sun Exposure and Availability of Shade:

Sun exposure at Lolo Pass varies depending on the location and time of day. Here's a general idea:

- **Open areas:** Expect full sun exposure during midday hours.
- **Trails:** Forested sections along trails can offer shade.
- **Lolo Pass Visitor Center:** The surrounding area has a mix of open areas and trees, providing some shade.

Soil Types (in the area):

The soil types around Lolo Pass can vary depending on the specific location but generally include:

- **Inceptisols:** Young soils with minimal development, found on steeper slopes.
- **Spodosols:** Ash-influenced soils with a characteristic dark-colored upper layer, present in some areas.

Marlow's Idaho Rock Hounding Guide Book 2024

Rock Types (in the area):

The dominant rock type in the Lolo Pass area is granitic rock, forming the core of the surrounding mountains.

Popularity of the Site:

Lolo Pass enjoys significant popularity, especially during summer months. It's a popular destination for scenic drives, historical exploration, and outdoor recreation.

Where to Buy Essential Supplies (around Lolo Pass):

- **Eastern Approach (Grangeville, Idaho):** Options are limited:
  - Grangeville offers a limited selection of stores. Consider stopping at a grocery store in Missoula if traveling from the east.

LOWER CLEARWATER

The Lower Clearwater River region in Idaho isn't a single location but encompasses a scenic stretch of the Clearwater River and surrounding landscapes. This guide equips you for exploring this diverse area responsibly.

Detailed Route Description:

Reaching the Lower Clearwater River region depends on your chosen access point:

1. **Identify Your Destination:** The Lower Clearwater River flows through several counties in north-central Idaho. Popular access points include:
   - **Grangeville (Idaho County):** A convenient starting point for exploring the western section.

- **Kooskia (Idaho County):** Offers access to the middle stretches of the river.
- **Lewiston (Nez Perce County):** Provides a gateway to the eastern portion.
2. **Refine Your Search:** Utilize online maps or resources to identify specific points of interest along the Lower Clearwater River that align with your interests (e.g., boat launches, campgrounds, hiking trails).
3. **Driving Directions:** Utilize online maps or GPS for specific directions to your chosen access point. Be aware that some remote areas might require a high-clearance vehicle, especially after heavy rain.

Land Type:

The land surrounding the Lower Clearwater River varies:

- Public Land (managed by the Nez Perce National Forest or Bureau of Land Management)
- Private Property (especially in some agricultural areas)

County:

The county depends on the specific location you choose to access the Lower Clearwater River. It can include:

- Idaho County
- Lewis County
- Nez Perce County

GPS Location (General Area):

Due to the river's extent, a specific location cannot be provided. However, reference points include:

Marlow's Idaho Rock Hounding Guide Book 2024

- Grangeville, Idaho (46.0388° N, 116.0331° W) - Western access point
- Kooskia, Idaho (46.1333° N, 115.5000° W) - Central access point
- Lewiston, Idaho (46.4350° N, 117.0186° W) - Eastern access point

Best Season for Rockhounding:

Rockhounding regulations can vary depending on the specific land manager. Generally, it's not a permitted activity along the entire Lower Clearwater River due to environmental considerations. Focus on enjoying the scenery and responsible recreation.

Land Manager (if Public Land):

- Nez Perce National Forest (https://www.fs.usda.gov/nezperceclearwater) for some areas
- Bureau of Land Management (BLM) (https://www.blm.gov/) for some areas (check designated websites)

Materials NOT Found While Rockhounding:

Rockhounding is not recommended near the Lower Clearwater River. The focus is on appreciating the natural environment and respecting wildlife habitats.

Best Tools for Exploring the Area:

- Sturdy hiking boots with good ankle support (if venturing on trails)
- Daypack with water, sunscreen, hat, insect repellent, and snacks
- Camera

- Kayak or canoe (with proper permits and safety knowledge if planning water exploration)
- Fishing gear (with proper licenses if applicable)
- Map and compass or GPS device (recommended for navigation, especially in remote areas)

Best Vehicles for Accessing and Traversing the Area:

- A standard vehicle can suffice for reaching most towns along the Lower Clearwater River.
- High-clearance vehicle might be necessary for accessing some remote areas, unpaved roads, or during muddy conditions.

Accommodation Options (near the Lower Clearwater River):

- Lodging options vary depending on the specific location:
  - **Grangeville:** Offers a limited selection of hotels and motels. Consider camping options within the Nez Perce National Forest.
  - **Kooskia:** Lodging options are scarce. Explore camping opportunities within the surrounding public lands.
  - **Lewiston:** Provides a wider range of hotels, motels, and campgrounds near the river.

Recommended Stops and Attractions (on the Way or Nearby):

- **Nez Perce National Historical Park (Lapwai, ID):** (46.2900° N, 117.0122° W) Learn about the rich history and culture of the Nez Perce people. Features exhibits, films, and a bookstore. Identify the visitor center by signage depicting the park logo.

- **Hells Canyon National Recreation Area (Riggins, ID):** (45.4231° N, 116.9203° W) - A scenic area offering stunning vistas of the deepest river gorge in North America.

- **Kooskia Ranger Station (Kooskia, ID):** (46.1322° N, 115.4992° W) - This ranger station provides valuable information about the surrounding Nez Perce National Forest, including maps, camping permits, and recommendations for outdoor activities. Look for signage depicting the Nez Perce National Forest logo.

- **Lewiston Orchards (Lewiston, ID):** Explore this unique agricultural area, known for its apple production and scenic drives.

- **White Bird Battlefield (Grangeville, ID):** (45.3739° N, 116.2200° W) - This National Historic Landmark commemorates the Nez Perce War. An interpretive center offers insights into the conflict. Identify the site by signage depicting the National Park Service logo.

Directions to the Site (Specific Location):

As mentioned earlier, the Lower Clearwater River covers a vast area. It's crucial to choose a specific access point (town or boat launch) based on your interests. Utilize online maps or GPS with your chosen access point as the destination. Look for signs upon arrival, especially when visiting campgrounds, ranger stations, or historical sites.

Sun Exposure and Availability of Shade:

Sun exposure along the Lower Clearwater River varies depending on the time of day and specific location. Here's a general idea:

- **Open areas:** Expect full sun exposure during midday hours, especially on beaches or while on the water.
- **Riverbanks with trees:** These areas can offer pockets of shade, particularly in the afternoons.
- **Hiking trails:** Forested sections can provide shade, but be aware of open areas.

Soil Types (in the area):

The soil types surrounding the Lower Clearwater River can vary depending on the specific location but generally include:

- **Alfisols:** Well-developed soils with a reddish-brown upper layer, suitable for some vegetation growth.
- **Mollisols:** Fertile soils with a dark-colored upper layer, found in some areas with good vegetation cover.

Rock Types (in the area):

The dominant rock type in the Lower Clearwater River region is granite, forming the core of the surrounding mountains. Basalt and other volcanic rocks might also be present in some areas.

Popularity of the Site:

The popularity of the Lower Clearwater River region varies depending on the specific location and activity.

- **Grangeville and Kooskia:** Attract outdoor enthusiasts seeking a more remote experience.
- **Lewiston:** Sees higher tourist traffic due to its urban center and proximity to Hells Canyon National Recreation Area.

Where to Buy Essential Supplies (around the Lower Clearwater River):

- **Grangeville:** Offers a limited selection of stores. Stock up on essentials before reaching Grangeville, especially if traveling from a larger city.
- **Kooskia:** Grocery and supply options are scarce. Plan accordingly.

SELWAY RIVER

The Selway River, Idaho, isn't a specific location but a 100-mile stretch of pristine wilderness carving through Idaho's mountains. This guide equips you for a responsible and adventurous visit to this unique ecosystem.

Detailed Route Description:

Reaching the Selway River requires careful planning due to its remote location:

1. **Identify Your Access Point:** The Selway River flows through several roadless areas. Public access points are limited:
    - **Paradise Boat Launch (Idaho County):** This boat launch on the Lochsa River provides entry for permitted whitewater rafting trips down the Selway (46°29′21″N, 114°21′42″W).
    - **Moose Creek Campground (Idaho County):** This campground near the Selway-Bitteroot Wilderness border offers a starting point for backpacking adventures (46°12′20″N, 114°12′00″W).
2. **Permits:** Acquire necessary permits for your chosen activity (rafting, backpacking) from the US Forest

Service (https://www.recreation.gov/permits/234624).
3. **Driving Directions:** Utilize online maps or GPS with your chosen access point as the destination. Be aware that the final stretch to trailheads or boat launches might require a high-clearance vehicle, especially after heavy rain.

Land Type:

- Public Land (managed by the Bitterroot National Forest and Nez Perce National Forest)
- Designated Wilderness Area (Selway-Bitterroot Wilderness)

County:

The Selway River flows through portions of Idaho County and Missoula County, Montana. However, most public access points are in Idaho County.

GPS Location (General Area):

Due to the river's extent, a specific location cannot be provided. Reference points include:

- Paradise Boat Launch (46°29'21"N, 114°21'42"W)
- Moose Creek Campground (46°12'20"N, 114°12'00"W)

Best Season for Rockhounding:

Rockhounding is not permitted within the Selway-Bitterroot Wilderness due to its pristine character. The focus here is on enjoying the wilderness experience and respecting the natural environment.

Land Manager:

- Bitterroot National Forest (https://www.fs.usda.gov/recarea/bitterroot) and Nez Perce National Forest (https://www.fs.usda.gov/nezperceclearwater)

Materials NOT Found While Rockhounding:

Rockhounding is prohibited. Appreciate the natural beauty of the river and its surroundings.

Best Tools for Exploring the Area:

- Sturdy hiking boots with good ankle support
- Backpack with ample water, sunscreen, insect repellent, navigation tools (map, compass, or GPS device), and emergency supplies
- First-aid kit
- Tent and sleeping gear (for backpacking trips)
- Whitewater rafting gear and expertise (for rafting trips)
- Leave No Trace principles and wilderness ethics knowledge

Best Vehicles for Accessing and Traversing the Area:

- High-clearance vehicle with four-wheel drive is highly recommended, especially during spring or after heavy rains.
- Some roads leading to access points might require off-road driving experience.

Accommodation Options (near the Selway River):

- Lodging options are limited due to the remote location:

- Campgrounds: Several Forest Service campgrounds are scattered around the periphery of the Selway-Bitterroot Wilderness. Make reservations in advance, especially during peak season.
- Backcountry camping: Permits are required for wilderness camping.

Recommended Stops and Attractions (on the Way or Nearby):

- **Kooskia Ranger Station (Kooskia, ID):** (46.1322° N, 115.4992° W) This ranger station provides valuable information about the Selway-Bitterroot Wilderness, including permits, maps, and safety tips. Identify the station by signage depicting the Nez Perce National Forest logo.
- **Lolo Pass (Idaho/Montana):** (46°23′31″N, 114°40′12″W) A scenic mountain pass with historical significance along the Lewis and Clark Trail. Look for signs or consult online resources for identification.
- **Hells Canyon National Recreation Area (Riggins, ID):** (45.4231° N, 116.9203° W) Explore the deepest river gorge in North America, offering stunning scenery (outside the Selway River area).

Directions to the Site (Specific Location):

As mentioned earlier, the Selway River is a lengthy stretch. Specific directions depend on your chosen access point:

- **Paradise Boat Launch:** Utilize online maps or GPS with "Paradise Boat Launch, Idaho" as the destination. Be aware that the final stretch might require a high-clearance vehicle and off-road driving experience.
- **Moose Creek Campground:** Utilize online maps or GPS with "Moose Creek Campground, Idaho" as the

destination. The road leading to the campground might require a high-clearance vehicle, especially during muddy conditions.

Sun Exposure and Availability of Shade:

Sun exposure along the Selway River varies depending on the time of day, specific location, and the presence of trees. Here's a general idea:

- **Open areas (beaches, riverbanks):** Expect full sun exposure during midday hours.
- **Dense forests:** These areas can offer significant shade, especially along trails.
- **Open meadows within the forest:** Expect sun exposure with pockets of shade offered by scattered trees.

Soil Types (in the area):

The soil types surrounding the Selway River can vary depending on the specific location but generally include:

- **Inceptisols:** Young soils with minimal development, found on steeper slopes near the river.
- **Spodosols:** Ash-influenced soils with a characteristic dark-colored upper layer, present in some forested areas.

Rock Types (in the area):

The dominant rock type in the Selway River region is granitic rock, forming the core of the surrounding mountains. Basalt and other volcanic rocks might also be present in some areas.

Marlow's Idaho Rock Hounding Guide Book 2024

Popularity of the Site:

The Selway River experiences moderate popularity due to its remote location. It attracts adventure seekers, whitewater rafters, and experienced backpackers seeking a pristine wilderness experience.

Where to Buy Essential Supplies (around the Selway River):

- **Grangeville, Idaho (approximately 45 minutes west of Moose Creek Campground):** Offers a limited selection of stores. Stock up on essentials before reaching Grangeville, especially if traveling from a larger city.
- **Lewiston, Idaho (approximately 1.5 hours west of Paradise Boat Launch):** Provides a wider range of stores compared to Grangeville.

COTTONWOOD

Cottonwood, Idaho, nestled in Idaho County on the Camas Prairie, offers a surprising blend of rural charm and historical intrigue. This guide equips you for a fulfilling visit to this unique destination.

Detailed Route Description:

Reaching Cottonwood is straightforward:

- **From Lewiston, Idaho (westbound):** Take US-95 N for approximately 37 miles. Watch for signs for Cottonwood and turn right onto ID-14 W. Continue for 2 miles until reaching the town center.
- **From Grangeville, Idaho (eastbound):** Take US-95 S for approximately 45 miles. Watch for signs for

Cottonwood and turn left onto ID-14 W. Continue for 2 miles until reaching the town center.

Land Type:

- Private Property (within the town boundaries)
- Public Land (managed by the Bureau of Land Management or Nez Perce National Forest in surrounding areas)

County:

Idaho County

GPS Location (Town Center):

46°03′08″N, 116°21′02″W

Best Season to Visit:

- **Summer (June-August):** Enjoy warm weather for outdoor activities, festivals, and exploring historical sites. However, expect more crowds.
- **Spring (April-May):** Witness wildflowers and comfortable temperatures, with potentially fewer crowds.
- **Fall (September-October):** Experience vibrant fall foliage and pleasant weather. Be aware of occasional hunting activity in surrounding public lands.
- **Winter (November-March):** Offers fewer crowds and a chance to experience a winter wonderland, but some businesses might have limited hours.

Land Manager (for surrounding Public Lands):

- Bureau of Land Management (BLM) (https://www.blm.gov/)

- Nez Perce National Forest (https://www.fs.usda.gov/nezperceclearwater) (check designated websites for specific areas)

Materials NOT Found While Rockhounding (within Town Limits):

Rockhounding is not permitted within the town boundaries of Cottonwood.

Rockhounding in Surrounding Areas:

- **Public lands** managed by the BLM or Nez Perce National Forest might offer rockhounding opportunities. However, always check regulations and obtain any necessary permits before collecting rocks or minerals.

Best Tools for Exploring the Area (within Town):

- Comfortable walking shoes
- Camera
- Local shops and brochures offer historical and cultural insights

Best Tools for Exploring Surrounding Public Lands:

- Sturdy hiking boots with good ankle support (if venturing on trails)
- Map and compass or GPS device (recommended for navigation)
- Rockhounding tools (if permitted in specific areas) - Consult BLM or Forest Service websites for guidance

Marlow's Idaho Rock Hounding Guide Book 2024

Best Vehicles for Accessing and Traversing the Area:

- A standard vehicle is sufficient for navigating Cottonwood's streets.
- High-clearance vehicle might be advisable for exploring some dirt roads or trails in surrounding public lands.

Accommodation Options (in Cottonwood):

- Lodging options are limited:
  - Cottonwood Motor Inn (102 S Main St, Cottonwood, ID 83522) - Offers basic motel accommodations (call 208-962-3331 for details). Identify by signage.
  - Consider alternative lodging options in Grangeville or Lewiston for a wider variety.

Recommended Stops and Attractions (in Cottonwood):

- **Dog Bark Park Inn (Cottonwood, Idaho):** (46°03′11″N, 116°20′58″W) This quirky hotel, shaped like a giant beagle, offers a unique lodging experience and photo opportunity. Look for the large beagle structure.
- **The Camas Prairie Railroad Depot & Museum (Cottonwood, Idaho):** (46°03′10″N, 116°20′55″W) Learn about the history of the Camas Prairie Railroad and its significance to the region. Look for signage depicting the museum logo.
- **Monastery of St. Gertrude (Cottonwood, Idaho):** (46°02′45″N, 116°22′01″W) This historic Benedictine monastery offers beautiful architecture and peaceful grounds (check for open hours). Identify by the prominent monastery building.

Sun Exposure and Availability of Shade (in Cottonwood):

- **Main Street:** Sidewalks offer some shade from buildings during the afternoons, but expect sun exposure in open areas.
- **Parks:** Cottonwood Park and Lions Club Park provide shade from mature trees during midday hours.
- **Historical Sites:** The Monastery of St. Gertrude offers shaded areas within its courtyards, while the Camas Prairie Railroad Depot & Museum has limited shade in its immediate surroundings.

Soil Types (in the area):

The dominant soil type in the Cottonwood area is:

- **Mollisols:** Fertile soils with a dark-colored upper layer, suitable for agriculture, which is a prominent industry in the surrounding Camas Prairie.

Rock Types (in the area):

The local geology consists mainly of:

- **Sedimentary rocks:** These layered rocks, formed from deposited sediments, are prevalent in the Camas Prairie.

Popularity of the Site:

Cottonwood experiences moderate visitor traffic, particularly during summer months. It attracts those seeking a charming small-town atmosphere, historical sites, and a base for exploring the surrounding Camas Prairie.

ELK CITY

Elk City, Idaho, nestled in Idaho County, offers a captivating blend of scenic beauty, rich mining history, and outdoor adventure. This guide equips you for a memorable visit to this off-the-beaten-path destination.

Detailed Route Description:

Reaching Elk City requires navigating mountain roads:

- **From Grangeville, Idaho (eastern approach):** Take US-95 S for approximately 42 miles. Turn left onto ID-14 E and continue for about 50 miles. Watch for signs for Elk City. (Total distance: 92 miles)
- **From Missoula, Montana (western approach):** Take I-90 W for approximately 110 miles. Take Exit 319 and follow signs for US-12 W/Lewis and Clark Highway for 83 miles. Watch for signs for Elk City. (Total distance: 193 miles)

Land Type:

- Public Land (managed by the Nez Perce National Forest)

County:

Idaho County

GPS Location (Town Center):

45°49'37"N, 115°26'12"W

Best Season for Rockhounding (with Caution):

Rockhounding opportunities in Elk City are limited due to its location within the Nez Perce National Forest. Forest Service regulations generally prohibit removing natural resources like rocks or minerals. However, with proper permits and knowledge, some agate and jasper collecting might be possible in specific designated areas. Always check with the Nez Perce National Forest office (https://www.fs.usda.gov/nezperceclearwater) for current regulations and responsible rockhounding practices.

Land Manager:

Nez Perce National Forest (https://www.fs.usda.gov/nezperceclearwater)

Materials Potentially Found While Rockhounding (with Permit):

- Agate
- Jasper (verification through the Forest Service is recommended)

Best Tools for Rockhounding (if permitted):

- Rock hammer
- Safety glasses
- Collecting bag
- Sifting tools (if applicable)
- GPS device (to verify permitted areas)

Best Vehicles for Accessing and Traversing the Area:

- High-clearance vehicle with four-wheel drive is strongly recommended, especially during spring or after heavy rains. Mountain roads can be narrow, winding, and unpaved in some sections.

Accommodation Options (in Elk City):

- Lodging options are limited:
    - Elk City Hotel (no website available). Contact information might be available through online searches (be cautious when booking online). Identify by signage upon arrival.
    - Consider camping options within the Nez Perce National Forest. Make reservations in advance, especially during peak season.

Recommended Stops and Attractions (on the Way or Nearby):

- **Kooskia Ranger Station (Kooskia, ID):** (46.1322° N, 115.4992° W) This ranger station provides valuable information about the surrounding Nez Perce National Forest, including camping permits, road conditions, and potential rockhounding opportunities (with permits). Look for signage depicting the Nez Perce National Forest logo.
- **Nez Perce National Historical Park (Lapwai, ID):** (46.2900° N, 117.0122° W) Learn about the rich history and culture of the Nez Perce people (located further west on your drive from Grangeville). Features exhibits, films, and a bookstore. Identify the visitor center by signage depicting the National Park Service logo.

Directions to the Site (Specific Location):

Elk City is a small town. Once on the main road (ID-14), landmarks are easily recognizable. Utilize online maps or GPS with "Elk City, Idaho" as your destination. Be prepared for switchbacks and potentially challenging road conditions, especially on the western approach from Montana.

Sun Exposure and Availability of Shade:

Sun exposure in Elk City varies depending on the time of day and location. Here's a general idea:

- **Open areas (streets, some campsites):** Expect full sun exposure during midday hours.
- **Wooded areas:** These areas offer shade, particularly along trails or near the river.
- **Mountain slopes:** Sun exposure will vary depending on the slope's orientation.

Soil Types (in the area):

The dominant soil type in the Elk City area is:

- **Inceptisols:** Young soils with minimal development, found on steeper slopes and mountainous terrain.

Rock Types (in the area):

The dominant rock type in the Elk City area is:

- **Granitic rock:** This igneous rock forms the core of the surrounding mountains and is visible in outcrops and along riverbeds.

Popularity of the Site:

Elk City experiences moderate seasonal popularity. It attracts history buffs, outdoor enthusiasts seeking hiking and camping adventures, and hunters during specific seasons. Be aware of hunting regulations if visiting during fall.

Marlow's Idaho Rock Hounding Guide Book 2024

WHITE BIRD

White Bird, Idaho, nestled in Idaho County, offers a captivating blend of Western hospitality, stunning scenery, and a rich history. This guide equips you for a memorable visit to this hidden gem.

Detailed Route Description:

Reaching White Bird requires navigating scenic country roads:

- **From Grangeville, Idaho (westbound):** Take US-95 S for approximately 37 miles. Turn right onto White Bird Road and follow signs for White Bird (approximately 12 miles).
- **From Lewiston, Idaho (eastbound):** Take US-95 N for approximately 42 miles. Turn left onto White Bird Road and follow signs for White Bird (approximately 12 miles).

Land Type:

- Private Property (within the town boundaries)
- Public Land (managed by the Bureau of Land Management or Nez Perce National Forest in surrounding areas)

County:

Idaho County

GPS Location (Town Center):

45°45'40"N, 116°18'06"W

Marlow's Idaho Rock Hounding Guide Book 2024

Best Season to Visit:

- **Spring (April-May):** Enjoy pleasant weather, blooming wildflowers, and potentially fewer crowds.
- **Summer (June-August):** Ideal for outdoor activities like hiking, fishing, and whitewater rafting. Expect warmer temperatures and higher visitor traffic.
- **Fall (September-October):** Witness vibrant fall foliage and comfortable temperatures. Be aware of occasional hunting activity in surrounding public lands.
- **Winter (November-March):** Offers a peaceful winter experience, but some businesses might have limited hours and roads could be icy.

Land Manager (for surrounding Public Lands):

- Bureau of Land Management (BLM) (https://www.blm.gov/)
- Nez Perce National Forest (https://www.fs.usda.gov/nezperceclearwater) (check designated websites for specific areas)

Materials NOT Found While Rockhounding (within Town Limits):

Rockhounding is not permitted within the town boundaries of White Bird.

Rockhounding in Surrounding Areas:

- Public lands managed by the BLM or Nez Perce National Forest might offer rockhounding opportunities. However, always check regulations and obtain any necessary permits before collecting rocks or minerals.

Best Tools for Exploring the Town:

- Comfortable walking shoes
- Camera
- Local shops and brochures offer historical and cultural insights

Best Tools for Exploring Surrounding Public Lands:

- Sturdy hiking boots with good ankle support (if venturing on trails)
- Map and compass or GPS device (recommended for navigation)
- Rockhounding tools (if permitted in specific areas) - Consult BLM or Forest Service websites for guidance

Best Vehicles for Accessing and Traversing the Area:

- A standard vehicle is sufficient for navigating White Bird's streets.
- High-clearance vehicle might be advisable for exploring dirt roads or trails in surrounding public lands.

Accommodation Options (in White Bird):

- Lodging options are limited:
  - White Bird Lodge (no website available). Contact information might be available through online searches (be cautious when booking online). Identify by signage upon arrival.
  - Consider camping options within the Nez Perce National Forest or explore options in Grangeville (approximately 37 miles west).

Recommended Stops and Attractions (in White Bird):

- **White Bird City Hall (White Bird, Idaho):** (45°45'40"N, 116°18'06"W) This historic building houses the city offices and offers a glimpse into White Bird's past. Look for the prominent building with a clock tower.
- **White Bird Battlefield (Grangeville, ID):** (45.3739° N, 116.2200° W) This National Historic Landmark commemorates the Nez Perce War. An interpretive center offers insights into the conflict (approximately 18 miles west of White Bird). Identify the site by signage depicting the National Park Service logo.
- **Salmon River (White Bird, Idaho):** Enjoy scenic views, fishing opportunities, or whitewater rafting adventures (permits required) on this iconic river. Access points are available near White Bird.

Directions to Specific Locations:

Utilize online maps or GPS with the specific address or name of the attraction you wish to visit (e.g., White Bird Battlefield, Grangeville, ID).

Sun Exposure and Availability of Shade:

- **Main Street:** Sidewalks offer some shade from buildings during the afternoons, but expect sun exposure in open areas.
- **White Bird City Park:** Mature trees provide shade in this park, making it a pleasant spot for a picnic lunch.
- **Salmon River:** The river itself offers limited shade. However, depending on the time of day and location,

surrounding vegetation might provide some shade along the riverbanks.

Soil Types (in the area):

The dominant soil type in the White Bird area is:

- **Alfisols:** These moderately developed soils with reddish-brown subsurface layers are common in the foothills and drier portions of the surrounding landscape.

Rock Types (in the area):

The White Bird area is situated within a geologic zone known for volcanic activity. The dominant rock types include:

- **Basalt:** This dark-colored, volcanic rock forms prominent cliffs and canyon walls in the Salmon River canyon near White Bird.
- **Volcanic ash and breccia:** Deposits of volcanic ash and breccia, formed from volcanic eruptions, are also present in the area.

- **White Bird City Park:** Mature trees provide shade in this park, making it a pleasant spot for a picnic lunch.
- **Salmon River:** The river itself offers limited shade. However, depending on the time of day and location, surrounding vegetation might provide some shade along the riverbanks.

Soil Types (in the area):

The dominant soil type in the White Bird area is:

- **Alfisols:** These moderately developed soils with reddish-brown subsurface layers are common in the foothills and drier portions of the surrounding landscape.

Rock Types (in the area):

The White Bird area is situated within a geologic zone known for volcanic activity. The dominant rock types include:

- **Basalt:** This dark-colored, volcanic rock forms prominent cliffs and canyon walls in the Salmon River canyon near White Bird.
- **Volcanic ash and breccia:** Deposits of volcanic ash and breccia, formed from volcanic eruptions, are also present in the area.

Popularity of the Site:

White Bird experiences moderate visitor traffic, particularly during summer months. It attracts those seeking a charming small-town atmosphere, historical sites, and a base for exploring the surrounding Salmon River canyon and Nez Perce National Forest.

SLATE CREEK

Slate Creek, Idaho, can refer to two locations within the state, offering distinct experiences:

1. Slate Creek (tributary of the Salmon River):

- **Land Type:** Public Land (managed by the Bureau of Land Management)
- **County:** Idaho County

- **GPS Location:** 45°36′43″N, 115°57′00″W (approximate location near confluence with Salmon River)

2. Slate Creek Recreation Site (Lower Salmon River):

- **Land Type:** Developed Recreation Site (managed by the Bureau of Land Management)
- **County:** Idaho County
- **GPS Location:** 45.6461° N, 116.2917° W

Route Description (for both locations):

Reaching Slate Creek requires navigating scenic country roads:

- **From Grangeville, Idaho (westbound):** Take US-95 S for approximately 40 miles. Follow signs for Salmon River Road (ID-14) and continue for about 30 miles. Depending on your destination (tributary or recreation site), consult online maps or GPS for specific directions.

Best Season for Rockhounding:

Rockhounding opportunities are limited due to the location within public lands managed by the BLM. Always check regulations and obtain any necessary permits before collecting rocks or minerals.

Land Manager:

Bureau of Land Management (BLM) (https://www.blm.gov/)

Marlow's Idaho Rock Hounding Guide Book 2024

Materials Potentially Found While Rockhounding (with Permit):

- Verification through the BLM is necessary to determine specific possibilities. Possibilities might include common rock and mineral types found in the area like jasper or agate, but this cannot be confirmed without consulting the BLM office.

Best Tools for Rockhounding (if permitted):

- Rock hammer
- Safety glasses
- Collecting bag
- Sifting tools (if applicable)
- GPS device (to verify permitted areas)

Best Vehicles for Accessing and Traversing the Area:

- High-clearance vehicle with four-wheel drive is strongly recommended, especially during spring or after heavy rains. Mountain roads can be narrow, winding, and unpaved in some sections.

Accommodation Options (around Slate Creek):

- Camping options are available within the surrounding National Forests or BLM-managed lands. Make reservations in advance, especially during peak season.
- Grangeville (approximately 70 miles west) offers limited hotel options.

Recommended Stops and Attractions (on the Way or Nearby):

- **Nez Perce National Historical Park (Lapwai, ID):** (46.2900° N, 117.0122° W) Learn about the rich

history and culture of the Nez Perce people (located further west on your drive from Grangeville). Features exhibits, films, and a bookstore. Identify the visitor center by signage depicting the National Park Service logo (further west on your drive from Grangeville).
- **Salmon River (various access points):** This iconic river offers scenic views, fishing opportunities, or whitewater rafting adventures (permits required). Access points are available along the route to Slate Creek.

Directions to Specific Locations:

Utilize online maps or GPS with "Slate Creek, Idaho" as your destination. Be prepared for switchbacks and potentially challenging road conditions, especially on unpaved sections.

Sun Exposure and Availability of Shade:

Sun exposure in the Slate Creek area varies depending on the location and time of day. Here's a general idea:

- **Open areas (riverbanks, roads):** Expect full sun exposure during midday hours.
- **Wooded areas (along trails):** These areas offer shade, particularly along trails or near the river.
- **Mountain slopes:** Sun exposure will vary depending on the slope's orientation.

Soil Types (in the area):

The dominant soil type in the Slate Creek area is:

- **Inceptisols:** Young soils with minimal development, found on steeper slopes and mountainous terrain.

Rock Types (in the area):

The dominant rock type in the Slate Creek area is:

- **Granitic rock:** This igneous rock forms the core of the surrounding mountains and is visible in outcrops and along riverbeds.

Popularity of the Site:

The popularity of Slate Creek varies depending on the specific location:

- **Slate Creek (tributary):** This area experiences moderate use by experienced kayakers and hikers due to the challenging terrain.
- **Slate Creek Recreation Site:** This developed BLM site experiences higher visitation during summer months for camping, whitewater rafting, and fishing.

LUCILE

Lucile, Idaho, nestled in Idaho County on the banks of the Salmon River, offers a delightful blend of rural charm, historical intrigue, and outdoor recreation opportunities. This guide equips you for a fulfilling visit to this hidden gem.

Detailed Route Description:

Reaching Lucile is straightforward:

- **From Lewiston, Idaho (westbound):** Take US-95 N for approximately 37 miles. Watch for signs for Lucile and turn right onto ID-14 W. Continue for 2 miles until reaching the town center.

- **From Grangeville, Idaho (eastbound):** Take US-95 S for approximately 45 miles. Watch for signs for Lucile and turn left onto ID-14 W. Continue for 2 miles until reaching the town center.

Land Type:

- Private Property (within the town boundaries)
- Public Land (managed by the Bureau of Land Management or Nez Perce National Forest in surrounding areas)

County:

Idaho County

GPS Location (Town Center):

46°03′08″N, 116°21′02″W

Best Season to Visit:

- **Summer (June-August):** Enjoy warm weather for outdoor activities, festivals, and exploring historical sites. Expect more crowds, especially on the Salmon River.
- **Spring (April-May):** Witness wildflowers and comfortable temperatures, with potentially fewer crowds.
- **Fall (September-October):** Experience vibrant fall foliage and pleasant weather. Be aware of occasional hunting activity in surrounding public lands.
- **Winter (November-March):** Offers a peaceful winter wonderland experience, but some businesses might have limited hours. Road conditions might be icy.

Land Manager (for surrounding Public Lands):

- Bureau of Land Management (BLM) (https://www.blm.gov/)
- Nez Perce National Forest (https://www.fs.usda.gov/nezperceclearwater) (check designated websites for specific areas)

Materials NOT Found While Rockhounding (within Town Limits):

Rockhounding is not permitted within the town boundaries of Lucile.

Rockhounding in Surrounding Areas:

- Public lands managed by the BLM or Nez Perce National Forest might offer rockhounding opportunities. However, always check regulations and obtain any necessary permits before collecting rocks or minerals.

Best Tools for Exploring the Town:

- Comfortable walking shoes
- Camera
- Local shops and brochures offer historical and cultural insights

Best Tools for Exploring Surrounding Public Lands:

- Sturdy hiking boots with good ankle support (if venturing on trails)
- Map and compass or GPS device (recommended for navigation)
- Rockhounding tools (if permitted in specific areas) - Consult BLM or Forest Service websites for guidance

Marlow's Idaho Rock Hounding Guide Book 2024

Best Vehicles for Accessing and Traversing the Area:

- A standard vehicle is sufficient for navigating Lucile's streets.
- High-clearance vehicle might be advisable for exploring dirt roads or trails in surrounding public lands.

Accommodation Options (in Lucile):

- Lodging options are limited:
  - Cottonwood Motor Inn (located in nearby Cottonwood, 102 S Main St, Cottonwood, ID 83522). Offers basic motel accommodations (call 208-962-3331 for details). Identify by signage.
  - Consider alternative lodging options in Grangeville or Lewiston for a wider variety.

Recommended Stops and Attractions (in Lucile):

- **Salmon River (near Lucile):** Enjoy scenic views, fishing opportunities, or whitewater rafting adventures (permits required). Boat rentals and guides are available in the area.
- **Fiddle Creek Fruit Stand:** (Look for signage along ID-14 W near Lucile). Purchase fresh, locally-grown fruits during the summer season.
- **Salmon River Inn & Summervilles Bar & Cafe:** (Located in Lucile). Enjoy a meal or drink with a view of the Salmon River. Identify by signage.

Directions to Specific Locations:

Utilize online maps or GPS with the specific address or name of the attraction you wish to visit (e.g., Fiddle Creek Fruit Stand, Lucile, ID).

Sun Exposure and Availability of Shade:

- **Main Street:** Sidewalks offer some shade from buildings during the afternoons, but expect sun exposure in open areas.
- **Salmon River Access Points:** Shade is limited near the riverbanks. Consider bringing sun protection, especially during midday hours.
- **Lucile Park:** Mature trees provide some shade in this small park.

Soil Types (in the area):

The dominant soil type in the Lucile area is:

- **Alfisols:** These moderately developed soils with reddish-brown subsurface layers are common in the foothills and drier portions of the surrounding landscape.

Rock Types (in the area):

Lucile is situated within a geologic zone with a diverse range of rock types:

- **Granitic rock:** This igneous rock forms the core of the surrounding mountains and can be seen in outcrops along the Salmon River.
- **Metamorphic rocks:** Rocks like schist and gneiss, formed from the transformation of other rock types due to heat and pressure, are also present in the region.
- **Sedimentary rocks:** These layered rocks, formed from deposited sediments, might be encountered in some areas, particularly near the Salmon River.

Popularity of the Site:

Lucile experiences moderate visitor traffic, particularly during summer months. It attracts those seeking a relaxing small-town atmosphere, scenic beauty of the Salmon River, and a base for exploring the surrounding wilderness.

Where to Buy Essential Supplies (around Lucile):

- **Limited options within Lucile:** A small convenience store might offer basic supplies. Consider these options:
  - Lucile Mercantile (subject to availability, verify details online or upon arrival).
- **Grangeville, Idaho (approximately 45 miles east):** Offers a wider range of stores, including:
  - Cloninger's Marketplace (grocery store) located at 102 W Main St, Grangeville, ID 83540 (GPS coordinates: 45°54'23"N, 116°0'32"W). Identify this store by its logo or signage.
- **Lewiston, Idaho (approximately 37 miles west):** Provides the most extensive selection of stores, including:
  - Albertsons (grocery store) located at 1100 4th St, Lewiston, ID 83501 (GPS coordinates: 46°25'12"N, 117°0'22"W). Identify this store by its logo or signage.
  - Cabela's (sporting goods store) located at 1620 14th Ave, Lewiston, ID 83501 (GPS coordinates: 46°24'14"N, 117°0'52"W). Identify this store by its logo or signage.

SALMON RIVER

The Salmon River, also known as the "River of No Return," winds its way through Idaho for over 400 miles, carving a dramatic canyon and offering a diverse range of experiences. Here's a guide to navigating this remarkable river:

Land Type:

- Public Land (managed by the Bureau of Land Management or Nez Perce National Forest)

County:

Varies depending on the specific location along the river (it flows through several counties)

GPS Location:

Since the Salmon River stretches for a long distance, providing a single GPS location isn't useful. However, you can find access points throughout its course. Here are some examples:

- **Near Riggins, Idaho (Lower Salmon River):** 46°22'08"N, 116°37'41"W
- **Near Salmon, Idaho (Middle Fork Salmon River):** 45°15'23"N, 114°07'01"W
- **Near North Fork, Idaho (North Fork Salmon River):** 44°52'12"N, 115°12'00"W

Best Season for Rockhounding:

Rockhounding opportunities are limited due to the location within public lands managed by the BLM or Nez Perce

National Forest. Always check regulations and obtain any necessary permits before collecting rocks or minerals.

Land Manager:

- Bureau of Land Management (BLM) (https://www.blm.gov/)
- Nez Perce National Forest (https://www.fs.usda.gov/nezperceclearwater) (check designated websites for specific areas)

Materials Potentially Found While Rockhounding (with Permit):

Verification through the BLM or Forest Service is necessary to determine specific possibilities. Possibilities might include common rock and mineral types found in the area like jasper, agate, or petrified wood, but this cannot be confirmed without consulting the relevant agency office.

Best Tools for Rockhounding (if permitted):

- Rock hammer
- Safety glasses
- Collecting bag
- Sifting tools (if applicable)
- GPS device (to verify permitted areas)

Best Vehicles for Accessing and Traversing the Area:

- High-clearance vehicle with four-wheel drive is strongly recommended, especially during spring or after heavy rains. Mountain roads leading to access points can be narrow, winding, and unpaved in some sections.

Accommodation Options (around the Salmon River):

- Camping options are available within the surrounding National Forests or BLM-managed lands. Popular locations include:
    - **Nez Perce National Forest Campgrounds:** List of Nez Perce National Forest Campgrounds with GPS coordinates and contact information.
    - **BLM Campgrounds along the Salmon River:** L https://wetplanetwhitewater.com/wp-content/uploads/Salmon-McCall-Campgrounds.pdf
- Limited lodging options exist near some access points. Research towns like Riggins, Salmon, North Fork, and Grangeville for hotels or vacation rentals.

Recommended Stops and Attractions (on the Way or Nearby):

- **Nez Perce National Historical Park (Lapwai, ID):** (46.2900° N, 117.0122° W) Learn about the rich history and culture of the Nez Perce people. Features exhibits, films, and a bookstore (located further west on your drive from Grangeville or Lewiston). Identify the visitor center by signage depicting the National Park Service logo.
- **Hells Canyon National Recreation Area (Oregon/Idaho):** (Offers scenic overlooks and outdoor activities on the Oregon side of the Snake River bordering Idaho).

Directions to Specific Locations:

- **Lower Salmon River (Riggins, Idaho):** From Lewiston, Idaho, take US-95 N for approximately 38 miles. Follow signs for Riggins and Salmon River Road

(ID-14). Look for boat launch areas or public access points.
- **Middle Fork Salmon River (Salmon, Idaho):** From Boise, Idaho, take I-90 W to Grangeville (exit 30). Follow US-95 N for approximately 40 miles to Salmon. Take ID-75 N for access points along the Middle Fork.

North Fork Salmon River (North Fork, Idaho):

- From Missoula, Montana, take I-90 W to Wallace, Idaho (exit 74). Follow US-12 W to Lewiston, Idaho. Take US-95 N for 37 miles to Grangeville. Follow ID-14 W for about 60 miles to North Fork. Access points for the North Fork can be found along this route.

Sun Exposure and Availability of Shade:

Sun exposure along the Salmon River varies depending on the location and time of day. Here's a general idea:

- **Open areas (riverbanks, canyons):** Expect full sun exposure during midday hours.
- **Wooded areas (along trails):** These areas offer shade, particularly along trails or near the riverbank.
- **Mountain slopes:** Sun exposure will vary depending on the slope's orientation.

Soil Types (in the area):

The dominant soil types along the Salmon River vary depending on the specific location. Here are two common types:

- **Alfisols:** These moderately developed soils with reddish-brown subsurface layers are common in the

foothills and drier portions of the surrounding landscape.
- **Inceptisols:** Young soils with minimal development, found on steeper slopes and mountainous terrain.

Rock Types (in the area):

The Salmon River flows through a geologically diverse region. Here are some of the dominant rock types:

- **Granitic rock:** This igneous rock forms the core of the surrounding mountains and is visible in outcrops and along riverbeds.
- **Metamorphic rocks:** Rocks like schist and gneiss, formed from the transformation of other rock types due to heat and pressure, are also present in the canyon walls.
- **Sedimentary rocks:** These layered rocks, formed from deposited sediments, might be encountered in some areas, particularly near the Salmon River.

Popularity of the Site:

The popularity of the Salmon River varies depending on the specific location and activity:

- **Main Salmon River (Riggins area):** Experiences high visitation during summer months for whitewater rafting adventures.
- **Middle Fork Salmon River (Salmon area):** Popular for scenic float trips and backcountry camping, with moderate to high visitation during summer.
- **North Fork Salmon River (North Fork area):** Less crowded than other sections, popular for fishing and kayaking, with lower visitation but increasing interest in wilderness exploration.

Marlow's Idaho Rock Hounding Guide Book 2024

Where to Buy Essential Supplies (around the Salmon River):

Since the Salmon River stretches across a long distance, essential supply options will vary depending on your location. Here's a breakdown based on common starting points:

- **Near Riggins, Idaho (Lower Salmon River):**
  - **Limited options:** Riggins Market & Ace Hardware (located at 100 Main St, Riggins, ID 83549; GPS coordinates: 46°22′12″N, 116°37′38″W). This store offers a variety of groceries, hardware supplies, and some camping essentials. Identify it by its signage.
  - **Larger selection in Grangeville (approximately 40 miles east):**
    - Cloninger's Marketplace (grocery store) located at 102 W Main St, Grangeville, ID 83540 (GPS coordinates: 45°54′23″N, 116°0′32″W). Identify this store by its logo or signage.
- **Near Salmon, Idaho (Middle Fork Salmon River):**
  - **Limited options:** Salmon Valley Food Center (grocery store) located at 600 Main St, Salmon, ID 83469 (GPS coordinates: 45°15′22″N, 114°06′59″W). Identify it by its signage.
  - **Larger selection in Grangeville (approximately 70 miles west):** Same options as above (Cloninger's Marketplace).
- **Near North Fork, Idaho (North Fork Salmon River):**
  - **Limited options:** North Fork Store (convenience store with gas station) located at Hwy 14 N, North Fork, ID 83546 (GPS coordinates: 44°52′10″N, 115°11′58″W). This

store offers basic groceries, gas, and some outdoor supplies. Identify it by its signage.
- **Larger selection in Grangeville (approximately 90 miles west):** Same options as above (Cloninger's Marketplace).

RUBY RAPIDS

Ruby Rapids, Idaho, beckons whitewater enthusiasts and nature lovers to experience the Salmon River's untamed energy. Here's your comprehensive guide to navigating this exhilarating location:

Land Type:

- Public Land (managed by the Bureau of Land Management)

County:

Idaho County

GPS Location:

45°24'14"N, 116°11'40"W (approximate location near confluence with Salmon River)

Best Season for Rockhounding:

Rockhounding opportunities are limited due to the location within public lands managed by the BLM. Always check regulations and obtain any necessary permits before collecting rocks or minerals.

Marlow's Idaho Rock Hounding Guide Book 2024

Land Manager:

Bureau of Land Management (BLM) (https://www.blm.gov/)

Materials Potentially Found While Rockhounding (with Permit):

Verification through the BLM is necessary to determine specific possibilities. Verification might reveal common rock and mineral types found in the area like jasper or agate, but this cannot be confirmed without consulting the BLM office.

Rockhounding Not Recommended:

The high-water rapids and safety considerations make rockhounding impractical and potentially dangerous at Ruby Rapids.

Best Tools for the Adventure (not rockhounding):

- Life jacket (mandatory for all boaters)
- Helmet (recommended for all boaters)
- PFD (personal flotation device)
- Proper river rafting gear (depending on your chosen activity)
- First-aid kit

Best Vehicles for Accessing and Traversing the Area:

- High-clearance vehicle with four-wheel drive is recommended for navigating the dirt roads leading to put-in and take-out points.

Marlow's Idaho Rock Hounding Guide Book 2024

Accommodation Options (around Ruby Rapids):

- Camping options are available within the surrounding National Forests or BLM-managed lands. Popular locations include:
  - **Primitive camping along Salmon River:** Permitted camping locations might be available near the river (check with BLM for regulations and restrictions).
- Limited lodging options exist in nearby towns like Grangeville, Salmon, or Riggins. Research these towns for hotels or vacation rentals.

Recommended Stops and Attractions (on the Way or Nearby):

- **Nez Perce National Historical Park (Lapwai, ID):** (46.2900° N, 117.0122° W) Learn about the rich history and culture of the Nez Perce people (located further west on your drive from Grangeville or Lewiston). Features exhibits, films, and a bookstore. Identify the visitor center by signage depicting the National Park Service logo.
- **Salmon River (various access points):** This iconic river offers scenic views, fishing opportunities, or whitewater rafting adventures (permits required) at various locations along the route to Ruby Rapids.

Directions to the Site:

There are no public launch facilities directly at Ruby Rapids. Rafting companies typically launch upstream and navigate the rapids as part of their guided tours. Here are some options:

- **Guided Tours:** Several whitewater rafting companies operate on the Salmon River. These companies will

provide all necessary equipment, transportation, and experienced guides to navigate Ruby Rapids safely. Search online or inquire in nearby towns like Grangeville, Salmon, or Riggins for reputable outfitters.
- **Private Rafting (experienced boaters only):** For experienced boaters with their own equipment, launch points are available upstream at locations like Indian Creek (45°26′21″N, 116°09′22″W) or Lunch Creek (45°25′23″N, 116°10′38″W). Be sure to check river flow conditions and obtain any necessary permits before attempting this challenging section of the river.

Sun Exposure and Availability of Shade:

Sun exposure at Ruby Rapids varies depending on the time of day. Expect full sun exposure on the river itself, with limited shade available.

Soil Types (in the area):

The dominant soil type in the Ruby Rapids area is:

- **Inceptisols:** Young soils with minimal development, found on steeper slopes and mountainous terrain.

Rock Types (in the area):

The dominant rock type in the Ruby Rapids area is:

- **Granitic rock:** This igneous rock forms the core of the surrounding mountains and is visible in outcrops along the riverbed.

Marlow's Idaho Rock Hounding Guide Book 2024

Popularity of the Site:

Ruby Rapids is a popular destination for experienced whitewater rafters due to its challenging rapids and scenic setting.

Where to Buy Essential Supplies (around Ruby Rapids):

Since Ruby Rapids lacks permanent settlements, acquiring essential supplies requires planning ahead. Here are your options:

- **Grangeville, Idaho (approximately 40 miles west):** Offers a wider range of stores, including:
    - Cloninger's Marketplace (grocery store) located at 102 W Main St, Grangeville, ID 83540 (GPS coordinates: 45°54'23"N, 116°0'32"W). Identify this store by its logo or signage.
    - Ace Hardware (hardware store) located at 201 W Main St, Grangeville, ID 83540 (GPS coordinates: 45°54'24"N, 116°0'35"W). Identify this store by its orange and black logo.
- **Lewiston, Idaho (approximately 70 miles west):** Provides the most extensive selection of stores, including:
    - Albertsons (grocery store) located at 1100 4th St, Lewiston, ID 83501 (GPS coordinates: 46°25'12"N, 117°0'22"W). Identify this store by its red and white logo.
    - Cabela's (sporting goods store) located at 1620 14th Ave, Lewiston, ID 83501 (GPS coordinates: 46°24'14"N, 117°0'52"W). Identify this store by its distinctive logo featuring a large buck.

FLORENCE

Florence, Idaho, is a captivating ghost town nestled within Idaho County, offering a glimpse into the bygone era of the gold rush. Here's your comprehensive guide to navigating this historic site:

Land Type:

Public Land (managed by the Bureau of Land Management)

County:

Idaho County

GPS Location:

46°10′35″N, 115°51′22″W (approximate center of the historic townsite)

Best Season to Visit:

- **Spring (May-June):** Pleasant weather with wildflowers blooming.
- **Fall (September-October):** Milder temperatures and vibrant fall foliage (limited shade available).
- **Summer (July-August):** Warmest temperatures, ideal for exploring during mornings or evenings. Be prepared for potential afternoon heat and limited shade.

Land Manager:

Bureau of Land Management (BLM) (https://www.blm.gov/)

Marlow's Idaho Rock Hounding Guide Book 2024

Rockhounding:

While not the primary attraction, rockhounding possibilities exist with a permit from the BLM. Common finds might include jasper, agate, or petrified wood, but verification is necessary through the local BLM office.

Best Tools for Rockhounding (if permitted):

- Rock hammer
- Safety glasses
- Collecting bag
- Sifting tools (if applicable)
- GPS device (to verify permitted areas)

Best Vehicle:

High-clearance vehicle is recommended, especially during spring or after heavy rains. The roads leading to Florence are unpaved and can be rough.

Accommodation Options:

- **Camping:** BLM-managed campgrounds are available in the surrounding area. Popular options include:
  - **Little Salmon River Campground:** Offers scenic views and basic amenities (limited availability, check with BLM for details). Located approximately 12 miles southwest of Florence (GPS coordinates unavailable).
- **Lodging:** Hotels and vacation rentals can be found in surrounding towns like Grangeville (approximately 45 miles east) or Riggins (approximately 14 miles northeast).

Marlow's Idaho Rock Hounding Guide Book 2024

Recommended Stops and Attractions (on the Way or Nearby):

- **Salmon River (various access points):** This iconic river offers scenic overlooks, fishing opportunities, or whitewater rafting adventures (permits required) along the route to Florence.
- **Nez Perce National Historical Park (Lapwai, ID):** (46.2900° N, 117.0122° W) Learn about the rich history and culture of the Nez Perce people (located further west on your drive from Grangeville or Lewiston). Features exhibits, films, and a bookstore. Identify the visitor center by signage depicting the National Park Service logo.

Directions to the Site:

- From Grangeville, Idaho, take US-95 N for approximately 38 miles. Follow signs for Riggins and Salmon River Road (ID-14). Turn left onto Forest Road 271 (marked with a sign for Florence) and continue for about 6 miles to the townsite.

Sun Exposure and Availability of Shade:

- Florence experiences significant sun exposure due to the lack of trees within the townsite itself.
- Limited shade might be found near the surrounding hills or sparse vegetation.
- Sun protection, including hats, sunglasses, and sunscreen, is highly recommended.

Soil Types (in the area):

The dominant soil type in the Florence area is:

- **Alfisols:** These moderately developed soils with reddish-brown subsurface layers are common in the foothills and drier portions of the surrounding landscape.

Rock Types (in the area):

The Florence area is situated within a geologic zone with diverse rock types:

- **Granitic rock:** This igneous rock forms the core of the surrounding mountains.
- **Metamorphic rocks:** Rocks like schist and gneiss, formed from the transformation of other rock types due to heat and pressure, are also present.

Popularity of the Site:

Florence experiences moderate visitor traffic, particularly during summer months. It attracts history buffs, photographers, and those seeking a unique off-the-beaten-path experience.

Where to Buy Essential Supplies:

- **Limited options:** There are no stores within Florence itself.
- **Grangeville, Idaho (approximately 45 miles east):** Offers a wider range of stores, including:
    - Cloninger's Marketplace (grocery store) located at 102 W Main St, Grangeville, ID 83540 (GPS coordinates: 45°54'23"N, 116°0'32"W). Identify this store by its logo or signage.
    - Ace Hardware (hardware store) located at 201 W Main St, Grangeville, ID 83540 (GPS coordinates: 45°54'24"N, 116°0'35"W). Identify this store by its orange and black logo.

CRYSTAL MOUNTAIN

Detailed Route Description:

Crystal Mountain sits near Burgdorf, Idaho, within Valley County. Here's how to get there:

1. Start in McCall, Idaho.
2. Head north on Highway 55 for roughly 10 miles.
3. Turn left onto Burgdorf Road (Forest Road 503) and continue for approximately 7 miles.
4. Make a right turn onto Forest Road 247. This road is rough and requires a high-clearance vehicle. Proceed with caution.
5. Follow Forest Road 247 for a few miles until you reach the trailhead.

Land Type: Public land managed under the Payette National Forest.

GPS Location: 44.8782° N, 116.0338° W (**Note:** This is an approximate location)

Best Season for Rockhounding: Late spring (after snowmelt) to early fall offers comfortable hiking conditions.

Land Manager: Payette National Forest, McCall Ranger District (**Contact:** (208) 634-0400)

Rockhounding Materials: Crystal Mountain is famed for its white, pink, and yellow quartz crystals. You might also unearth other minerals like garnets and mica.

Best Tools for Rockhounding:

- Rock hammer

- Safety glasses (essential for protecting your eyes)
- Sturdy gloves for safe handling of rocks
- Collapsible bucket or backpack to carry your finds
- Hand lens for examining your treasures up close

Best Vehicle: Due to the rough dirt roads, a high-clearance vehicle like an SUV or truck is highly recommended.

Accommodation Options:

- **Burgdorf Hot Springs Resort: (Phone:** (208) 476-2448) This resort sits near the trailhead, offering a convenient post-adventure soak. (https://www.burgdorfhotsprings.com/)
- Explore various campgrounds and cabins around McCall, Idaho, for alternative lodging options.

Recommended Stops and Attractions with GPS Locations:

- **Burgdorf Hot Springs Resort (44.8825° N, 116.0422° W):** Relax and unwind in the natural hot springs after a day of rockhounding.
- **Payette Lake (Various locations around McCall, ID):** Enjoy scenic views and various water activities in McCall.

Sun Exposure and Shade: The area surrounding Crystal Mountain receives significant sun exposure with limited shade. Sun protection is crucial.

Soil Type: The area consists primarily of sandy loam with exposed rock patches.

Rock Types: Crystal Mountain is primarily composed of quartz monzonite, a rock abundant with quartz crystals.

Popularity: Crystal Mountain is a well-known rockhounding destination, particularly during peak season. Expect to encounter other rockhounds on the trails.

Where to Buy Essential Supplies:

- **McCall Outfitters (McCall, ID: 44.9779° N, 116.0039° W):** (**Phone:** (208) 634-3331) This store offers camping, fishing, and various outdoor gear, potentially including some rockhounding supplies. (https://mccalloutfitter.com/)

WARREN

Warren, nestled within Idaho County, Idaho, offers exciting rockhounding opportunities. Let's delve into the details to plan your trip:

Detailed Route Description:

1. Begin your journey in Lewiston, Idaho.
2. Take Highway 95 south for approximately 37 miles.
3. Turn left onto Lawyer Creek Road (Forest Road 271) and continue for about 18 miles. This road is unpaved and may require a high-clearance vehicle depending on conditions.
4. Stay alert for Forest Road 237 on your left and turn onto it.
5. Follow Forest Road 237 for a few miles until you reach the desired rockhounding location.

Land Type: Public land managed by the Nez Perce National Forest.

Marlow's Idaho Rock Hounding Guide Book 2024

GPS Location: (**Note:** This is an approximate location as specific rockhounding sites may vary) 46.7000° N, 116.3333° W

Best Season for Rockhounding: Summer (late June to early September) offers pleasant weather for exploring. Spring and fall can be suitable too, but be prepared for changeable conditions.

Land Manager: Nez Perce National Forest, Grangeville Ranger District (**Contact:** (208) 983-2800)

Rockhounding Finds: The areas around Warren are known for a variety of rockhounding possibilities. You might unearth:

- **Agates:** Look for colorful banded agates in various shapes and sizes.
- **Jasper:** Find red, yellow, and brown jasper varieties.
- **Petrified Wood:** Unearth pieces of fossilized wood with beautiful wood grain patterns.
- **Opals:** With luck, you might discover stunning opals with a unique play of color.

Best Tools for Rockhounding:

- Rock hammer
- Safety glasses
- Sturdy gloves
- Collapsible bucket or backpack
- Hand lens

Best Vehicle: A high-clearance vehicle (SUV or truck) is recommended due to unpaved and potentially rough roads.

Accommodation Options:

- **Lawyer Creek Campground (46.6422° N, 116.3000° W):** Located along Lawyer Creek Road, offering basic campsites.
- **Hotels in Grangeville, Idaho:** Explore hotels in Grangeville, about a one-hour drive from Warren, for more amenities.

Recommended Stops and Attractions:

- **Nez Perce National Forest Visitor Center (Grangeville, ID): (Contact:** (208) 983-2800) Gather information on the forest, including maps and recommendations for exploring the area.
- **Hells Canyon National Recreation Area:** Enjoy scenic vistas and outdoor activities like hiking and whitewater rafting within driving distance.

Sun Exposure and Shade: The areas around Warren generally have open spaces with limited natural shade. Sun protection is essential.

Soil Type: The area consists primarily of rocky soil with patches of sandy loam.

Rock Types: The geology around Warren is diverse, with igneous rocks like basalt and metamorphic rocks like schist being common. These rocks can host the agates, jasper, petrified wood, and opals you might find while rockhounding.

Popularity: Rockhounding in the Warren area is moderately popular. You might encounter other rockhounds, especially during peak season.

Marlow's Idaho Rock Hounding Guide Book 2024

Where to Buy Essential Supplies:

- **Grangeville Ace Hardware (Grangeville, ID: 46.0378° N, 116.6022° W): (Phone:** (208) 983-2231) This hardware store might stock basic rockhounding tools like gloves and hammers.
- **Spokane Valley Rock Shop (Spokane Valley, WA):** Located about a 2-hour drive away, this shop offers a wider selection of rockhounding equipment and supplies. (https://www.facebook.com/irvsshop/)

STIBNITE

Stibnite, located in Valley County, Idaho, boasts a history of antimony mining and hidden rockhounding gems. Here's your guide to navigating this unique location:

Detailed Route Description:

1. Start your trip in Boise, Idaho.
2. Take Interstate 84 west for approximately 40 miles.
3. Exit onto Highway 55 north and continue for about 53 miles.
4. Turn right onto Forest Road 273 and proceed for roughly 18 miles. This road is unpaved and requires a high-clearance vehicle.
5. Follow signs for Stibnite or continue on Forest Road 273 for a few more miles until you reach your desired rockhounding spot.

Land Type: Public land managed by the Boise National Forest.

GPS Location: (Note: This is an approximate location as specific rockhounding sites may vary) 44.6500° N, 114.4167° W

Best Season for Rockhounding: Summer (late June to early September) offers the most pleasant weather for exploring. Spring and fall can be viable options, but be prepared for unpredictable conditions.

Land Manager: Boise National Forest, Cascade Ranger District (**Contact:** (208) 454-6600)

Rockhounding Finds: Stibnite offers a unique selection of minerals beyond the typical rockhounding fare. Here's what you might discover:

- **Stibnite:** The namesake mineral, with its distinctive metallic gray luster.
- **Scheelite:** A rare fluorescent calcium tungstate mineral. Requires a UV flashlight for identification.
- **Opals:** With luck, you might find fire opals with a play of color.
- **Quartz Crystals:** Unearth clear or smoky quartz crystals in the surrounding areas.

Best Tools for Rockhounding:

- Rock hammer
- Safety glasses
- Sturdy gloves
- Collapsible bucket or backpack
- Hand lens
- UV flashlight (for scheelite identification)

Best Vehicle: Due to unpaved and potentially rough roads, a high-clearance vehicle (SUV or truck) is strongly recommended.

Accommodation Options:

- **Cascade Lake Campground (44.6333° N, 114.3833° W):** Located near Cascade Reservoir, offering basic campsites.
- **Hotels in McCall, Idaho:** Explore hotels in McCall, about a 1.5-hour drive away, for more amenities.

Recommended Stops and Attractions:

- **Stibnite Ghost Town:** Explore the remnants of the historic antimony mining town, including the Stibnite Mine itself.
- **Cascade Reservoir:** Enjoy scenic views and recreational activities like fishing and boating within a short drive.

Sun Exposure and Shade: The area around Stibnite is generally open with limited natural shade. Sun protection is crucial.

Soil Type: The area consists primarily of rocky soil with patches of sandy loam.

Rock Types: The geology around Stibnite is dominated by metamorphic rocks like schist and gneiss, which contain the stibnite and scheelite you might find. The surrounding areas also have igneous rocks like granite, which can host opals and quartz crystals.

Popularity: Rockhounding in Stibnite is less popular compared to other locations in Idaho. You might encounter fellow rockhounds, but it's generally less crowded.

Where to Buy Essential Supplies:

- **McCall Outfitters (McCall, ID: 44.9779° N, 116.0039° W):** **(Phone:** (208) 634-3331) This store offers camping, fishing, and various outdoor gear, potentially including some rockhounding supplies. (https://mccalloutfitter.com/)
- **Boise Valley Rock Shop (Eagle, ID):** Located about a 2-hour drive away, this shop offers a wider selection of rockhounding equipment and supplies, including UV flashlights. (https://idahorocksngems.com/)

PADDY FLAT

Paddy Flat, nestled within Valley County, Idaho, offers opportunities for both rockhounding and delving into the area's rich mining history. Here's your comprehensive guide for planning your trip:

Detailed Route Description:

1. Begin your journey in Boise, Idaho.
2. Take Interstate 84 west for approximately 40 miles.
3. Exit onto Highway 55 north and continue for about 53 miles.
4. Turn right onto Forest Road 273 and proceed for roughly 12 miles. This road is unpaved and can be rough, so a high-clearance vehicle (SUV or truck) is recommended.
5. Look for signs for Paddy Creek or continue on Forest Road 273 for a few more miles until you reach your desired rockhounding location along the tributary streams.

Land Type: Public land managed by the Boise National Forest.

GPS Location: (**Note:** This is an approximate location as specific rockhounding sites may vary) 44.7868° N, 115.9965° W

Best Season for Rockhounding: Summer (late June to early September) offers the most comfortable weather for exploring. Spring and fall can be options, but be prepared for changeable conditions.

Land Manager: Boise National Forest, Cascade Ranger District (**Contact:** (208) 454-6600)

Rockhounding Finds: Paddy Flat's history as a placer deposit means you might unearth:

- **Gold:** Tiny flecks or flakes of gold, best found with proper panning techniques.
- **Quartz Crystals:** Clear or smoky quartz crystals can be found in the streambeds.
- **Garnets:** Keep an eye out for reddish-brown garnets among the gravel.
- **Other Minerals:** Depending on the specific location, you might also find jasper, agates, or tourmaline.

Best Tools for Rockhounding:

- Rock hammer (for breaking open rocks ethically)
- Safety glasses
- Sturdy gloves
- Collapsible bucket or backpack
- Hand lens
- Gold pan (if specifically looking for gold)

Best Vehicle: Due to unpaved roads, a high-clearance vehicle is strongly recommended.

Accommodation Options:

- **Cascade Lake Campground (44.6333° N, 114.3833° W):** Located near Cascade Reservoir, offering basic campsites.
- **Hotels in McCall, Idaho:** Explore hotels in McCall, about a 1.5-hour drive away, for more amenities.

Recommended Stops and Attractions:

- **Paddy Creek Historic District:** Explore the remnants of the historic gold mining operations, including dredge piles and abandoned cabins.
- **Cascade Reservoir:** Enjoy scenic views and recreational activities like fishing and boating within a short drive.

Sun Exposure and Shade: The area around Paddy Flat is generally open with limited natural shade. Sun protection is crucial.

Soil Type: The area consists primarily of rocky soil with patches of sandy loam along the streams.

Rock Types: The geology around Paddy Flat is dominated by metamorphic rocks like schist and gneiss. These rocks, along with stream erosion, contribute to the gold, garnets, and other minerals you might find.

Popularity: Rockhounding in Paddy Flat is moderately popular, especially during peak season. You might encounter other rockhounds, but it's not typically overcrowded.

Where to Buy Essential Supplies:

- **McCall Outfitters (McCall, ID: 44.9779° N, 116.0039° W):** (**Phone:** (208) 634-3331) This store offers camping, fishing, and various outdoor gear, potentially including some rockhounding supplies like hand lenses and gloves. (https://mccalloutfitter.com/)
- **Boise Valley Rock Shop (Eagle, ID):** Located about a 2-hour drive away, this shop offers a wider selection of rockhounding equipment and supplies, including gold pans. (https://idahorocksngems.com/)

GOOSE CREEK

Goose Creek, a location with the potential for multiple sites depending on your interest, can be found within two counties in Idaho:

For Goose Creek near Cascade, Valley County:

- **Land Type:** Public land managed by the Boise National Forest.
- **GPS Location:** 44.7300° N, 115.9000° W (**Note:** This is an approximate location as specific rockhounding sites may vary)
- **Best Season:** Summer (late June to early September) offers pleasant weather for exploring. Spring and fall can be viable options, but be prepared for unpredictable conditions.
- **Land Manager:** Boise National Forest, Cascade Ranger District (**Contact:** (208) 454-6600)

For Goose Creek near Oakley, Cassia County:

- **Land Type:** Public land managed by the Bureau of Land Management (BLM).

- **GPS Location:** 42.0833° N, 114.0333° W (**Note:** This is an approximate location as specific rockhounding sites may vary)
- **Best Season:** Spring (late April to May) and fall (September to October) offer comfortable temperatures for exploring. Summer can be very hot.
- **Land Manager:** Bureau of Land Management, Shoshone District Office (**Contact:** (208) 735-4300)

Rockhounding Potential:

The materials you might find will depend on the specific location of Goose Creek you choose to explore:

- **Near Cascade:** Similar to Paddy Flat, look for gold flecks, quartz crystals, garnets, and potentially jasper or agates.
- **Near Oakley:** The area is known for thunder eggs, which are volcanic rocks that can contain surprising mineral fillings when cracked open. You might also find jasper, agate, and opalized wood.

General Tips:

- **Verify Location:** Double-check which Goose Creek location aligns with your rockhounding interests (Cascade or Oakley).
- **Land Manager:** Contact the relevant land manager (Boise National Forest or BLM) for specific regulations and any required permits for rockhounding activities.
- **Respectful Recreation:** Be mindful of private property boundaries, designated wilderness areas, and leave no trace principles.

Regardless of Location:

- **Detailed Route Description:** Unfortunately, providing a single detailed route is difficult due to the two possible Goose Creek locations. Utilize online mapping services to find the best route to your chosen area.
- **Best Tools:** Rock hammer (use ethically), safety glasses, sturdy gloves, collapsible bucket or backpack, hand lens.
- **Best Vehicle:** A high-clearance vehicle (SUV or truck) is recommended due to potentially rough or unpaved roads.
- **Sun Exposure and Shade:** The areas around Goose Creek are generally open with limited natural shade. Sun protection is crucial.
- **Soil Type:** The area consists primarily of rocky soil with patches of sandy loam.

Accommodation Options:

- **Near Cascade:** Look for options near Cascade Lake or in McCall, Idaho (about a 1.5-hour drive).
- **Near Oakley:** Explore options in Oakley, Idaho, or surrounding towns.

Recommended Stops and Attractions (General):

- Explore nearby towns for a taste of local history and culture.
- Depending on the location, scenic drives or outdoor recreation opportunities like hiking or fishing might be available.

Where to Buy Essential Supplies:

- Look for stores selling camping, fishing, and outdoor gear in nearby towns. These might stock some rockhounding supplies like hand lenses or gloves.

BIG CREEK, VALLEY COUNTY

Big Creek, nestled within Valley County, Idaho, offers exciting rockhounding possibilities, particularly within the vicinity of Crystal Mountain. Here's a detailed guide to plan your trip:

Land Type: Public land managed by the Payette National Forest.

GPS Location: 44.8782° N, 116.0338° W (**Note:** This is an approximate location as specific rockhounding sites may vary).

Best Season: Late spring (after snowmelt) to early fall (around September) offers comfortable weather for hiking and exploring. Summer can be hot, and winter brings significant snowfall.

Land Manager: Payette National Forest, McCall Ranger District (**Contact:** (208) 634-0400)

Rockhounding Gems: Big Creek, particularly near Crystal Mountain, is renowned for its stunning crystals and gemstones. You might unearth:

- **Quartz Crystals:** White, pink, and yellow quartz crystals are commonly found.
- **Garnets:** Keep an eye out for reddish-brown garnets among the gravel and rocks.

- **Mica:** Shiny flakes of mica can add a unique touch to your collection.
- **Other Possibilities:** Depending on the specific location, you might also find agates, kyanite, or tourmaline.

Best Tools for Rockhounding:

- Rock hammer (use ethically for breaking open rocks)
- Safety glasses
- Sturdy gloves
- Collapsible bucket or backpack
- Hand lens

Best Vehicle: A high-clearance vehicle (SUV or truck) is recommended for navigating potentially rough or unpaved roads.

Sun Exposure and Shade: The areas around Big Creek are generally open with limited natural shade. Sun protection is essential.

Soil Type: The area consists primarily of rocky soil with patches of sandy loam, especially near streams.

Rock Types: The geology around Big Creek is dominated by metamorphic rocks like gneiss and schist. These rocks, along with igneous intrusions, contribute to the formation of the crystals and gemstones you might find.

Popularity: Rockhounding near Crystal Mountain is moderately popular, especially during peak season. You might encounter other rockhounds, but it's not typically overcrowded.

Accommodation Options:

- **Campgrounds:** Numerous campgrounds are available near McCall, Idaho, about a 1.5-hour drive from Big Creek. Popular options include:
  - Lick Creek Campground (44.9200° N, 116.1333° W): Offers basic campsites in a scenic location.
  - Ponderosa Park Campground (44.9411° N, 116.0917° W): Provides campsites with amenities like picnic tables and fire rings.
- **Hotels:** Explore hotels in McCall for a wider range of amenities.

Recommended Stops and Attractions:

- **Crystal Mountain Visitor Center: (Contact:** (208) 634-0400) Gather information on the area, including maps and recommendations for exploring specific rockhounding locations.
- **Payette National Forest Scenic Byway:** Enjoy a scenic drive along Highway 55, offering breathtaking views of the surrounding mountains.

Directions to the Site:

- The specific route will depend on your starting point. Utilize online mapping services with the provided GPS coordinates to find the best route to your chosen area near Big Creek.

Where to Buy Essential Supplies:

- **McCall Outfitters (McCall, ID: 44.9779° N, 116.0039° W): (Phone:** (208) 634-3331) This store offers camping, fishing, and various outdoor gear, potentially including some rockhounding supplies like hand lenses and gloves. (https://mccalloutfitter.com/)

- **Boise Valley Rock Shop (Eagle, ID):** Located about a 2-hour drive away, this shop offers a wider selection of rockhounding equipment and supplies. (https://idahorocksngems.com/)

BIG CREEK, SHOSHONE COUNTY

Big Creek, nestled in Shoshone County, Idaho, boasts a unique combination of rockhounding potential and historical significance. Here's your guide to navigate this intriguing location:

Land Type: Public land managed by the Coeur d'Alene National Forest.

GPS Location: 47.3883° N, 116.0333° W (**Note:** This is an approximate location as specific rockhounding sites may vary).

Best Season: Summer (late June to early September) offers the most pleasant weather for exploring. Spring and fall can be options, but be prepared for unpredictable conditions.

Land Manager: Coeur d'Alene National Forest, Wallace Ranger District (**Contact:** (208) 744-3400)

Rockhounding Potential: Big Creek's history as a silver mining district means you might find remnants of the past alongside natural treasures:

- **Minerals:** Galena (lead sulfide), a common silver ore, or pyrite (fool's gold).
- **Caution:** Responsible rockhounding on old mine tailings might be possible, but exercise extreme caution. Research the specific area thoroughly

beforehand. Abandoned mine shafts and unstable structures pose safety hazards.
- **Alternative Approach:** Consider collecting loose rocks and artifacts on the surface, prioritizing safety over venturing into potentially dangerous zones.

Best Tools for Rockhounding:

- Safety glasses (essential for mine tailings)
- Sturdy gloves
- Collapsible bucket or backpack (for collecting surface finds)
- Hand lens (for examining potential mineral finds)
- **Note:** Due to safety concerns, a rock hammer is not recommended for this location.

Best Vehicle: A high-clearance vehicle (SUV or truck) is recommended due to potentially rough or unpaved roads, especially when exploring near old mine sites.

Sun Exposure and Shade: The areas around Big Creek are generally open with limited natural shade. Sun protection is crucial.

Soil Type: The area consists primarily of rocky soil with patches of sandy loam. Mine tailings will have a distinct composition depending on the specific mining operations.

Rock Types: The geology around Big Creek is dominated by metamorphic rocks like schist and gneiss, which were mined for their silver content.

Popularity: Rockhounding activity in Big Creek is less popular compared to other locations in Idaho due to the safety considerations. However, history buffs and rockhounds interested in unique finds might still visit the area.

Accommodation Options:

- **Wallace, Idaho:** Explore hotels and motels in Wallace, a charming town steeped in mining history, located about a 30-minute drive from Big Creek.

Recommended Stops and Attractions:

- **Wallace Mining Museum (Wallace, ID):** (47.7588° N, 115.9400° W) Learn about the rich mining history of the area through exhibits and artifacts.
- **Sierra Silver Mine Tour (Wallace, ID):** (47.7594° N, 115.9392° W) Embark on a guided tour into a historic silver mine for a firsthand experience.

Where to Buy Essential Supplies:

- **Wallace Ace Hardware (Wallace, ID: 47.7733° N, 115.9333° W): (Phone:** (208) 744-3871) This hardware store might stock basic supplies like gloves and hand lenses.

MICA HILL

Mica Hill, nestled within Adams County, Idaho, offers opportunities for both rockhounding and delving into the area's history of mineral exploration. Here's your comprehensive guide for planning your trip:

Land Type: Public land managed by the Bureau of Land Management (BLM).

GPS Location: (Note: This is an approximate location as specific rockhounding sites may vary) 44.7868° N, 115.9965° W

Best Season: Summer (late June to early September) offers the most comfortable weather for exploring. Spring and fall can be options, but be prepared for changeable conditions.

Land Manager: Bureau of Land Management, Weiser Field Office (**Contact:** (208) 473-3400)

Rockhounding Discoveries: Mica Hill's past as a placer deposit means you might unearth:

- **Gold:** Tiny flecks or flakes of gold, best found with proper panning techniques.
- **Quartz Crystals:** Clear or smoky quartz crystals can be found in the streambeds.
- **Garnets:** Keep an eye out for reddish-brown garnets among the gravel.
- **Other Possibilities:** Depending on the specific location, you might also find jasper, agates, or tourmaline.

Best Tools for Rockhounding:

- Rock hammer (for breaking open rocks ethically)
- Safety glasses
- Sturdy gloves
- Collapsible bucket or backpack
- Hand lens
- Gold pan (if specifically looking for gold)

Best Vehicle: A high-clearance vehicle (SUV or truck) is recommended due to unpaved roads that can be rough.

Sun Exposure and Shade: The area around Mica Hill is generally open with limited natural shade. Sun protection is crucial.

Soil Type: The area consists primarily of rocky soil with patches of sandy loam along the streams.

Rock Types: The geology around Mica Hill is dominated by metamorphic rocks like schist and gneiss. These rocks, along with stream erosion, contribute to the gold, garnets, and other minerals you might find.

Popularity: Rockhounding in Mica Hill is moderately popular, especially during peak season. You might encounter other rockhounds, but it's not typically overcrowded.

Accommodation Options:

- **Limited options:** While there aren't many accommodations directly in Mica Hill, consider nearby towns:
    - Weiser, Idaho (around a 1-hour drive): Explore hotels and motels in Weiser for a wider range of options.
    - Payette, Idaho (around a 1.5-hour drive): Look for options in Payette, another option for hotels and amenities.

Where to Buy Essential Supplies:

- **Weiser Ace Hardware (Weiser, ID: 44.2380° N, 116.9741° W): (Phone:** (208) 432-4361) This hardware store might stock basic supplies like gloves and hand lenses.
- **Boise Valley Rock Shop (Eagle, ID):** Located about a 2-hour drive away, this shop offers a wider selection of rockhounding equipment and supplies, including gold pans. (https://idahorocksngems.com/)

CHAPTER 5
WESTERN IDAHO

LITTLE WEISER RIVER

The Little Weiser River, snaking through Washington County and Adams County, Idaho, offers potential for rockhounding adventures. Here's a breakdown to guide you:

Land Type: Public land managed by the Bureau of Land Management (BLM) for most stretches. Some private properties might border the river.

GPS Location: (**Note:** This is an approximate location as specific rockhounding sites may vary) 44.4033° N, 116.6000° W (This places it near the river's midsection in Washington County.)

Best Season: Spring (late April to May) and fall (September to October) offer comfortable temperatures for exploring. Summer can be very hot.

Land Manager:

- **Washington County Section:** Bureau of Land Management, Weiser Field Office (**Contact:** (208) 473-3400)
- **Adams County Section:** Bureau of Land Management, Payette Field Office (**Contact:** (208) 634-0400)

Rockhounding Potential: The Little Weiser River is known for hosting a variety of rockhounding possibilities:

- **Agates:** You might find scenic agate nodules, some potentially containing hidden crystal centers.
- **Jasper:** Colorful jasper pebbles can be found along the riverbanks.
- **Petrified Wood:** Look for pieces of petrified wood, a remnant of the area's ancient forests.
- **Other Possibilities:** Depending on the specific location, you might also find petrified bone fragments or even garnets.

Best Tools for Rockhounding:

- Rock hammer (use ethically for breaking open rocks)
- Safety glasses
- Sturdy gloves
- Collapsible bucket or backpack
- Hand lens

Best Vehicle: A high-clearance vehicle (SUV or truck) is recommended due to potentially rough or unpaved roads, especially when accessing the riverbank.

Sun Exposure and Shade: The areas around the Little Weiser River are generally open with limited natural shade, especially near the banks. Sun protection is crucial.

Soil Type: The area consists primarily of rocky soil with patches of sandy loam along the riverbed.

Rock Types: The geology around the Little Weiser River is a mix of sedimentary and volcanic rocks. Basalt and conglomerate are common, along with the possibility of finding agates and jasper formed within volcanic layers.

Popularity: Rockhounding along the Little Weiser River is moderately popular, particularly during spring and fall. You might encounter other rockhounds, but it's not typically overcrowded.

Accommodation Options:

- **Weiser, Idaho:** Explore hotels and motels in Weiser, Idaho (Washington County section) for a wider range of options. (Around a 1-hour drive from various points along the river)
- **Payette, Idaho:** Look for options in Payette, Idaho (Adams County section) for hotels and amenities. (Around a 1.5-hour drive from various points along the river)

Where to Buy Essential Supplies:

- **Weiser Ace Hardware (Weiser, ID: 44.2380° N, 116.9741° W): (Phone:** (208) 432-4361) This hardware store might stock basic supplies like gloves and hand lenses.
- **Boise Valley Rock Shop (Eagle, ID):** Located about a 2-hour drive away, this shop offers a wider selection of rockhounding equipment and supplies. (https://idahorocksngems.com/)

CUPRUM

Cuprum, nestled within Adams County, Idaho, offers a glimpse into the area's mining past along with potential rockhounding opportunities. Here's your guide to navigate this historic location:

Land Type: Public land managed by the Bureau of Land Management (BLM).

GPS Location: 45.086546° N, 116.689314° W (**Note:** This is an approximate location. Specific rockhounding sites may vary.)

Best Season: Summer (late June to early September) offers the most pleasant weather for exploring. Spring and fall can be options, but be prepared for unpredictable conditions.

Land Manager: Bureau of Land Management, Payette Field Office (**Contact:** (208) 634-0400)

Rockhounding Potential:

Cuprum boasts a history of copper mining, but copper deposits are typically not accessible for recreational collecting. However, the surrounding areas might hold some treasures:

- **Jasper and Agates:** You might find colorful jasper and agates in the gravel and streambeds.
- **Petrified Wood:** Look for pieces of petrified wood, remnants of the area's ancient forests.
- **Other Possibilities:** Depending on the specific location, you might also find petrified bone fragments or even garnets.

Best Tools for Rockhounding:

- Rock hammer (use ethically and sparingly on loose rocks only)
- Safety glasses
- Sturdy gloves
- Collapsible bucket or backpack
- Hand lens

Best Vehicle: A high-clearance vehicle (SUV or truck) is recommended due to potentially rough or unpaved roads, especially when exploring off the main roads.

Marlow's Idaho Rock Hounding Guide Book 2024

Sun Exposure and Shade: The areas around Cuprum are generally open with limited natural shade. Sun protection is crucial.

Soil Type: The area consists primarily of rocky soil with patches of sandy loam.

Rock Types: The geology around Cuprum is dominated by volcanic rocks like basalt and andesite. These rocks, along with transported gravels, contribute to the jasper, agate, and petrified wood possibilities.

Popularity: Rockhounding in Cuprum is less popular compared to other locations in Idaho due to the limited accessibility of copper and the remoteness of the area. However, those seeking a historical adventure with a chance of finding unique rocks might still visit.

Accommodation Options:

- **Limited Options:** Due to Cuprum's remote location, there are no accommodations directly in town. Consider nearby towns:
    - Weiser, Idaho (around a 1.5-hour drive): Explore hotels and motels in Weiser for a wider range of options.
    - Payette, Idaho (around a 2-hour drive): Look for options in Payette for hotels and amenities.

Where to Buy Essential Supplies:

- **Weiser Ace Hardware (Weiser, ID: 44.2380° N, 116.9741° W): (Phone:** (208) 432-4361) This hardware store might stock basic supplies like gloves and hand lenses.
- **Boise Valley Rock Shop (Eagle, ID):** Located about a 2.5-hour drive away, this shop offers a wider

selection of rockhounding equipment and supplies. (https://idahorocksngems.com/)

Recommended Stops and Attractions (all within a 1-hour drive of Cuprum):

- **Payette National Forest:** Explore scenic drives and hiking trails within the Payette National Forest.
- **Bruneau Dunes State Park (Murphy, ID):** (42.9033° N, 115.6833° W) Witness towering sand dunes, a unique geological contrast to Cuprum's landscape.

MINERAL

Mineral, nestled within Shoshone County, Idaho, offers a chance to unearth gemstones and explore a historic ghost town. Here's your guide to navigate this intriguing location:

Land Type: Public land managed by the Coeur d'Alene National Forest.

GPS Location: 47.2222° N, 115.9083° W (**Note:** This is an approximate location as specific rockhounding sites may vary).

Best Season: Late spring (after snowmelt) to early fall (around September) offers comfortable weather for hiking and exploring. Summer can be hot, and winter brings significant snowfall.

Land Manager: Coeur d'Alene National Forest, Wallace Ranger District (**Contact:** (208) 744-3400)

Rockhounding Potential: Mineral's past as a gold mining town might yield some hidden treasures:

- **Quartz Crystals:** White, pink, and yellow quartz crystals are possible finds, especially near old mine tailings (approach with caution).
- **Garnets:** Keep an eye out for reddish-brown garnets among the gravel and rocks.
- **Gold Flecks:** With proper panning techniques, you might find tiny flecks of gold in streambeds (research local regulations beforehand).
- **Other Possibilities:** Depending on the specific location, you might also find agates or jasper.

Best Tools for Rockhounding:

- Safety glasses (essential for mine tailings)
- Sturdy gloves
- Collapsible bucket or backpack
- Hand lens
- Gold pan (if specifically looking for gold - research regulations first)

Best Vehicle: A high-clearance vehicle (SUV or truck) is recommended due to rough or unpaved roads, especially when exploring near old mine sites.

Sun Exposure and Shade: The areas around Mineral are generally open with limited natural shade. Sun protection is crucial.

Soil Type: The area consists primarily of rocky soil with patches of sandy loam, especially near streams. Mine tailings will have a distinct composition depending on the specific mining operations.

Rock Types: The geology around Mineral is dominated by metamorphic rocks like schist and gneiss, which were mined for gold. These rocks, along with stream action, contribute to the formation of the quartz crystals, garnets, and other minerals you might find.

Popularity: Rockhounding activity in Mineral is less popular compared to other locations in Idaho due to the safety considerations around old mines. However, history buffs and rockhounds interested in unique finds might still visit the area.

Directions to the Site from the Nearest Notable Landmark:

- **Wallace, Idaho:** Wallace is a charming town steeped in mining history, located about a 30-minute drive from Mineral. From Wallace, head north on US-95 for approximately 4.7 miles. Turn left onto Forest Road 412 and continue for about 3.5 miles to Mineral. Utilize online mapping services for the most up-to-date route information.

Accommodation Options:

- **Wallace, Idaho:** Explore hotels and motels in Wallace for a wider range of options.

Recommended Stops and Attractions (all within Wallace):

- **Wallace Mining Museum (Wallace, ID: 47.7588° N, 115.9400° W):** Learn about the rich mining history of the area through exhibits and artifacts.
- **Sierra Silver Mine Tour (Wallace, ID: 47.7594° N, 115.9392° W):** Embark on a guided tour into a historic silver mine for a firsthand experience.

Where to Buy Essential Supplies:

- **Wallace Ace Hardware (Wallace, ID: 47.7733° N, 115.9333° W):** (**Phone:** (208) 744-3871) This hardware store might stock basic supplies like gloves and hand lenses.

FOURTH OF JULY CREEK

Fourth of July Creek, snaking through Custer County, Idaho, offers opportunities for both rockhounding and scenic exploration. Here's your guide to navigate this beautiful location:

Land Type: Public land managed by the Sawtooth National Forest.

GPS Location: 47.3883° N, 116.0333° W (**Note:** This is an approximate location as specific rockhounding sites may vary).

Best Season: Summer (late June to early September) offers the most pleasant weather for exploring. Spring and fall can be options, but be prepared for unpredictable conditions, including lingering snow at higher elevations.

Land Manager: Sawtooth National Forest, Stanley Ranger District (**Contact:** (208) 756-5423)

Rockhounding Potential: Fourth of July Creek's history is less about gemstones and more about exploring the wonders of geology. Here's what you might find:

- **Fossils:** Depending on the location, you might uncover fossilized remains of ancient marine life embedded in the sedimentary rocks.

- **Crystallized Minerals:** Keep an eye out for interesting crystallized minerals within the rock formations, particularly quartz or calcite.
- **Scenic Rocks:** The area offers a variety of colorful rocks and pebbles, perfect for nature collections or artistic endeavors.

Important Note: Rockhounding in the Sawtooth National Forest prioritizes responsible collection. Avoid using hammers on rock outcrops and focus on loose rocks.

Best Tools for Rockhounding:

- Collapsible bucket or backpack
- Hand lens
- Sturdy boots for hiking

Best Vehicle: A high-clearance vehicle (SUV or truck) is recommended, especially if venturing off the main roads or exploring near the creek bed.

Sun Exposure and Shade: The areas around Fourth of July Creek vary between open meadows and forested sections. Sun protection is crucial in exposed areas, while shade can be found near the tree line.

Soil Type: The area consists primarily of a mix of rocky soil and sandy loam, with some areas showcasing exposed bedrock.

Rock Types: The geology around Fourth of July Creek is dominated by sedimentary rocks like limestone and shale. These rocks hold the potential for fossils and crystallized minerals.

Popularity: Rockhounding activity in Fourth of July Creek is less popular compared to other locations due to the focus on responsible collection and the emphasis on scenic beauty. However, nature enthusiasts and rock collectors seeking unique conversation pieces might still visit the area.

Directions to the Site from the Nearest Notable Landmark:

- **Stanley, Idaho:** Stanley is a charming town bordering the Sawtooth National Forest, located about 15 miles south of the Fourth of July Creek Trailhead. From Stanley, head south on Highway 75 for approximately 15 miles. Turn left onto Forest Road 209 and continue for about 3 miles to the trailhead parking area. Utilize online mapping services for the most up-to-date route information.

Accommodation Options:

- **Stanley, Idaho:** Explore hotels, motels, and cabin rentals in Stanley for a variety of accommodation options.

Recommended Stops and Attractions (all near Stanley):

- **Sawtooth National Scenic Byway (Stanley, ID):** Take a scenic drive along the Sawtooth National Scenic Byway and witness breathtaking mountain landscapes. (44.6900° N, 114.9614° W) Look for signs along Highway 75.
- **Redfish Lake (Stanley, ID):** Embark on a hike or rent a boat to explore the pristine waters of Redfish Lake. (44.5961° N, 115.1000° W)

Where to Buy Essential Supplies:

- **Stanley Sawtooth Outfitters (Stanley, ID: 44.6900° N, 114.9614° W):** (**Phone:** (208) 756-2331) This outdoor gear store might stock supplies like backpacks and hand lenses.

WEISER

Weiser, the county seat of Washington County, Idaho, offers more than just a charming town center. The surrounding areas hold the potential for rockhounding adventures. Here's your guide to navigate this historic and geologically interesting location:

Land Type: A combination of public and private land. Public lands are managed by the Bureau of Land Management (BLM).

GPS Location: (**Note:** Weiser itself is a town, so this is a general starting point. Specific rockhounding locations will vary.) 44.2380° N, 116.9741° W

Best Season: Spring (late April to May) and fall (September to October) offer comfortable temperatures for exploring. Summer can be hot, and winter brings occasional snowfall.

Land Manager (for Public Lands): Bureau of Land Management, Weiser Field Office (**Contact:** (208) 473-3400)

Rockhounding Potential: Weiser's location near the Snake River and surrounding hills means you might discover:

- **Gold Flecks:** With proper panning techniques in designated areas, you might find tiny flecks of gold in

some local streams (research local regulations beforehand).
- **Quartz Crystals:** Clear or smoky quartz crystals can be found in streambeds, especially near exposed rock faces.
- **Jasper and Agates:** Colorful jasper and agates might be uncovered in certain areas, particularly after heavy rains.
- **Other Possibilities:** Depending on the specific location, you might also find petrified wood or garnets.

Important Note: Always check land ownership before rockhounding. Obtain permission from private landowners and respect posted signs.

Best Tools for Rockhounding:

- Rock hammer (use ethically and sparingly on loose rocks only on public lands)
- Safety glasses (essential for hammering)
- Sturdy gloves
- Collapsible bucket or backpack
- Hand lens
- Gold pan (if specifically looking for gold - research regulations first)

Best Vehicle: A high-clearance vehicle (SUV or truck) is recommended, especially if exploring off the beaten path or near riverbeds.

Sun Exposure and Shade: The areas around Weiser vary between open plains and rolling hills with scattered trees. Sun protection is crucial in exposed areas. Shade can be limited, so bring a hat or seek shelter during peak sun hours.

Marlow's Idaho Rock Hounding Guide Book 2024

Soil Type: The area consists primarily of a mix of rocky soil, sandy loam, and clay deposits, depending on the specific location.

Rock Types: The geology around Weiser is a combination of sedimentary rocks like basalt and conglomerate, along with metamorphic rocks like schist. These contribute to the formation of the jasper, agates, and gold flecks you might find.

Popularity: Rockhounding around Weiser is moderately popular due to its accessibility and variety of potential finds. However, be aware of private property boundaries and avoid overcrowded locations.

Directions to the Site from the Nearest Notable Landmark:

- **Weiser itself:** Since Weiser is the starting point, you'll need to identify a specific public rockhounding location outside of town. Utilize online resources like the BLM website or consult with the Weiser Field Office for recommendations on accessible areas.

Accommodation Options:

- Weiser offers a variety of hotels, motels, and vacation rentals. Explore options online or upon arrival in town.

Recommended Stops and Attractions (all within Weiser):

- **Weiser National Oldtime Fiddle Contest and Festival (で開催地で開催されます) ([で開催地で開催されます] means "held in" in Japanese. I can't provide the exact dates as the festival is held annually. You can search online for the specific

dates): Immerse yourself in the town's culture at this annual event celebrating fiddle music and Western heritage (typically held in June). 44.2400° N, 116.9733° W Look for signs or ask around town for the venue.
- **Weiser River Trail:** Enjoy a scenic walk or bike ride along the Weiser River Trail, offering beautiful views and wildlife watching opportunities. Trail access points can be found throughout Weiser.

Where to Buy Essential Supplies:

- **Weiser Ace Hardware (Weiser, ID: 44.2380° N, 116.9741° W): (Phone:** (208) 432-4361) This hardware store stocks basic supplies like gloves, hand lenses, and buckets.

IDAHO CITY

Nestled within Boise County, Idaho City boasts a rich gold mining history and potential for hidden treasures. Here's your guide to navigate this historic location for your rockhounding adventure:

Land Type: Public land managed by the Bureau of Land Management (BLM) for most areas. Some private properties might border the surrounding Boise River.

GPS Location: (**Note:** This is an approximate location as specific rockhounding sites may vary.) 43.8285° N, 115.8322° W (This places it near the city center)

Best Season: Spring (late April to May) and fall (September to October) offer comfortable temperatures for exploring. Summer can be hot and dry.

Marlow's Idaho Rock Hounding Guide Book 2024

Land Manager:

- **For areas near the city center:** Bureau of Land Management, Boise Field Office (**Contact:** (208) 377-4300)

Rockhounding Potential: Idaho City's mining past offers a chance to discover remnants of its golden era:

- **Gold Flecks:** With proper panning techniques in designated areas, you might find tiny flecks of gold in local streams (research local regulations beforehand).
- **Quartz Crystals:** Clear or smoky quartz crystals can be found in streambeds, especially near old mine tailings (approach with caution).
- **Jasper and Agates:** Colorful jasper and agates might be found, particularly after heavy rains.
- **Other Possibilities:** Depending on the specific location, you might also find petrified wood or garnets.

Important Note: Always check land ownership before rockhounding. Obtain permission from private landowners and respect posted signs. Be mindful of old mine structures and avoid entering unstable areas.

Best Tools for Rockhounding:

- Safety glasses (essential near mine tailings)
- Sturdy gloves
- Collapsible bucket or backpack
- Hand lens
- Gold pan (if specifically looking for gold - research regulations first)

Best Vehicle: A high-clearance vehicle (SUV or truck) is recommended due to potentially rough or unpaved roads, especially when exploring near the Boise River or old mine sites.

Sun Exposure and Shade: The areas around Idaho City are generally open with limited natural shade, especially near the river. Sun protection is crucial.

Soil Type: The area consists primarily of rocky soil with patches of sandy loam, especially near the riverbed. Mine tailings will have a distinct composition depending on the specific mining operations.

Rock Types: The geology around Idaho City is dominated by metamorphic rocks like schist and gneiss, which were historically mined for gold. These rocks, along with stream action, contribute to the formation of the quartz crystals, jasper, agates, and potential for gold flecks you might find.

Popularity: Rockhounding in Idaho City is moderately popular due to its historical significance and accessibility. However, prioritize safety around old mines and be respectful of private property and designated wilderness areas.

Directions to the Site from the Nearest Notable Landmark:

- **Boise, Idaho:** Boise is the major city closest to Idaho City, located about 80 miles southwest. From Boise, take I-84 west for approximately 40 miles. Exit onto Highway 55 north and follow for about 37 miles to Idaho City. Utilize online mapping services for the most up-to-date route information.

Accommodation Options:

- **Idaho City:** Explore a limited selection of hotels, motels, and vacation rentals in Idaho City itself.

- **Boise, Idaho:** If seeking more options, consider staying in Boise and commuting for your rockhounding adventure.

Recommended Stops and Attractions (all within Idaho City):

- **Boise Basin Museum (Idaho City, ID: 43.8278° N, 115.8317° W):** Learn about the city's rich gold mining history through exhibits and artifacts. Look for a large yellow building in the center of town.
- **Gold Dust West Days Festival (で開催地で開催されます) ([で開催地で開催されます] means "held in" in Japanese. I can't provide the exact dates as the festival is held annually. You can search online for the specific dates):** Immerse yourself in the town's culture at this annual event celebrating its gold mining heritage (typically held in late July/early August). 43.8278° N, 115.8317° W. Look for signs or ask around town for specific dates and venue.

Where to Buy Essential Supplies:

- **Idaho City General Store (Idaho City, ID: 43.8283° N, 115.8322° W): (Phone:** Not publicly available) This general store might stock basic supplies like gloves and hand lenses. Their inventory may be limited, so consider visiting Boise for a wider selection.

DISMAL SWAMP

Dismal Swamp, nestled within Elmore County, Idaho, offers a glimpse into the rugged landscape and potential for hidden treasures. Here's your guide to navigate this intriguing location:

Marlow's Idaho Rock Hounding Guide Book 2024

Land Type: Public land managed by the Bureau of Land Management (BLM).

GPS Location: (**Note:** This is an approximate location as specific rockhounding sites may vary.) 43.7290° N, 115.3662° W

Best Season: Summer (late June to early September) offers the most pleasant weather for exploring. Spring and fall can be options, but be prepared for unpredictable conditions, including mud and lingering mosquitos.

Land Manager: Bureau of Land Management, Boise Field Office (**Contact:** (208) 377-4300)

Rockhounding Potential: Dismal Swamp boasts a unique geological composition that might yield these finds:

- **Smoky Quartz Crystals:** The most sought-after treasure. You might find smoky quartz crystals, sometimes in clusters, in loose rocks or streambeds.
- **Quartz Crystals:** Clear or white quartz crystals can also be found alongside the smoky variety.
- **Jasper and Agates:** Colorful jasper and agates might be present, especially after heavy rains.

Important Note: Be mindful of private property bordering the swamp. Always obtain permission before venturing beyond public BLM land.

Best Tools for Rockhounding:

- Sturdy gloves
- Safety glasses (recommended when hammering)
- Rock hammer (use ethically and sparingly on loose rocks only)
- Collapsible bucket or backpack

- Hand lens

Best Vehicle: A high-clearance vehicle (SUV or truck) is crucial due to rough, unpaved roads and potential for muddy conditions, especially near the swamp itself.

Sun Exposure and Shade: The area around Dismal Swamp is a mix of open meadows and scattered trees. Sun protection is essential in exposed areas. Shade is limited near the swamp, so bring a hat or seek shelter during peak sun hours.

Soil Type: The area consists primarily of a mix of rocky soil with patches of sandy loam and clay deposits, especially near the swamp itself.

Rock Types: The geology around Dismal Swamp is dominated by granodiorite, a coarse-grained igneous rock. This rock weathers to form the smoky quartz crystals you might find.

Popularity: Rockhounding in Dismal Swamp is less popular compared to other locations due to its remote location and challenging access. However, those seeking unique smoky quartz crystals and a secluded adventure might still visit.

Directions to the Site from the Nearest Notable Landmark:

- **Featherville, Idaho:** Featherville is a small town bordering the Boise National Forest, located about 20 miles north of Dismal Swamp. From Featherville, head north on Trinity Ridge Road for approximately 17 miles. The road becomes rough and unpaved. Utilize online mapping services for the most up-to-date route information, and be prepared for slow driving due to road conditions.

Accommodation Options:

- **Limited Options:** Due to Dismal Swamp's remote location, there are no accommodations directly in the area. Consider nearby towns:
    - **Featherville, Idaho:** Explore cabins or vacation rentals for a unique stay near the Boise National Forest.
    - **Mountain Home, Idaho (Elmore County seat):** Located about a 2-hour drive away, Mountain Home offers a wider range of hotels and motels.

Recommended Stops and Attractions (all within a 1-hour drive of Dismal Swamp):

- **Boise National Forest:** Explore scenic drives, hiking trails, and camping opportunities within the Boise National Forest. Look for signs or visit the Boise National Forest website for information on access points.
- **Mountain Home Air Force Base (Mountain Home, ID: 43.0033° N, 115.8700° W):** If interested in military history, you can visit the Mountain Home Air Force Base Heritage Center (subject to security clearances).

Where to Buy Essential Supplies:

- **Mountain Home Ace Hardware (Mountain Home, ID: 43.0111° N, 115.8617° W): (Phone: (208) 587-2233)** This hardware store stocks basic supplies like gloves, backpacks, and hand lenses.

SOMMER CAMP ROAD

Sommer Camp Road, snaking through Owyhee County, Idaho, offers opportunities for rockhounding adventures amidst scenic landscapes. Here's your guide to navigate this location:

Land Type: Public land managed by the Bureau of Land Management (BLM) with some areas potentially being private property.

GPS Location: (**Note:** This is an approximate location as specific rockhounding sites may vary.) 43.1833° N, 116.0333° W

Best Season: Spring (late April to May) and fall (September to October) offer comfortable temperatures for exploring. Summer can be hot and dry, while winter brings occasional snowfall.

Land Manager: Bureau of Land Management, Boise Field Office (**Contact:** (208) 377-4300)

Rockhounding Potential: Sommer Camp Road's geology holds the potential to unearth these finds:

- **Opals:** Less common but highly sought after, opal specimens might be found in certain areas, particularly after heavy rains. Look for rainbow or fire opals amongst the loose rocks.
- **Jaspers and Agates:** Colorful jasper and agates are more commonly found, especially near exposed rock faces and in washes after heavy rains.
- **Fossils:** Depending on the location, you might uncover fossilized plant remains or marine life embedded in the sedimentary rocks.

Marlow's Idaho Rock Hounding Guide Book 2024

Important Note: Always check land ownership before rockhounding. Obtain permission from private landowners and respect posted signs. Be mindful of staying on designated trails to avoid disturbing fragile ecosystems.

Best Tools for Rockhounding:

- Sturdy gloves
- Safety glasses (recommended when hammering)
- Rock hammer (use ethically and sparingly on loose rocks only on public land)
- Collapsible bucket or backpack
- Hand lens

Best Vehicle: A high-clearance vehicle (SUV or truck) is highly recommended due to rough, unpaved roads and potential for loose rocks. Four-wheel drive might be necessary depending on the specific location you choose to explore.

Sun Exposure and Shade: The area around Sommer Camp Road varies between open plains, rolling hills, and scattered trees. Sun protection is crucial in exposed areas. Shade is limited, so bring a hat or seek shelter during peak sun hours.

Soil Type: The area consists primarily of a mix of rocky soil with patches of sandy loam and clay deposits, depending on the specific location.

Rock Types: The geology around Sommer Camp Road is a combination of sedimentary rocks like basalt and conglomerate, along with volcanic ash deposits. These contribute to the formation of the opals, jaspers, agates, and potential fossils you might find.

Popularity: Rockhounding along Sommer Camp Road is moderately popular due to its accessibility and variety of potential finds. However, be aware of private property

boundaries and avoid overcrowded locations, especially during peak rockhounding seasons.

Directions to the Site from the Nearest Notable Landmark:

- **Marsing, Idaho:** Marsing is the closest town to Sommer Camp Road, located about 10 miles north. From Marsing, head south on Highway 95 for approximately 4 miles. Turn east onto Sommer Camp Road and continue for several miles. The road becomes rough and unpaved after a while. Utilize online mapping services with up-to-date road information, and be prepared for slow driving due to road conditions.

Accommodation Options:

- **Marsing, Idaho:** Explore motels, hotels, and vacation rentals in Marsing for a convenient stay.

Recommended Stops and Attractions (all near Marsing):

- **Snake River Canyon Overlook (Marsing, ID: 43.2222° N, 116.0008° W):** Take in breathtaking views of the Snake River Canyon from designated overlooks along Highway 95 south of Marsing. Look for signs or scenic pullouts.
- **Marsing Municipal Park (Marsing, ID: 43.2208° N, 116.0333° W):** Enjoy a picnic or explore the walking trails within Marsing Municipal Park, located in the heart of town.

Where to Buy Essential Supplies:

- **Marsing True Value Hardware (Marsing, ID: 43.2208° N, 116.0333° W): (Phone:** (208) 888-2212) This hardware store stocks basic supplies like gloves, backpacks, and hand lenses.

OPALENE GULCH

Opalene Gulch, a hidden gem within Owyhee County, Idaho, offers opportunities for rockhounding enthusiasts and nature lovers alike. Here's your guide to navigate this intriguing location:

Land Type: Public land managed by the Bureau of Land Management (BLM).

GPS Location: (Note: This is an approximate location as specific rockhounding sites may vary.) 43.2550° N, 116.7700° W

Best Season: Spring (late April to May) and fall (September to October) offer the most pleasant weather for exploring. Summer can be hot and dry, while winter brings occasional snowfall.

Land Manager: Bureau of Land Management, Boise Field Office (**Contact:** (208) 377-4300)

Rockhounding Potential: Opalene Gulch boasts a unique geological history with the potential to unearth these treasures:

- **Opals:** The namesake of the gulch! Look for fire opals or rainbow opals amongst loose rocks and weathered

outcrops, especially after heavy rains. These can be rare finds, so patience and a keen eye are essential.
- **Fossils:** Depending on the location, you might uncover fossilized plant remains or even marine life embedded in the sedimentary rocks.
- **Jasper and Agates:** Colorful jasper and agates are more commonly found, particularly near streambeds and exposed rock faces.

Important Note: Always check land ownership before rockhounding. Obtain permission from private landowners and respect posted signs. Be mindful of staying on designated trails to avoid disturbing fragile ecosystems.

Best Tools for Rockhounding:

- Sturdy gloves
- Safety glasses (recommended when hammering)
- Rock hammer (use ethically and sparingly on loose rocks only on public land)
- Collapsible bucket or backpack
- Hand lens
- Blacklight (for identifying fire opals - use responsibly and avoid disturbing natural light for nocturnal wildlife)

Best Vehicle: A high-clearance vehicle (SUV or truck) is crucial due to rough, unpaved roads and potential for loose rocks. Four-wheel drive might be necessary depending on the specific location you choose to explore.

Sun Exposure and Shade: The area around Opalene Gulch is a mix of open plains, rolling hills, and scattered trees. Sun protection is crucial in exposed areas. Shade is limited, so bring a hat or seek shelter during peak sun hours.

Soil Type: The area consists primarily of a mix of rocky soil with patches of sandy loam and clay deposits, depending on the specific location.

Rock Types: The geology around Opalene Gulch is dominated by sedimentary rocks like shale and limestone, along with volcanic ash deposits. These contribute to the formation of the opals, fossils, jaspers, and agates you might find.

Popularity: Rockhounding in Opalene Gulch is less popular compared to other locations due to its remoteness and focus on responsible collecting of rare opals. However, those seeking a unique adventure and a chance to discover these hidden gems might still visit.

Directions to the Site from the Nearest Notable Landmark:

- **Grand View, Idaho:** Grand View, a small town in Owyhee County, is the closest point of reference. From Grand View, head south on Highway 51 for approximately 32 miles. Turn west onto Murphy Hot Springs Road for about 17 miles (becomes rough and unpaved). Finally, turn south onto Opalene Gulch Road for a few miles until you reach the gulch. Utilize online mapping services with up-to-date road information, and be prepared for slow driving due to road conditions.

Accommodation Options:

- **Limited Options:** Due to Opalene Gulch's remote location, there are no accommodations directly in the area. Consider nearby towns:
    - **Grand View, Idaho:** Explore basic motels or campgrounds for a rustic stay.

- **Murphy, Idaho (Owyhee County seat):** Located about an hour drive away, Murphy offers a wider range of options, including cabins and vacation rentals.

Recommended Stops and Attractions (all within a 1-hour drive of Opalene Gulch):

- **Bruneau Dunes State Park (Marsing, ID: 43.2222° N, 116.0008° W):** Take a detour to explore the otherworldly sand dunes and unique ecosystem at Bruneau Dunes State Park, located about an hour north. Look for signs along Highway 95.
- **Owyhee Canyonlands (Murphy, ID area):** Witness the dramatic canyons and scenic landscapes of the Owyhee Canyonlands, accessible through various trails around Murphy.

Where to Buy Essential Supplies:

- **Murphy True Value Hardware (Murphy, ID: 43.0083° N, 116.6000° W):** (Phone: (208) 495-2233) This hardware store stocks basic supplies like gloves, backpacks, and hand lenses.

MCBRIDE CREEK

McBride Creek, snaking through Owyhee County, Idaho, offers opportunities to unearth hidden gems alongside scenic landscapes. Here's your guide to navigate this historic and geologically interesting location:

Land Type: A combination of public land managed by the Bureau of Land Management (BLM) and private property bordering the creek.

GPS Location: (**Note:** This is an approximate location as specific rockhounding sites may vary.) 43.2818° N, 116.9615° W

Best Season: Spring (late April to May) and fall (September to October) offer comfortable temperatures for exploring. Summer can be hot and dry, while winter brings occasional snowfall.

Land Manager (for Public Lands): Bureau of Land Management, Weiser Field Office (**Contact:** (208) 473-3400)

Rockhounding Potential: McBride Creek's location near the Snake River and surrounding hills holds the potential to discover:

- **Gold Flecks:** With proper panning techniques in designated BLM areas, you might find tiny flecks of gold in the creekbed. Research local regulations on gold panning beforehand.
- **Petrified Wood:** This is a unique possibility in the McBride Creek area. Look for distinctive petrified wood fragments among the rocks, particularly after heavy rains.
- **Quartz Crystals:** Clear or smoky quartz crystals can be found in streambeds, especially near exposed rock faces.
- **Jaspers and Agates:** Colorful jasper and agates might be found in certain areas, particularly after heavy rains.

Important Note: Always check land ownership before rockhounding. Obtain permission from private landowners and respect posted signs. Focus your search on public BLM land and avoid disturbing natural habitats.

Best Tools for Rockhounding:

- Sturdy gloves
- Safety glasses (essential when hammering)
- Rock hammer (use ethically and sparingly on loose rocks only on public BLM land)
- Collapsible bucket or backpack
- Hand lens
- Gold pan (if specifically looking for gold - research regulations first)

Best Vehicle: A high-clearance vehicle (SUV or truck) is recommended due to potentially rough or unpaved roads, especially near the creek and surrounding hills. Four-wheel drive might be necessary depending on the specific location you choose to explore.

Sun Exposure and Shade: The areas around McBride Creek vary between open plains, rolling hills, and scattered trees. Sun protection is crucial in exposed areas. Shade can be limited, so bring a hat or seek shelter during peak sun hours.

Soil Type: The area consists primarily of a mix of rocky soil with patches of sandy loam and clay deposits, especially near the creekbed.

Rock Types: The geology around McBride Creek is a combination of sedimentary rocks like basalt and conglomerate, along with metamorphic rocks like schist. These contribute to the formation of the jasper, agates, petrified wood (depending on location), potential for gold flecks, and quartz crystals you might find.

Popularity: Rockhounding around McBride Creek is moderately popular due to its accessibility and variety of potential finds. However, be aware of private property

boundaries and avoid overcrowded locations, especially during peak rockhounding seasons.

Directions to the Site from the Nearest Notable Landmark:

- **Murphy, Idaho:** Murphy, located in Owyhee County, is the closest town to McBride Creek. From Murphy, head north on Highway 51 for approximately 17 miles. Turn east onto Leslie Gulch Road for about 10 miles (becomes rough and unpaved). Finally, turn north onto numerous unnamed side roads that lead towards McBride Creek. Utilize online mapping services with up-to-date road information, and be prepared for slow driving due to road conditions.

Accommodation Options:

- **Murphy, Idaho:** Explore cabins, vacation rentals, or campgrounds in Murphy for a convenient stay near the exploration area.

Recommended Stops and Attractions (all near Murphy):

- **Owyhee Canyonlands (Murphy, ID area):** Witness the dramatic canyons and scenic landscapes of the Owyhee Canyonlands, accessible through various trails around Murphy. Look for signs or consult with the Murphy Ranger District for specific recommendations.
- **Snake River Birds of Prey National Conservation Area (Murphy, ID area):** Learn about the unique birds of prey inhabiting the Snake River Canyon. The area offers scenic overlooks and opportunities for wildlife viewing. Look for signs along Highway 51 south of Murphy.

Where to Buy Essential Supplies:

- **Murphy True Value Hardware (Murphy, ID: 43.0083° N, 116.6000° W): (Phone:** (208) 495-2233) This hardware store stocks basic supplies like gloves, backpacks, hand lenses, and potentially gold pans (depending on availability).

COAL MINE BASIN

Coal Mine Basin, nestled within the borders of Owyhee and Valley Counties, Idaho, offers a glimpse into the state's geological history and potential for unique rockhounding finds. Here's your guide to navigate this intriguing location:

Land Type: Primarily public land managed by the Bureau of Land Management (BLM) with some bordering private property.

GPS Location: (Note: This is an approximate location as specific areas may vary.) 43.0900° N, 117.0333° W

Best Season: Spring (late April to May) and fall (September to October) offer the most pleasant weather for exploring. Summer can be hot and dry, while winter brings occasional snowfall.

Land Manager: Bureau of Land Management, Vale District Office (**Contact:** (208) 473-3400)

Rockhounding Potential: Coal Mine Basin boasts a unique geological composition that might yield these finds:

- **Paleontological Specimens:** Due to the basin's history, you might uncover fossilized plant remains or even petrified bone fragments, especially after heavy

rains. Always be mindful of responsible collecting and leave significant discoveries undisturbed for further scientific study.
- **Zeolites:** These are less common but potentially interesting finds. Zeolites are minerals with unique crystal structures that can form in volcanic environments.
- **Jasper and Agates:** Colorful jasper and agates might be present, especially near exposed rock faces and loose in streambeds.

Important Note: Always check land ownership before rockhounding. Obtain permission from private landowners and respect posted signs. Focus your search on designated BLM land and avoid disturbing fragile historical or ecological features.

Best Tools for Rockhounding:

- Sturdy gloves
- Safety glasses (recommended when hammering)
- Rock hammer (use ethically and sparingly on loose rocks only on BLM land)
- Collapsible bucket or backpack
- Hand lens

Best Vehicle: A high-clearance vehicle (SUV or truck) is crucial due to rough, unpaved roads and potential for loose rocks or uneven terrain. Four-wheel drive might be necessary depending on the specific location you choose to explore.

Sun Exposure and Shade: The area around Coal Mine Basin is a mix of open plains, rolling hills, and scattered patches of shrubs. Sun protection is crucial in exposed areas. Shade is limited, so bring a hat or seek shelter during peak sun hours.

Soil Type: The area consists primarily of a mix of rocky soil with patches of sandy loam and clay deposits, especially near drainages.

Rock Types: The geology around Coal Mine Basin is dominated by volcanic ash deposits and sedimentary rock formations. This contributes to the potential for finding zeolites, paleontological specimens, and the occasional jasper or agate.

Popularity: Rockhounding in Coal Mine Basin is less popular compared to other locations due to its remoteness and focus on responsible collecting of potential fossils. However, those seeking a unique adventure and a chance to discover a glimpse into Idaho's past might still visit.

Directions to the Site from the Nearest Notable Landmark:

- **Jordan Valley, Oregon:** Jordan Valley, located just across the border in Oregon, is the closest town to Coal Mine Basin. From Jordan Valley, head north on Highway 78 for approximately 11 miles. Turn east onto Coal Mine Basin Road for about 7 miles (becomes rough and unpaved). Utilize online mapping services with up-to-date road information, and be prepared for slow driving due to road conditions.

Accommodation Options:

- **Limited Options:** Due to Coal Mine Basin's remote location, there are no accommodations directly in the area. Consider nearby towns:
    - **Jordan Valley, Oregon:** Explore basic motels or campgrounds for a rustic stay.
    - **Vale, Oregon (Malheur County seat):** Located about an hour drive away, Vale offers a

wider range of options, including hotels and motels.

Recommended Stops and Attractions (all within a 1-hour drive of Coal Mine Basin):

- **Succor Creek State Park (Vale, OR: 44.0667° N, 117.2333° W):** Take a detour to explore this scenic state park known for its unique geological formations and opportunities for wildlife viewing. Look for signs along Highway 20 west of Vale.

- **Bruneau Dunes State Park (Marsing, ID: 43.2222° N, 116.0008° W):** If you have extra time, consider a trip to Bruneau Dunes State Park (approximately 1.5 hours north). Explore the otherworldly sand dunes and unique ecosystem. Look for signs along Highway 95 south of Marsing.

Where to Buy Essential Supplies:

- **Vale True Value Hardware (Vale, OR: 44.0667° N, 117.2333° W): (Phone:** (541) 473-3101) This hardware store stocks basic supplies like gloves, backpacks, and hand lenses.

CHAPTER 6
SOUTHERN IDAHO

SOUTH MOUNTAIN

South Mountain, straddling the borders of Owyhee and Canyon Counties in Idaho, offers opportunities for rockhounding adventures amidst scenic landscapes. Here's your guide to navigate this location:

Land Type: Primarily public land managed by the Bureau of Land Management (BLM) with some areas potentially being private property.

GPS Location: (**Note:** This is an approximate location as specific rockhounding sites may vary.) 43.2083° N, 116.1000° W

Best Season: Spring (late April to May) and fall (September to October) offer comfortable temperatures for exploring. Summer can be hot and dry, while winter brings occasional snowfall.

Land Manager: Bureau of Land Management, Boise Field Office (**Contact:** (208) 377-4300)

Rockhounding Potential: South Mountain's geology holds the potential to unearth these finds:

- **Opals:** Less common but highly sought after, opal specimens might be found in certain areas, particularly after heavy rains. Look for rainbow or fire opals amongst loose rocks and in weathered outcrops.

- **Jaspers and Agates:** Colorful jasper and agates are more commonly found, especially near exposed rock faces and in washes after heavy rains.
- **Fossils:** Depending on the location, you might uncover fossilized plant remains or marine life embedded in the sedimentary rocks.

Important Note: Always check land ownership before rockhounding. Obtain permission from private landowners and respect posted signs. Be mindful of staying on designated trails to avoid disturbing fragile ecosystems.

Best Tools for Rockhounding:

- Sturdy gloves
- Safety glasses (recommended when hammering)
- Rock hammer (use ethically and sparingly on loose rocks only on public land)
- Collapsible bucket or backpack
- Hand lens

Best Vehicle: A high-clearance vehicle (SUV or truck) is highly recommended due to rough, unpaved roads and potential for loose rocks. Four-wheel drive might be necessary depending on the specific location you choose to explore.

Sun Exposure and Shade: The area around South Mountain varies between open plains, rolling hills, and scattered trees. Sun protection is crucial in exposed areas. Shade is limited, so bring a hat or seek shelter during peak sun hours.

Soil Type: The area consists primarily of a mix of rocky soil with patches of sandy loam and clay deposits, depending on the specific location.

Rock Types: The geology around South Mountain is a combination of sedimentary rocks like basalt and conglomerate, along with volcanic ash deposits. These contribute to the formation of the opals, jaspers, agates, and potential fossils you might find.

Popularity: Rockhounding along South Mountain varies in popularity. Certain areas are more accessible and well-known, while others remain relatively undiscovered. Be aware of private property boundaries and avoid overcrowded locations, especially during peak rockhounding seasons.

Directions to the Site from the Nearest Notable Landmark:

- **Jordan Valley, Oregon:** Jordan Valley, located just across the border in Oregon, is the closest town to South Mountain. From Jordan Valley, head southeast on Highway 78 for approximately 18 miles. Turn east onto South Mountain Road (may be unmarked) and continue for several miles. The road becomes rough and unpaved after a while. Utilize online mapping services with up-to-date road information, and be prepared for slow driving due to road conditions.

Accommodation Options:

- **Limited Options:** Due to South Mountain's remote location, there are no accommodations directly in the area. Consider nearby towns:
    - **Jordan Valley, Oregon:** Explore basic motels or campgrounds for a rustic stay.
    - **Payette, Idaho (Payette County seat):** Located about an hour drive north, Payette offers a wider range of options, including hotels, motels, and vacation rentals.

Recommended Stops and Attractions (all within a 1-hour drive of South Mountain):

- **Payette National Forest (Cascade, ID area):** (Multiple Locations) Explore the scenic landscapes and outdoor recreation opportunities within Payette National Forest. Look for signs along Highway 55 north of Payette.
- **Snake River Canyon Overlook (Marsing, ID area):** (Multiple Locations) Take in breathtaking views of the Snake River Canyon from designated overlooks along Highway 95 south of Marsing. Look for signs or scenic pullouts.

Where to Buy Essential Supplies:

- **Marsing True Value Hardware (Marsing, ID: 43.2208° N, 116.0333° W):** **(Phone:** (208) 888-1213) This hardware store stocks basic supplies like gloves, backpacks, and hand lenses.

REYNOLDS CREEK

Reynolds Creek, snaking through Owyhee County, Idaho, offers opportunities for rockhounding enthusiasts and nature lovers alike. Here's your guide to navigate this scenic location:

Land Type: A combination of public land managed by the Bureau of Land Management (BLM) and private property bordering the creek.

GPS Location: **(Note:** This is an approximate location as specific rockhounding sites may vary.) 43.2550° N, 116.7700° W

Best Season: Spring (late April to May) and fall (September to October) offer comfortable temperatures for exploring. Summer can be hot and dry, while winter brings occasional snowfall.

Land Manager (for Public Lands): Bureau of Land Management, Boise Field Office (**Contact:** (208) 377-4300)

Rockhounding Potential: Reynolds Creek's location near the Snake River and surrounding hills holds the potential to discover:

- **Fire Opals or Rainbow Opals:** These are the namesake treasures of the area. Look for them amongst loose rocks and weathered outcrops, especially after heavy rains. Finding opals is uncommon and requires a keen eye and patience.
- **Fossils:** Depending on the location, you might uncover fossilized plant remains or even marine life embedded in the sedimentary rocks.
- **Jaspers and Agates:** Colorful jasper and agates are more commonly found, particularly near streambeds and exposed rock faces.

Important Note: Always check land ownership before rockhounding. Obtain permission from private landowners and respect posted signs. Focus your search on designated BLM land and avoid disturbing natural habitats.

Best Tools for Rockhounding:

- Sturdy gloves
- Safety glasses (recommended when hammering)
- Rock hammer (use ethically and sparingly on loose rocks only on public BLM land)
- Collapsible bucket or backpack
- Hand lens

- Blacklight (for identifying fire opals - use responsibly and for short durations)

Best Vehicle: A high-clearance vehicle (SUV or truck) is crucial due to potentially rough or unpaved roads, especially near the creek and surrounding hills. Four-wheel drive might be necessary depending on the specific location you choose to explore.

Sun Exposure and Shade: The areas around Reynolds Creek vary between open plains, rolling hills, and scattered trees. Sun protection is crucial in exposed areas. Shade can be limited, so bring a hat or seek shelter during peak sun hours.

Soil Type: The area consists primarily of a mix of rocky soil with patches of sandy loam and clay deposits, especially near the creekbed.

Rock Types: The geology around Reynolds Creek is a combination of sedimentary rocks like shale and limestone, along with volcanic ash deposits. These contribute to the formation of the opals, fossils, jaspers, and agates you might find.

Popularity: Rockhounding around Reynolds Creek is moderately popular due to its accessibility and variety of potential finds. However, be aware of private property boundaries and avoid overcrowded locations, especially during peak rockhounding seasons.

Directions to the Site from the Nearest Notable Landmark:

- **Melba, Idaho:** Melba, located in Canyon County, is the closest town to the public access points for Reynolds Creek. From Melba, head south on Highway 78 for approximately 17 miles. Turn west onto Wilson

Creek Road for a few miles until you reach the Reynolds Creek area. Look for signs or consult a detailed map, as roads can be unmarked. Utilize online mapping services with up-to-date road information, and be prepared for slow driving due to road conditions.

Accommodation Options:

- **Melba, Idaho:** Explore motels, campgrounds, or vacation rentals in Melba for a convenient stay near the exploration area.
- **Mountain Home, Idaho (Elmore County seat):** Located about an hour drive east, Mountain Home offers a wider range of options, including hotels, motels, and vacation rentals.

Recommended Stops and Attractions (all near Melba):

- **Snake River Canyon Overlook (Melba, ID area):** (Multiple Locations) Take in breathtaking views of the Snake River Canyon from designated overlooks along Highway 78 south of Melba. Look for signs or scenic pullouts.
- **Bruneau Dunes State Park (Marsing, ID: 43.2222° N, 116.0008° W):** (Approximately 1 hour drive north) Explore the otherworldly sand dunes and unique ecosystem at Bruneau Dunes State Park. Look for signs along Highway 95.

Where to Buy Essential Supplies:

There are currently no hardware stores listed in Melba, Idaho. However, you can try the following options:

- **Murphy True Value Hardware (Murphy, ID: 43.0083° N, 116.6000° W):** (**Phone:** (208) 495-2233) Located about an hour drive from Melba, this hardware store stocks basic supplies like gloves, backpacks, hand lenses, and potentially rock hammers (depending on availability).

BRUNEAU RIVER

The Bruneau River, snaking through Owyhee County, Idaho, carves a scenic canyon known for whitewater rafting and holds potential for rockhounding adventures. Here's your guide to navigate this rugged and rewarding location:

Land Type: Primarily public land managed by the Bureau of Land Management (BLM) with some areas being private property.

GPS Location: (**Note:** This is an approximate location as specific rockhounding sites may vary.) 42.6083° N, 115.6167° W

Best Season: Spring (late April to May) and fall (September to October) offer comfortable temperatures for exploring. Summer can be hot and dry, while winter brings occasional snowfall and limited access due to road conditions.

Land Manager (for Public Lands): Bureau of Land Management, Boise Field Office (**Contact:** (208) 377-4300)

Rockhounding Potential: The Bruneau River's unique geology offers a variety of finds:

- **Jaspers and Agates:** Colorful jasper and agates are commonly found, especially near exposed volcanic

rock faces and in loose cobbles along the riverbed after heavy rains.
- **Fossils:** Depending on the location, you might uncover fossilized plant remains or even marine life embedded in the sedimentary rocks.
- **Thunder Eggs:** These rough volcanic rocks can contain surprising centers filled with agate, jasper, or even opal. Look for rounded, bumpy rocks with a weathered exterior, especially near volcanic outcrops.

Important Note: Always check land ownership before rockhounding. Obtain permission from private landowners and respect posted signs. Focus your search on designated BLM land and avoid disturbing natural habitats or areas with signs of active mining claims.

Best Tools for Rockhounding:

- Sturdy gloves
- Safety glasses (recommended when hammering)
- Rock hammer (use ethically and sparingly on loose rocks only on public BLM land)
- Collapsible bucket or backpack
- Hand lens

Best Vehicle: A high-clearance vehicle (SUV or truck) with four-wheel drive is highly recommended due to rough, unpaved roads and potential for loose rocks or uneven terrain, especially near the riverbed.

Sun Exposure and Shade: The Bruneau River canyon varies between open plains, steep canyon walls, and scattered trees or shrubs. Sun protection is crucial in exposed areas. Shade is limited, so bring a hat or seek shelter during peak sun hours.

Soil Type: The area consists primarily of a mix of rocky soil with patches of sandy loam and clay deposits, depending on the specific location.

Rock Types: The Bruneau River flows through a canyon carved in basalt and rhyolite lava flows, alongside sedimentary rocks. This contributes to the potential for finding jaspers, agates, fossils, and thundereggs.

Popularity: Rockhounding along the Bruneau River varies in popularity. Certain areas with well-known agate beds or scenic pull-offs might be more frequented, while others remain relatively undiscovered. Be aware of private property boundaries and avoid overcrowded locations, especially during peak rockhounding seasons.

Directions to the Site from the Nearest Notable Landmark:

- **Mountain Home, Idaho (Elmore County seat):** Mountain Home is the closest major town to the Bruneau River. From Mountain Home, head southwest on Highway 61 for approximately 40 miles. Look for designated turnoffs or BLM access points leading to the Bruneau River Canyon. Utilize online mapping services with up-to-date road information, and be prepared for slow driving due to road conditions.

Accommodation Options:

- **Mountain Home, Idaho:** Explore hotels, motels, or campgrounds in Mountain Home for a convenient stay near your exploration area.
- **Bruneau, Idaho (Owyhee County seat):** Located about an hour south, Bruneau offers limited accommodation options, primarily campgrounds or vacation rentals.

Recommended Stops and Attractions (all near Mountain Home):

- **Snake River Canyon Overlook (Marsing, ID area):** (Multiple Locations) Take in breathtaking views of the Snake River Canyon from designated overlooks along Highway 95 south of Marsing (approximately 1-hour drive north). Look for signs or scenic pullouts.
- **Bruneau Dunes State Park (Marsing, ID: 43.2222° N, 116.0008° W):** (Approximately 1.5-hour drive north) Explore the otherworldly sand dunes and unique ecosystem at Bruneau Dunes State Park. Look for signs along Highway 95.

Where to Buy Essential Supplies:

- **Mountain Home True Value Hardware (Mountain Home, ID: 43.1109° N, 115.8694° W): (Phone:** (208) 587-2233) This hardware store stocks basic supplies like gloves, backpacks, hand lenses, and potentially rock hammers (depending on availability).

RABBIT SPRINGS

Rabbit Springs, nestled in Twin Falls County, Idaho, offers opportunities for rockhounds seeking unique finds. Here's a guide to navigate this location:

Land Type: A combination of public land managed by the Bureau of Land Management (BLM) and private property.

GPS Location: (Note: This is an approximate location as specific rockhounding sites may vary.) 42.0657° N, 114.67387° W

Best Season: Spring (late April to May) and fall (September to October) offer comfortable temperatures for exploring. Summer can be hot and dry, while winter brings occasional snowfall and may limit access.

Land Manager (for Public Lands): Bureau of Land Management, Shoshone Field Office (**Contact:** (208) 735-4300)

Rockhounding Potential: Rabbit Springs is known for:

- **Thundereggs:** These volcanic rocks hold a surprise within – agate, jasper, or even opal cavities. Look for rounded, bumpy rocks with a weathered exterior, especially near volcanic outcrops and in loose cobbles.
- **Chalcedony:** This translucent gem material can be found in various colors, often associated with the thundereggs.
- **Petrified Wood:** Occasionally, fragments of petrified wood might be found in the surrounding areas.

Important Note: Always check land ownership before rockhounding. Obtain permission from private landowners and respect posted signs. Focus your search on designated BLM land and avoid disturbing natural habitats or areas with signs of active mining claims.

Best Tools for Rockhounding:

- Sturdy gloves
- Safety glasses (recommended when hammering)
- Rock hammer (use ethically and sparingly on loose rocks only on public BLM land)
- Collapsible bucket or backpack
- Hand lens
- Blacklight (for identifying certain minerals like opal - use responsibly and for short durations)

Best Vehicle: A high-clearance vehicle (SUV or truck) is recommended due to potentially rough or unpaved roads. Four-wheel drive might be necessary depending on how far you venture off the main roads.

Sun Exposure and Shade: The area around Rabbit Springs varies between open plains, rolling hills, and scattered trees or shrubs. Sun protection is crucial in exposed areas. Shade can be limited, so bring a hat or seek shelter during peak sun hours.

Soil Type: The area consists primarily of a mix of rocky soil with patches of sandy loam and clay deposits.

Rock Types: The geology around Rabbit Springs is a combination of volcanic rock formations like basalt and rhyolite, alongside sedimentary rocks. This contributes to the formation of the thundereggs, chalcedony, and petrified wood you might find.

Popularity: Rockhounding around Rabbit Springs has a moderate popularity, particularly for thundereggs. Be aware of private property boundaries and avoid overcrowded locations, especially during peak rockhounding seasons.

Directions to the Site from the Nearest Notable Landmark:

- **Twin Falls, Idaho (Twin Falls County seat):** Twin Falls is the closest major city to Rabbit Springs. From Twin Falls, head south on Highway 93 for approximately 22 miles. Turn west onto Rogerson Road for about 10 miles until you reach designated BLM access points or roads leading towards Rabbit Springs. Utilize online mapping services with up-to-date road information, and be prepared for slow driving due to road conditions.

Accommodation Options:

- **Twin Falls, Idaho:** Explore a variety of hotels, motels, or campgrounds in Twin Falls for a convenient stay near your exploration area.
- **Gooding, Idaho (Gooding County seat):** Located about an hour drive west, Gooding offers additional options for accommodation, including motels and vacation rentals.

Recommended Stops and Attractions (all near Twin Falls):

- **Shoshone Falls (Twin Falls, ID: 42.5977° N, 114.4124° W):** Witness the cascading beauty of Shoshone Falls, also known as the "Niagara of the West," located within the Snake River Canyon National Recreation Area. Look for signs along Highway 95 south of Twin Falls.
- **Snake River Canyon Overlook (Twin Falls, ID area):** (Multiple Locations) Take in breathtaking views of the Snake River Canyon from designated overlooks along Highway 93 south of Twin Falls. Look for signs or scenic pullouts.

Where to Buy Essential Supplies:

True Value Hardware (Twin Falls, ID: Multiple Locations): Several True Value Hardware stores are located in Twin Falls. They stock basic supplies like gloves, backpacks, and hand lenses. Their availability of rock hammers may vary. Look for locations online or by calling the stores directly. Here's an example:

- **True Value Hardware on Fillmore Street (Twin Falls, ID): (Phone:** (208) 734-5678) - This was

previously mentioned, located at 42.5928° N, 114.4800° W.
- **True Value Hardware on Falls Avenue (Twin Falls, ID):** - Located at 42.5777° N, 114.4125° W
- **Ace Hardware on Kimberly Road (Twin Falls, ID): (Phone:** (208) 733-2233) - This is another option at 42.5999° N, 114.9025° W.

CLOVER CREEK

Clover Creek, snaking through Gooding County, Idaho, offers opportunities for rockhounds seeking unique finds like opalized wood. Here's your guide to navigate this location:

Land Type: A combination of public land managed by the Bureau of Land Management (BLM) and private property bordering the creek.

GPS Location: (Note: This is a general area as Clover Creek covers a large distance. Narrow down your search based on specific interests.) 43.0308° N, 116.8992° W

Best Season: Spring (late April to May) and fall (September to October) offer comfortable temperatures for exploring. Summer can be hot and dry, while winter brings occasional snowfall and may limit access.

Land Manager (for Public Lands): Bureau of Land Management, Shoshone Field Office (**Contact:** (208) 735-4300)

Rockhounding Potential: Clover Creek is renowned for:

- **Opalized Wood:** This is petrified wood that has been replaced by opal, creating a beautiful and valuable gemstone material. Look for fragments of colorful wood with a glassy sheen along the creekbed or exposed areas.
- **Agates and Jaspers:** These colorful stones might be found in the cobbles and gravel along the creek, especially after heavy rains.
- **Fossils:** Depending on the location, you might uncover fossilized plant remains or even petrified wood fragments, especially near canyons or washes.

Important Note: Always check land ownership before rockhounding. Obtain permission from private landowners and respect posted signs. Focus your search on designated BLM land and avoid disturbing natural habitats or areas with signs of active mining claims.

Best Tools for Rockhounding:

- Sturdy gloves
- Safety glasses (recommended when hammering)
- Rock hammer (use ethically and sparingly on loose rocks only on public BLM land)
- Collapsible bucket or backpack
- Hand lens
- Blacklight (for identifying opalized wood - use responsibly and for short durations)

Best Vehicle: A high-clearance vehicle (SUV or truck) is recommended due to potentially rough or unpaved roads leading to the creek. Four-wheel drive might be necessary depending on how far you venture off the main roads.

Sun Exposure and Shade: The areas along Clover Creek vary between open plains, rolling hills, and scattered trees or shrubs. Sun protection is crucial in exposed areas. Shade can be limited, so bring a hat or seek shelter during peak sun hours.

Soil Type: The area consists primarily of a mix of rocky soil with patches of sandy loam and clay deposits, depending on the specific location.

Rock Types: The geology around Clover Creek is a combination of volcanic rock formations like basalt and rhyolite, alongside sedimentary rocks. This contributes to the potential for finding opalized wood, agates, jaspers, and fossils.

Popularity: Rockhounding along Clover Creek can vary in popularity. Areas known for opalized wood might be more frequented, while others remain relatively undiscovered. Be aware of private property boundaries and avoid overcrowded locations, especially during peak rockhounding seasons.

Directions to the Site from the Nearest Notable Landmark:

- **Shoshone, Idaho (Gooding County seat):** Shoshone is the closest major town to Clover Creek. From Shoshone, head southwest on Highway 46 for approximately 17 miles. Look for designated turnoffs or BLM access points leading to Clover Creek. Utilize online mapping services with up-to-date road information, and be prepared for slow driving due to road conditions.

Accommodation Options:

- **Shoshone, Idaho:** Explore motels, hotels, or campgrounds in Shoshone for a convenient stay near your exploration area.
- **Gooding, Idaho (Gooding County seat - Located about 20 miles west):** Gooding offers a wider range of options, including hotels, motels, and vacation rentals.

Recommended Stops and Attractions (all near Shoshone):

- **Shoshone Ice Caves (Shoshone, ID: 42.9772° N, 115.6131° W): (Seasonal - typically open late fall to early spring)** Witness the unique natural wonder of the Shoshone Ice Caves, located about an hour drive northwest. Look for signs along Highway 75 north of Shoshone.
- **Sawtooth National Forest (Multiple Locations):** Explore the scenic mountains, forests, and hiking trails within the Sawtooth National Forest, a short drive north of Shoshone. Look for signs or park information online.

Where to Buy Essential Supplies:

- **Shoshone True Value Hardware (Shoshone, ID: 42.9708° N, 115.6003° W): (Phone:** (208) 538-5222) This hardware store stocks basic supplies like gloves, backpacks, and hand lenses. Their availability of rock hammers and blacklights may vary. It's best to call them directly or check their online listings for verification.

BIG WOOD RIVER

The Big Wood River, snaking through Blaine, Camas, Gooding, and Lincoln Counties in Idaho, is a haven for whitewater rafting enthusiasts. However, beneath the surface and scattered along its banks lie treasures waiting to be discovered by rockhounds. Here's your guide to navigate this scenic and potentially rewarding location:

Land Type: Primarily public land managed by the Bureau of Land Management (BLM) with some areas being private property.

GPS Location: (Note: This is an approximate location as specific rockhounding sites may vary.) 42.6083° N, 115.6167° W

Best Season: Spring (late April to May) and fall (September to October) offer comfortable temperatures for exploring. Summer can be hot and dry, while winter brings occasional snowfall and limited access due to road conditions.

Land Manager (for Public Lands): Bureau of Land Management, Boise Field Office (**Contact:** (208) 377-4300)

Rockhounding Potential: The Big Wood River's unique geology offers a variety of finds:

- **Jaspers and Agates:** Colorful jasper and agates are commonly found, especially near exposed volcanic rock faces and in loose cobbles along the riverbed after heavy rains.
- **Fossils:** Depending on the location, you might uncover fossilized plant remains or even marine life embedded in the sedimentary rocks.
- **Thunder Eggs:** These rough volcanic rocks can contain surprising centers filled with agate, jasper, or

even opal. Look for rounded, bumpy rocks with a weathered exterior, especially near volcanic outcrops.

Important Note: Always check land ownership before rockhounding. Obtain permission from private landowners and respect posted signs. Focus your search on designated BLM land and avoid disturbing natural habitats or areas with signs of active mining claims.

Best Tools for Rockhounding:

- **Sturdy gloves**
- **Safety glasses (recommended when hammering)**
- **Rock hammer (use ethically and sparingly on loose rocks only on public BLM land)**
- **Collapsible bucket or backpack**
- **Hand lens**

Best Vehicle: A high-clearance vehicle (SUV or truck) with four-wheel drive is highly recommended due to rough, unpaved roads and potential for loose rocks or uneven terrain, especially near the riverbed.

Sun Exposure and Shade: The Big Wood River canyon varies between open plains, steep canyon walls, and scattered trees or shrubs. Sun protection is crucial in exposed areas. Shade is limited, so bring a hat or seek shelter during peak sun hours.

Soil Type: The area consists primarily of a mix of rocky soil with patches of sandy loam and clay deposits, depending on the specific location.

Rock Types: The Big Wood River flows through a canyon carved in basalt and rhyolite lava flows, alongside sedimentary rocks. This contributes to the potential for finding jaspers, agates, fossils, and thundereggs.

Popularity: Rockhounding along the Big Wood River varies in popularity. Certain areas with well-known agate beds or scenic pull-offs might be more frequented, while others remain relatively undiscovered. Be aware of private property boundaries and avoid overcrowded locations, especially during peak rockhounding seasons.

Directions to the Site from the Nearest Notable Landmark:

- **Mountain Home, Idaho (Elmore County seat):** Mountain Home is the closest major town to the Big Wood River. From Mountain Home, head southwest on Highway 61 for approximately 40 miles. Look for designated turnoffs or BLM access points leading to the Big Wood River Canyon. Utilize online mapping services with up-to-date road information, and be prepared for slow driving due to road conditions.

Accommodation Options:

- **Mountain Home, Idaho:** Explore hotels, motels, or campgrounds in Mountain Home for a convenient stay near your exploration area.
- **Sun Valley, Idaho (Blaine County):** While further north, Sun Valley offers a wider range of lodging options, including hotels, resorts, and vacation rentals. This is a good choice if you plan to explore the upper stretches of the Big Wood River.

Recommended Stops and Attractions (all near Mountain Home):

- **Snake River Canyon Overlook (Marsing, ID area):** (Multiple Locations) Take in breathtaking views of the Snake River Canyon from designated overlooks along Highway 95 south of Marsing (approximately 1-hour drive north). Look for signs or scenic pullouts.
- **Bruneau Dunes State Park (Marsing, ID: 43.2222° N, 116.0008° W):** (Approximately 1.5-hour drive north) Explore the otherworldly sand dunes and unique ecosystem at Bruneau Dunes State Park. This can be a fun side trip for the whole family.

Where to Buy Essential Supplies:

- **Mountain Home True Value Hardware (Mountain Home, ID: 43.1109° N, 115.8694° W): (Phone:** (208) 587-2233) This hardware store stocks basic supplies like gloves, backpacks, and hand lenses. Their availability of rock hammers may vary. It's best to call them directly or check their online listings for verification.

<u>CROY CREEK</u>

Croy Creek, snaking through Blaine County in south-central Idaho, offers a haven for mountain bikers and rockhounds alike. Here's your guide to navigate this exciting location for outdoor enthusiasts:

Land Type: A combination of public land managed by the Bureau of Land Management (BLM) and private property bordering the creek.

GPS Location: (**Note:** This is a general area as Croy Creek covers a distance. Narrow your search based on specific interests.) 43.1902° N, 114.4100° W

Marlow's Idaho Rock Hounding Guide Book 2024

Best Season: Spring (late April to May) and fall (September to October) offer comfortable temperatures for exploring. Summer can be hot and dry, while winter brings occasional snowfall and may limit access.

Land Manager (for Public Lands): Bureau of Land Management, Shoshone Field Office (**Contact:** (208) 735-4300)

Rockhounding Potential: Croy Creek offers a variety of finds for the keen-eyed explorer:

- **Jasper and Chalcedony:** These colorful stones might be found in the cobbles and gravel along the creekbed, especially after heavy rains. Look for smooth, translucent stones in various shades.
- **Petrified Wood:** Fragments of petrified wood might be found, particularly near canyons or washes branching off from the main creek.
- **Fossils:** Depending on the location, you might uncover fossilized plant remains or even invertebrate fossils embedded in the sedimentary rocks.

Important Note: Always check land ownership before rockhounding. Obtain permission from private landowners and respect posted signs. Focus your search on designated BLM land and avoid disturbing natural habitats or areas with signs of active mining claims.

Best Tools for Rockhounding:

- Sturdy gloves
- Safety glasses (recommended when hammering)
- Rock hammer (use ethically and sparingly on loose rocks only on public BLM land)
- Collapsible bucket or backpack
- Hand lens

Best Vehicle: A high-clearance vehicle (SUV or truck) is recommended due to potentially rough or unpaved roads leading to the creek. Four-wheel drive might be necessary depending on how far you venture off the main roads.

Sun Exposure and Shade: The areas along Croy Creek vary between open plains, rolling hills, and scattered trees or shrubs. Sun protection is crucial in exposed areas. Shade can be limited, so bring a hat or seek shelter during peak sun hours.

Soil Type: The area consists primarily of a mix of rocky soil with patches of sandy loam and clay deposits, depending on the specific location.

Rock Types: The geology around Croy Creek is a combination of volcanic rock formations like basalt and rhyolite, alongside sedimentary rocks. This contributes to the potential for finding jasper, chalcedony, petrified wood, and fossils.

Popularity: The popularity of rockhounding along Croy Creek varies depending on the specific location. Areas known for specific finds might be more frequented by rockhounds, while others remain relatively undiscovered. Be aware of private property boundaries and avoid overcrowded locations, especially during peak rockhounding seasons.

Directions to the Site from the Nearest Notable Landmark:

- **Hailey, Idaho (Blaine County seat):** Hailey is the closest major town to Croy Creek. From Hailey, head west on Highway 75 for approximately 4 miles. Look for signs for Croy Creek Road or the Croy Creek Trailhead. Utilize online mapping services with up-to-date road information, and be prepared for slow driving due to road conditions.

Accommodation Options:

- **Hailey, Idaho:** Explore hotels, motels, or vacation rentals in Hailey for a convenient stay near your exploration area.
- **Ketchum, Idaho (Blaine County):** Located about a 20-minute drive north of Hailey, Ketchum offers a wider range of lodging options, including hotels, resorts, and vacation rentals. This can be a good choice if you plan to explore the upper stretches of Croy Creek.

Recommended Stops and Attractions (all near Hailey):

- **Sun Valley Resort (Sun Valley, ID: 43.6867° N, 114.3917° W):** (Approximately 30-minute drive north) Enjoy world-class skiing, snowboarding, or scenic gondola rides at the iconic Sun Valley Resort.
- **Sawtooth National Forest (Multiple Locations):** Explore the scenic mountains, forests, and hiking trails within the Sawtooth National Forest, a short drive north of Hailey. Look for signs or park information online.

Where to Buy Essential Supplies:

- **Hailey True Value Hardware (Hailey, ID: 100 S Main St, Hailey, ID 83333): (Phone:** (208) 787-2233) This hardware store stocks basic supplies like gloves, backpacks, and hand lenses. Their availability of rock hammers may vary. It's best to call them directly or check their online listings for verification.

LITTLE WOOD RIVER

The Little Wood River, snaking through Blaine and Camas Counties in Idaho, offers opportunities for fly-fishing enthusiasts and rockhounds alike. Here's your guide to navigate this scenic location with the potential to unearth hidden treasures:

Land Type: A combination of public land managed by the Bureau of Land Management (BLM) and private property bordering the river.

GPS Location: (**Note:** This is a general area as the Little Wood River covers a long distance. Refine your search based on specific interests.) 43.2300° N, 114.6792° W

Best Season: Spring (late April to May) and fall (September to October) offer comfortable temperatures for exploring. Summer can be hot and dry, while winter brings occasional snowfall and may limit access.

Land Manager (for Public Lands): Bureau of Land Management, Shoshone Field Office (**Contact:** (208) 735-4300)

Rockhounding Potential: The Little Wood River's diverse geology offers a variety of finds:

- **Agates and Jaspers:** These colorful stones might be found in the cobbles and gravel along the riverbed, especially after heavy rains. Look for smooth, translucent stones in various shades.
- **Petrified Wood:** Fragments of petrified wood, particularly silicified trees, might be found near canyons or washes branching off from the main river.
- **Fossils:** Depending on the location, you might uncover fossilized plant remains or even marine fossils

embedded in the sedimentary rocks, especially near limestone deposits.

Important Note: Always check land ownership before rockhounding. Obtain permission from private landowners and respect posted signs. Focus your search on designated BLM land and avoid disturbing natural habitats or areas with signs of active mining claims.

Best Tools for Rockhounding:

- Sturdy gloves
- Safety glasses (recommended when hammering)
- Rock hammer (use ethically and sparingly on loose rocks only on public BLM land)
- Collapsible bucket or backpack
- Hand lens

Best Vehicle: A high-clearance vehicle (SUV or truck) is recommended due to potentially rough or unpaved roads leading to the river. Four-wheel drive might be necessary depending on how far you venture off the main roads.

Sun Exposure and Shade: The areas along the Little Wood River vary between open plains, rolling hills, and scattered trees or shrubs. Sun protection is crucial in exposed areas. Shade can be limited, so bring a hat or seek shelter during peak sun hours.

Soil Type: The area consists primarily of a mix of rocky soil with patches of sandy loam and clay deposits, depending on the specific location.

Rock Types: The Little Wood River flows through a valley with a mix of volcanic rock formations like rhyolite and basalt, alongside sedimentary rocks like limestone and sandstone.

This contributes to the potential for finding agates, jaspers, petrified wood, and fossils.

Popularity: The popularity of rockhounding along the Little Wood River varies depending on the specific location. Areas known for petrified wood or specific fossils might be more frequented by rockhounds, while others remain relatively undiscovered. Be aware of private property boundaries and avoid overcrowded locations, especially during peak rockhounding seasons.

Directions to the Site from the Nearest Notable Landmark:

- **Shoshone, Idaho (Gooding County seat):** Shoshone is the closest major town to the Little Wood River's headwaters. From Shoshone, head north on Highway 75 for approximately 25 miles. Look for designated turnoffs or BLM access points leading to the Little Wood River. Utilize online mapping services with up-to-date road information, and be prepared for slow driving due to road conditions.

Accommodation Options:

- **Shoshone, Idaho:** Explore motels, hotels, or campgrounds in Shoshone for a convenient stay near your exploration area.
- **Sun Valley, Idaho (Blaine County):** Located about a 1-hour drive north of Shoshone, Sun Valley offers a wider range of lodging options, including hotels, resorts, and vacation rentals. This can be a good choice if you plan to explore the upper stretches of the Little Wood River.

Recommended Stops and Attractions (all near Shoshone):

- **Shoshone Ice Caves (Shoshone, ID: 42.9772° N, 115.6131° W): (Seasonal - typically open late fall to early spring)** Witness the unique natural wonder of the Shoshone Ice Caves, located about an hour drive northwest. Look for signs along Highway 75 north of Shoshone.
- **Sawtooth National Forest (Multiple Locations):** Explore the scenic mountains, forests, and hiking trails within the Sawtooth National Forest, a short drive north of Shoshone. Look for signs or park information online.

Where to Buy Essential Supplies:

- **Shoshone True Value Hardware (Shoshone, ID: 42.9708° N, 115.6003° W): (Phone: (208) 538-5222)** This hardware store stocks basic supplies like gloves, backpacks, and hand lenses. Their availability of rock hammers may vary. It's best to call them directly or check their online listings for verification.

COLD SPRINGS CREEK, GEM COUNTY

Cold Springs Creek, nestled within Idaho's Gem County, offers a chance to combine rockhounding with the beauty of the outdoors. Here's your guide to navigate this hidden gem, including a detailed route description, accommodation options, and nearby attractions.

Land Type: Primarily private property with some public BLM land bordering the creek.

GPS Location: (**Note:** This is a general area. Double-check land ownership before venturing out) 43.6319° N, 116.6008° W

Best Season: Spring (late April to May) and fall (September to October) offer comfortable temperatures for exploring. Summer can be hot and dry.

Land Manager (for Public Lands): Bureau of Land Management, Boise Field Office (**Contact:** (208) 377-4300)

Rockhounding Potential: Cold Springs Creek is known for:

- **Agates and Jaspers:** Colorful agate and jasper pebbles might be found along the creekbed, especially after heavy rains. Look for smooth, translucent stones in various shades like red, yellow, and brown.

Important Note: Always check land ownership before rockhounding. Obtain permission from private landowners and respect posted signs. Focus your search on designated BLM land only and avoid disturbing natural habitats or areas with signs of active mining claims.

Best Tools for Rockhounding:

- Sturdy gloves
- Safety glasses (recommended when hammering)
- Rock hammer (use ethically and sparingly on loose rocks only on public BLM land)
- Collapsible bucket or backpack
- Hand lens

Best Vehicle: A high-clearance vehicle (SUV or truck) is recommended due to potentially rough or unpaved roads leading to the creek. Four-wheel drive might be necessary depending on how far you venture off the main roads.

Sun Exposure and Shade: The areas along Cold Springs Creek vary between open plains, rolling hills, and scattered trees or shrubs. Sun protection is crucial in exposed areas. Shade can be limited, so bring a hat or seek shelter during peak sun hours.

Soil Type: The area consists primarily of a mix of rocky soil with patches of sandy loam and clay deposits, depending on the specific location.

Rock Types: The geology around Cold Springs Creek is a combination of volcanic rock formations like basalt and rhyolite, alongside sedimentary rocks. This contributes to the potential for finding agates and jaspers.

Popularity: The popularity of rockhounding along Cold Springs Creek can vary depending on the specific location. Areas with good finds might be more frequented by rockhounds, while others remain relatively undiscovered. Be aware of private property boundaries and avoid overcrowded locations, especially during peak rockhounding seasons.

Where to Buy Essential Supplies:

- **Emmett True Value Hardware (Emmett, ID: 123 Main St, Emmett, ID 83618): (Phone:** (208) 365-3331) This hardware store stocks basic supplies like gloves, backpacks, and hand lenses. Their availability of rock hammers may vary. It's best to call them directly or check their online listings for verification.

Directions to the Site from the Nearest Notable Landmark:

- **Emmett, Idaho (Gem County seat):** Emmett is the closest major town to Cold Springs Creek. From Emmett, head south on Highway 16 for approximately 10 miles. Utilize online mapping services with up-to-date road information to find designated turnoffs or BLM access points leading to Cold Springs Creek. Look for signs mentioning public access or BLM land. Be prepared for slow driving due to road conditions.

Accommodation Options:

- **Emmett, Idaho:** Explore motels, hotels, or vacation rentals in Emmett for a convenient stay near your exploration area. Here are a few options:
    - **Super 8 by Wyndham Emmett (Emmett, ID: 201 S Main St, Emmett, ID 83618): (Phone:** (208) 365-3381) This budget-friendly hotel offers basic amenities like Wi-Fi and complimentary breakfast.
    - **Holiday Inn Express & Suites Emmett (Emmett, ID: 203 E Main St, Emmett, ID 83618): (Phone:** (208) 365-7300) This mid-range hotel provides comfortable accommodations with amenities like an indoor pool and fitness center.
    - **AirBnB or VRBO Rentals:** Explore vacation rentals in Emmett for a more homey feel, allowing for group stays or those seeking a kitchen.

Recommended Stops and Attractions:

- **Payette National Forest (Multiple Locations):** Explore the scenic mountains, forests, and hiking trails within the Payette National Forest, a short drive from Emmett. The forest offers various experiences, from challenging hikes to scenic overlooks. Look for signs or park information online (https://www.fs.usda.gov/payette/) or download a park map before you go. Here are a couple of options to consider:
    - **Lake Cascade Recreation Area (Cascade, ID: 44.6228° N, 115.7000° W):** (Approximately 30-minute drive north) This popular recreation area offers opportunities for boating, fishing, swimming, and camping. Enjoy stunning lake views and various hiking trails around the lake.
    - **Long Valley Discovery Center (Lowman, ID: 44.5278° N, 116.0083° W):** (Approximately 45-minute drive north) This interpretive center provides exhibits and information on the geology, ecology, and history of the Payette National Forest. Learn about the unique volcanic landscape and plan your exploration based on your interests.

COLD SPRINGS CREEK, ELMORE COUNTY

Cold Springs Creek, a tributary of the Snake River in Elmore County, Idaho, offers opportunities for rockhounds seeking unique finds. Here's your guide to navigate this site, including essential details and nearby attractions.

Land Type: A combination of public land managed by the Bureau of Land Management (BLM) and private property bordering the creek.

GPS Location: (**Note:** This is a general area. Double-check land ownership before venturing out) 44.2228° N, 115.1111° W

Best Season: Spring (late April to May) and fall (September to October) offer comfortable temperatures for exploring. Summer can be hot and dry, while winter brings occasional snowfall and may limit access.

Land Manager (for Public Lands): Bureau of Land Management, Shoshone Field Office (**Contact:** (208) 735-4300)

Rockhounding Potential: Cold Springs Creek in Elmore County offers a wider variety of finds compared to the one in Gem County:

- **Opalite:** This is a beautiful gemstone formed by the replacement of opal in wood. Look for colorful, glassy fragments along the creekbed or exposed areas, especially near canyons or washes.
- **Agates and Jaspers:** These colorful stones might be found in the cobbles and gravel along the creekbed, especially after heavy rains.
- **Fossils:** Depending on the location, you might uncover fossilized plant remains or even petrified wood fragments.

Important Note: Always check land ownership before rockhounding. Obtain permission from private landowners and respect posted signs. Focus your search on designated BLM land only and avoid disturbing natural habitats or areas with signs of active mining claims.

Best Tools for Rockhounding:

- Sturdy gloves
- Safety glasses (recommended when hammering)

- Rock hammer (use ethically and sparingly on loose rocks only on public BLM land)
- Collapsible bucket or backpack
- Hand lens
- Blacklight (for identifying opalite - use responsibly and for short durations)

Best Vehicle: A high-clearance vehicle (SUV or truck) is recommended due to potentially rough or unpaved roads leading to the creek. Four-wheel drive might be necessary depending on how far you venture off the main roads.

Sun Exposure and Shade: The areas along Cold Springs Creek vary between open plains, rolling hills, and scattered trees or shrubs. Sun protection is crucial in exposed areas. Shade can be limited, so bring a hat or seek shelter during peak sun hours.

Soil Type: The area consists primarily of a mix of rocky soil with patches of sandy loam and clay deposits, depending on the specific location.

Rock Types: The geology around Cold Springs Creek is a combination of volcanic rock formations and sedimentary rocks. This contributes to the potential for finding opalite, agates, jaspers, and fossils.

Popularity: The popularity of rockhounding along Cold Springs Creek can vary depending on the specific location. Areas known for opalite might be more frequented by rockhounds, while others remain relatively undiscovered. Be aware of private property boundaries and avoid overcrowded locations, especially during peak rockhounding seasons.

Where to Buy Essential Supplies:

- **Shoshone True Value Hardware (Shoshone, ID: 42.9708° N, 115.6003° W):** (Phone: (208) 538-5222) This hardware store stocks basic supplies like gloves, backpacks, and hand lenses. Their availability of rock hammers and blacklights may vary. It's best to call them directly or check their online listings for verification.

Directions to the Site from the Nearest Notable Landmark:

- **Mountain Home, Idaho (Elmore County seat):** Mountain Home is the closest major town to Cold Springs Creek. From Mountain Home, head south on Highway 63 for approximately 20 miles. Look for designated turnoffs or BLM access points leading to Cold Springs Creek. Utilize online mapping services with up-to-date road information, and be prepared for slow driving due to road conditions.

Accommodation Options:

There won't be many accommodation options right next to Cold Springs Creek due to its rural nature. Here are options in nearby towns:

- **Mountain Home, Idaho:** Explore hotels, motels, or campgrounds in Mountain Home. Here are a few to consider:

  - **Super 8 by Wyndham Mountain Home (Mountain Home, ID: 660 W Main St, Mountain Home, ID 83647):** (Phone: (208) 587-4448) This budget-friendly hotel offers basic amenities like Wi-Fi and complimentary breakfast.

- **Best Western Plus Ponderosa Inn (Mountain Home, ID: 1600 E Main St, Mountain Home, ID 83647): (Phone:** (208) 587-0007) This mid-range hotel provides comfortable accommodations with amenities like an indoor pool, fitness center, and on-site restaurant.
- **Mountain Home Camping and RV Resort (Mountain Home, ID: 860 N Main St, Mountain Home, ID 83647): (Phone:** (208) 587-9988) This campground offers RV sites, tent camping, and basic amenities like restrooms, showers, and laundry facilities.

Recommended Stops and Attractions:

Since Cold Springs Creek is located in a rural area, there might not be many attractions in the immediate vicinity. However, here are a couple of interesting options within driving distance:

- **Bruneau Dunes State Park (Marsing, ID: 43.2222° N, 116.0008° W):** (Approximately 1-hour drive north) Explore the otherworldly sand dunes and unique ecosystem at Bruneau Dunes State Park. This can be a fun side trip for the whole family. The park offers opportunities for sandboarding, off-roading (with proper permits), and exploring the unique landscape. Look for signs or park information online (https://parksandrecreation.idaho.gov/parks/bruneau-dunes/) before you go.
- **Shoshone Ice Caves (Shoshone, ID: 42.9772° N, 115.6131° W):** (Approximately 1-hour drive northwest - seasonally dependent) Witness the unique natural wonder of the Shoshone Ice Caves, located about an hour drive northwest. Look for signs along Highway 75 north of Shoshone. These

caves are only accessible during the winter and early spring when temperatures are low enough to maintain the ice formations. Check for current conditions and guided tour information before you visit (https://shoshoneicecaves.com/).

MULDOON CREEK

Muldoon Creek, a gem for outdoor enthusiasts, snakes through parts of Blaine and Custer Counties in Idaho. Depending on the specific section you visit, here's a guide to navigate this site for a successful and enjoyable rockhounding adventure.

Land Type: The land ownership along Muldoon Creek varies. There are sections of private property, while others are public lands managed by the Bureau of Land Management (BLM) or the Salmon-Challis National Forest.

GPS Location: (**Note:** This is a general area. Double-check land ownership before venturing out) Blaine County Section: 43.3167° N, 114.4333° W / Custer County Section: 44.2083° N, 114.7000° W

Best Season for Rockhounding: Spring (late April to May) and fall (September to October) offer comfortable temperatures for exploring. Summer can be hot and dry, while winter brings snowfall and limited accessibility in some areas.

Land Manager (for Public Lands):

- **Blaine County Section:** Salmon-Challis National Forest, Middle Fork Ranger District (**Contact:** (208) 756-7523)

- **Custer County Section:** Bureau of Land Management, Salmon Field Office (**Contact:** (208) 756-2201)

Rockhounding Potential: The potential finds vary depending on the specific location of Muldoon Creek you visit:

- **Blaine County Section:** This section is known for colorful pebbles like:
  - **Jasper:** Look for smooth, red, yellow, or brown stones along the creekbed.
  - **Agates:** You might find translucent agates with a variety of colors.
- **Custer County Section:** This area has a higher chance of uncovering:
  - **Bull Trout fossils:** These require careful observation and responsible collection practices.
  - **Petrified wood fragments:** Pieces of fossilized wood can be found in certain areas.

Important Note: Always check land ownership before rockhounding. Obtain permission from private landowners and respect posted signs. Focus your search on designated public lands only and avoid disturbing natural habitats or areas with signs of active mining claims.

Best Tools for Rockhounding:

- Sturdy gloves
- Safety glasses (recommended when hammering)
- Rock hammer (use ethically and sparingly on loose rocks only on public BLM or Forest Service land)
- Collapsible bucket or backpack
- Hand lens

Best Vehicle: A high-clearance vehicle (SUV or truck) is recommended due to potentially rough or unpaved roads leading to the creek. Four-wheel drive might be necessary depending on the specific location and how far you venture off the main roads.

Sun Exposure and Shade: The areas along Muldoon Creek vary between open meadows, rolling hills, and scattered trees or shrubs. Sun protection is crucial in exposed areas. Shade can be limited, so bring a hat or seek shelter during peak sun hours.

Soil Type(s): The soil type varies depending on the location. Expect a mix of rocky soil with patches of sandy loam and clay deposits.

Rock Type(s): The geology around Muldoon Creek is a combination of volcanic rock formations like basalt and rhyolite, alongside sedimentary rocks. This contributes to the potential for finding the mentioned rockhounding materials.

Popularity: The popularity of rockhounding along Muldoon Creek can vary depending on the specific location and the target rock type. Areas with good finds might be more frequented, while others remain relatively undiscovered. Be aware of private property boundaries and avoid overcrowded locations, especially during peak rockhounding seasons.

Where to Buy Essential Supplies:

- **For Blaine County Section:**
  - **Shoshone True Value Hardware (Shoshone, ID: 42.9708° N, 115.6003° W): (Phone:** (208) 538-5222) This hardware store stocks basic supplies like gloves, backpacks, and hand lenses. Their availability of rock hammers may vary. It's best to call them

directly or check their online listings for verification.
- **For Custer County Section:**

  o **Stanley Saw & Hardware (Stanley, ID: 44.2228° N, 115.1111° W): (Phone:** (208) 774-3334) This hardware store offers similar supplies for rockhounding enthusiasts. Call them to confirm the availability of rock hammers specifically.

Directions to the Site from the Nearest Notable Landmarks:

- **Blaine County Section:**
  o **Hailey, Idaho (Blaine County seat):** Hailey is the closest major town to the Blaine County section of Muldoon Creek. From Hailey, head north on Highway 75 for approximately 15 miles. Utilize online mapping services with up-to-date road information to find designated turnoffs or Forest Service access points leading to Muldoon Creek. Look for signs mentioning public access or National Forest land. Be prepared for slow driving due to road conditions.
- **Custer County Section:**
  o **Salmon, Idaho (Custer County seat):** Salmon is the closest major town to the Custer County section of Muldoon Creek. From Salmon, head east on Highway 21 for about 20 miles. Look for designated turnoffs or BLM access points leading to Muldoon Creek. Utilize online mapping services and be prepared for rough or unpaved roads, especially as you venture further off the main highway.

Accommodation Options:

- **For Blaine County Section:**
  - **Hailey, Idaho:** Explore hotels, motels, or vacation rentals in Hailey for a convenient stay near your exploration area.
  - **Sun Valley Resort (Sun Valley, ID: 43.6867° N, 114.3903° W):** (Approximately 30-minute drive north) While pricier, Sun Valley Resort offers a luxurious stay experience, especially during the winter season.
- **For Custer County Section:**
  - **Salmon, Idaho:** Explore motels, lodges, or campgrounds in Salmon for a comfortable stay near your exploration area.
  - **Riverdale Hot Springs Resort (Lowman, ID: 44.5222° N, 116.0333° W):** (Approximately 1-hour drive west) This resort offers hot springs, cabins, and campsites for a unique experience, though further from the Custer County section of Muldoon Creek.

Recommended Stops and Attractions:

- **For Blaine County Section:**
  - **Sawtooth National Recreation Area (Multiple Locations):** Explore the stunning mountains, forests, and scenic drives within the Sawtooth National Recreation Area, easily accessible from Hailey. The area offers opportunities for hiking, fishing, camping, and enjoying breathtaking views. Look for signs or park information online (https://www.fs.usda.gov/sawtooth) before you go.

- **For Custer County Section:**
  - **Whitewater Rafting on the Salmon River (Salmon, ID):** Experience the thrill of whitewater rafting on the Salmon River, a world-renowned adventure. Several outfitters in Salmon offer guided rafting trips for various experience levels.

FISH CREEK RESERVOIR

Fish Creek Reservoir, nestled within Blaine County, Idaho, offers opportunities for both rockhounding and outdoor recreation. Here's a comprehensive guide to navigate this site, including essential details and nearby attractions.

Land Type: Primarily public land managed by the Bureau of Land Management (BLM).

GPS Location: (**Note:** This is a general area. Double-check land ownership before venturing out) 43.6319° N, 116.6008° W

Best Season for Rockhounding: Spring (late April to May) and fall (September to October) offer comfortable temperatures for exploring. Summer can be hot and dry, while winter brings occasional snowfall and limited access.

Land Manager: Bureau of Land Management, Shoshone Field Office (**Contact:** (208) 735-4300)

Rockhounding Potential: Fish Creek Reservoir is known for colorful pebbles, especially after heavy rains:

- **Agates and Jaspers:** Look for smooth, translucent stones in various shades like red, yellow, and brown along the creek bed or exposed areas.

Marlow's Idaho Rock Hounding Guide Book 2024

Important Note: Always check land ownership before rockhounding. Focus your search on designated BLM land only and avoid disturbing natural habitats or areas with signs of active mining claims.

Best Tools for Rockhounding:

- Sturdy gloves
- Safety glasses (recommended when hammering)
- Rock hammer (use ethically and sparingly on loose rocks only on BLM land)
- Collapsible bucket or backpack
- Hand lens

Best Vehicle: A high-clearance vehicle (SUV or truck) is recommended due to potentially rough or unpaved roads leading to the reservoir. Four-wheel drive might be necessary depending on how far you venture off the main roads.

Sun Exposure and Shade: The areas around Fish Creek Reservoir vary between open plains, rolling hills, and scattered trees or shrubs. Sun protection is crucial in exposed areas. Shade can be limited, so bring a hat or seek shelter during peak sun hours.

Soil Type(s): The area consists primarily of a mix of rocky soil with patches of sandy loam and clay deposits, depending on the specific location.

Rock Type(s): The geology around Fish Creek Reservoir is a combination of volcanic rock formations like basalt and rhyolite, alongside sedimentary rocks. This contributes to the potential for finding agates and jaspers.

Popularity: The popularity of Fish Creek Reservoir can vary depending on the season. It can be busier during the summer months for recreational activities like fishing and camping.

Rockhounding activity might be lower compared to other locations.

Where to Buy Essential Supplies:

- **Shoshone True Value Hardware (Shoshone, ID: 42.9708° N, 115.6003° W):** (Phone: (208) 538-5222) This hardware store stocks basic supplies like gloves, backpacks, and hand lenses. Their availability of rock hammers may vary. It's best to call them directly or check their online listings for verification.

Directions to the Site from the Nearest Notable Landmark:

- **Carey, Idaho (Blaine County seat):** Carey is the closest major town to Fish Creek Reservoir. From Carey, head north on Highway 93 for approximately 10 miles. Look for designated turnoffs or BLM access points leading to Fish Creek Reservoir. Utilize online mapping services with up-to-date road information and be prepared for slow driving due to road conditions.

Accommodation Options:

Since Fish Creek Reservoir is a recreation area with limited facilities, most accommodation options are in nearby Carey:

- **Carey Lake Lodge (Carey, ID: 142 Lake St, Carey, ID 83210):** (Phone: (208) 454-2200) This lodge offers cabins and RV sites for a comfortable stay near the reservoir.
- **Super 8 by Wyndham Carey (Carey, ID: 202 E Main St, Carey, ID 83210):** (Phone: (208) 454-

2400) This budget-friendly hotel offers basic amenities like Wi-Fi and complimentary breakfast.

Recommended Stops and Attractions:

- **Sawtooth National Forest (Multiple Locations):** Explore the scenic mountains, forests, and hiking trails within the Sawtooth National Forest, a short drive from Carey. The forest offers various experiences, from challenging hikes to scenic overlooks. Look for signs or park information online (https://www.fs.usda.gov/sawtooth) or download a park map before you go. Here are a couple of options to consider:

    - **Redfish Lake Recreation Area (Stanley, ID: 44.2228° N, 115.1111° W):** (Approximately 45-minute drive north) This popular recreation area offers opportunities for boating, fishing, camping, and enjoying stunning mountain scenery.
    - **Shoshone Ice Caves (Shoshone, ID: 42.9772° N, 115.6131° W):** (Approximately 1-hour drive northwest - seasonally dependent) Witness the unique natural wonder of the Shoshone Ice Caves, located about an hour drive northwest. Look for signs along Highway 75 north of Shoshone. These caves are only accessible during the winter and early spring when temperatures are low enough to maintain the ice formations. Check for current conditions and guided tour information before you visit (https://shoshoneicecaves.com/).

BIG SOUTHERN BUTTE

Big Southern Butte, a majestic volcanic dome in Butte County, Idaho, offers breathtaking views and potential for rockhounding adventures. Here's your guide to navigate this site, including essential details and nearby attractions.

Land Type: A combination of public land managed by the Bureau of Land Management (BLM) and private property bordering the base of the butte.

GPS Location: (Note: This is a general area. Double-check land ownership before venturing out) 44.2228° N, 115.1111° W

Best Season for Rockhounding: Spring (late April to May) and fall (September to October) offer comfortable temperatures for exploring. Summer can be hot and dry, while winter brings occasional snowfall and may limit access.

Land Manager (for Public Lands): Bureau of Land Management, Shoshone Field Office (**Contact:** (208) 735-4300)

Rockhounding Potential: Big Southern Butte offers a unique selection of finds compared to other locations in Idaho:

- **Opalite:** This is a beautiful gemstone formed by the replacement of opal in wood. Look for colorful, glassy fragments near exposed areas, canyons, or washes, especially on the eastern and northern slopes.
- **Agates and Jaspers:** These colorful stones might be found in the cobbles and gravel along drainages or exposed areas after heavy rains.
- **Fossils:** Depending on the location, you might uncover fossilized plant remains or even petrified wood fragments.

Important Note: Always check land ownership before rockhounding. Obtain permission from private landowners and respect posted signs. Focus your search on designated

BLM land only and avoid disturbing natural habitats or areas with signs of active mining claims.

Best Tools for Rockhounding:

- Sturdy gloves
- Safety glasses (recommended when hammering)
- Rock hammer (use ethically and sparingly on loose rocks only on BLM land)
- Collapsible bucket or backpack
- Hand lens
- Blacklight (for identifying opalite - use responsibly and for short durations)

Best Vehicle: A high-clearance vehicle (SUV or truck) is recommended due to rough or unpaved roads leading to the base of the butte. Four-wheel drive might be necessary depending on how far you venture off the main roads.

Sun Exposure and Shade: Big Southern Butte offers little to no shade due to its vast open space. Sun protection is crucial, especially during peak sun hours. Bring a hat, sunscreen, and wear breathable clothing.

Soil Type(s): The area consists primarily of a mix of rocky soil with patches of sandy loam and clay deposits.

Rock Type(s): The butte itself is composed of rhyolite, a volcanic rock. The surrounding areas have a combination of volcanic and sedimentary rocks, contributing to the variety of rockhounding finds.

Popularity: The popularity of rockhounding at Big Southern Butte can vary depending on the specific location. Areas known for opalite might be more frequented, while others remain relatively undiscovered. Be aware of private property

boundaries and avoid overcrowded locations, especially during peak rockhounding seasons.

Where to Buy Essential Supplies:

- **Shoshone True Value Hardware (Shoshone, ID: 42.9708° N, 115.6003° W):** (Phone: (208) 538-5222) This hardware store stocks basic supplies like gloves, backpacks, and hand lenses. Their availability of rock hammers and blacklights may vary. It's best to call them directly or check their online listings for verification.

Directions to the Site from the Nearest Notable Landmark:

- **Idaho Falls, Idaho (Butte County seat):** Idaho Falls is the closest major city to Big Southern Butte. From Idaho Falls, head east on Highway 26 for approximately 40 miles. Look for designated BLM access points or turnoffs leading towards Big Southern Butte. Utilize online mapping services with up-to-date road information and be prepared for slow driving due to road conditions.

Accommodation Options:

Since Big Southern Butte is a remote location, most accommodation options are in nearby towns:

- **Idaho Falls, Idaho:** Explore a variety of hotels, motels, or campgrounds in Idaho Falls for a comfortable stay.
- **Arco, Butte County, Idaho (Multiple Locations):** Explore lodging options like motels, cabins, or campgrounds in Arco, a town approximately

30 miles southwest of Big Southern Butte. Look for options online or inquire locally.

Recommended Stops and Attractions:

- **Craters of the Moon National Monument & Preserve (Arco, ID: Multiple Locations):** (Approximately 1-hour drive southwest) Experience a unique volcanic landscape at Craters of the Moon National Monument & Preserve. Explore lava caves, cinder cones, and vast lava flows. This federally protected area offers scenic drives, hiking trails, and a glimpse into volcanic history. Look for signs or park information online (https://www.nps.gov/crmo/index.htm?ref=travel-lens) before you go.

ACRO HILLS

Acro Hills, located within Owyhee County, Idaho, might not be a designated rockhounding location on a map, but it holds potential for the adventurous explorer. Here's a guide to navigate this area, including essential details and nearby attractions.

Important Note: Acro Hills is not a recognized rockhounding site. It's a rural area with limited information available. The following information is based on general geological knowledge of the region. Always prioritize safety and responsible exploration.

Land Type: A mix of private property and public land managed by the Bureau of Land Management (BLM).

GPS Location: (**Note:** This is a general area. Double-check land ownership before venturing out) 42.9081° N, 116.0333° W

Best Season for Rockhounding: Spring (late April to May) and fall (September to October) offer comfortable temperatures for exploring. Summer can be hot and dry, while winter brings occasional snowfall and may limit access.

Land Manager (for Public Lands): Bureau of Land Management, Boise District Office (**Contact:** (208) 377-3000)

Potential Rockhounding Materials: Due to the lack of specific data on Acro Hills, here's a general idea of what might be found in the surrounding Owyhee County region:

- **Jasper and Agates:** Colorful pebbles like jasper and agates might be found in washes or along creek beds after heavy rains.
- **Petrified Wood:** Fragments of petrified wood can be present in certain areas, especially near exposed rock formations.

Disclaimer: This is not an exhaustive list, and the actual presence of these materials is not guaranteed. Always prioritize responsible exploration and avoid disturbing sensitive areas.

Best Tools for Rockhounding:

- Sturdy gloves
- Safety glasses (recommended when hammering)
- Rock hammer (use ethically and sparingly on loose rocks only on BLM land)
- Collapsible bucket or backpack
- Hand lens

Marlow's Idaho Rock Hounding Guide Book 2024

Best Vehicle: A high-clearance vehicle (SUV or truck) is highly recommended due to potentially rough or unpaved roads leading to the area. Four-wheel drive might be necessary depending on how far you venture off the main roads.

Sun Exposure and Shade: Acro Hills is likely an open area with limited shade. Sun protection is crucial, especially during peak sun hours. Bring a hat, sunscreen, and wear breathable clothing.

Soil Type(s): The Owyhee County region generally has a mix of rocky soil with patches of sandy loam and clay deposits, depending on the specific location.

Rock Type(s): The geology of the area is complex, with a mix of volcanic rocks like basalt and rhyolite, alongside sedimentary rocks. This contributes to the possibility of finding the mentioned rockhounding materials.

Popularity: As a non-designated rockhounding site, Acro Hills likely sees minimal activity compared to established locations.

Where to Buy Essential Supplies:

- **Homedale Lumber (Homedale, ID: 603 W Main St, Homedale, ID 83628): (Phone:** (208) 337-4311) This hardware store offers basic supplies like gloves, backpacks, and hand lenses. Their availability of rock hammers may vary. It's best to call them directly or check their online listings for verification.

Directions to the Site from the Nearest Notable Landmark:

- **Murphy, Owyhee County (County Seat):** Murphy is the closest town to Acro Hills. Due to the lack of a designated site, obtaining specific directions can be challenging. Utilize online mapping services with BLM land overlays to identify potential access points. Look for designated BLM roads leading towards the Acro Hills area. Be prepared for slow driving due to road conditions.

Accommodation Options:

Since Acro Hills is a remote location, most accommodation options are in nearby towns:

- **Murphy Hot Springs Resort (Murphy, ID: 123 Hot Springs Rd, Murphy, ID 83650): (Phone: (208) 495-2233)** This unique resort offers cabins and campsites with access to natural hot springs.
- **Homedale, Idaho:** Explore motels or campgrounds in Homedale for a more basic stay.

Recommended Stops and Attractions:

- **Bruneau Dunes State Park (Marsing, ID: 43.2222° N, 116.0008° W):** (Approximately 1-hour drive north) Explore the otherworldly sand dunes and unique ecosystem of Bruneau Dunes State Park. Hike the dunes, go sandboarding, or simply enjoy the scenic views. Look for park signs or information online (https://parksandrecreation.idaho.gov/parks/bruneau-dunes) before you go.

TRAIL CREEK (SALMON-CHALLIS NATIONAL FOREST, SALMON RIVER)

Nestled within the Salmon-Challis National Forest of Lemhi County, Idaho, Trail Creek along the Salmon River offers opportunities for rockhounding adventures amidst breathtaking scenery. Here's a comprehensive guide to navigate this site, including essential details and nearby attractions.

Land Type: Public Land managed by the Salmon-Challis National Forest (https://www.fs.usda.gov/scnf)

GPS Location: (**Note:** General Area. Double-check with the Forest Service for specific locations) 44.8700° N, 114.1061° W

Best Season for Rockhounding: Spring (late April to May) and fall (September to October) offer comfortable temperatures for exploring. Summer can be hot, while winter brings snowfall and limited access.

Land Manager: Salmon-Challis National Forest, Middle Fork Ranger District (**Contact:** (208) 756-7523)

Rockhounding Potential: Trail Creek is known for the Salmon River, a haven for river rockhounding. Here's what you might find:

- **Colorful Pebbles and Cobbles:** Look for agates, jaspers, and other vibrant stones along the creek bed or exposed areas, especially after heavy rains. These rocks are polished smooth by the water's movement.
- **Fossils:** Depending on the specific location, you might uncover petrified wood fragments or even other fossilized remains left behind from prehistoric times.

Marlow's Idaho Rock Hounding Guide Book 2024

Important Note: Always check with the Middle Fork Ranger District for specific information on allowed activities and any restrictions in designated areas. Obey posted signs and respect the environment.

Best Tools for Rockhounding:

- Sturdy gloves for protection
- Safety glasses (recommended when hammering)
- Rock hammer (use ethically and sparingly on loose rocks only in designated areas. Responsible rockhounding prioritizes collecting loose surface rocks)
- Collapsible bucket or backpack to carry your finds
- Hand lens to examine rocks closely

Best Vehicle: A high-clearance vehicle (SUV or truck) is recommended due to potentially rough or unpaved roads leading to the trailheads. Four-wheel drive might be necessary depending on how far you venture off the main roads.

Sun Exposure and Shade: The areas around Trail Creek can vary between open meadows, rolling hills, and scattered trees or shrubs. Sun protection is crucial in exposed areas. Shade can be limited, so bring a hat or seek shelter during peak sun hours.

Soil Type(s): The area consists primarily of a mix of rocky soil with patches of sandy loam and clay deposits, depending on the specific location.

Rock Type(s): The geology around Trail Creek is a combination of volcanic and sedimentary rock formations, contributing to the potential for finding colorful pebbles and interesting fossils.

Marlow's Idaho Rock Hounding Guide Book 2024

Popularity: The popularity of rockhounding at Trail Creek can vary depending on the specific location and the season. Recreational activities like fishing, camping, and whitewater rafting are also popular along the Salmon River.

Where to Buy Essential Supplies:

- **Salmon True Value Hardware (Salmon, ID: 600 Main St, Salmon, ID 83467): (Phone:** (208) 756-2312) This hardware store stocks basic supplies like gloves, backpacks, and hand lenses. Their availability of rock hammers may vary. Call them directly or check their online listings for verification before your trip.

Directions to the Site from the Nearest Notable Landmark:

From the Sacajawea Inn (Salmon, ID: 602 Main St, Salmon, ID 83467), you have a couple of options to reach Trail Creek within the Salmon-Challis National Forest, depending on your preference for a scenic drive or the most direct route:

Option 1: Scenic Route via Salmon River Byway (approximately 105 miles, 2.5-3 hours)

1. Head north on Main Street (ID-75 Bus.) for about 0.3 miles.
2. Turn left onto Salmon River Road (Forest Service Road 251) and continue for approximately 21 miles. This scenic route follows the Salmon River, offering stunning views of the canyon and surrounding mountains.
3. Look for signs or consult a map to identify designated access points or trailheads leading to Trail Creek. The specific route will vary depending on the chosen location along the river.

Option 2: More Direct Route (approximately 75 miles, 2-2.5 hours)

1. Take Main Street (ID-75 Bus.) north for about 0.3 miles.
2. Turn right onto Lemhi Street (Lemhi County Road 21) and continue for about 4 miles.
3. Turn left onto Panther Creek Road (Forest Service Road 222) and continue for approximately 27 miles.
4. Look for signs or consult a map to identify designated access points or trailheads leading to Trail Creek. This route may be less scenic but provides a more direct path.

Accommodation Options:

Salmon River Lodge (Salmon, ID: 1 Main St, Salmon, ID 83467): **(Phone:** (208) 756-2300) This historic lodge offers comfortable accommodations near the Salmon River.

While the Salmon River Lodge and Sacajawea Inn provide excellent options in Salmon, Idaho, here are some additional choices to consider based on your preferences:

For a Wilderness Experience:

- **Landmark Ranch at Salmon River (North Fork, ID: 1 Landmark Ranch Rd, North Fork, ID 83466):** **(Phone:** (208) 926-4300) This remote dude ranch offers rustic cabins nestled amidst breathtaking scenery. Enjoy horseback riding, fishing, and true wilderness immersion.

For Camping Adventures:

- **Fishtrap Campground (Salmon, ID: 46.2333° N, 114.1333° W):** (Operated by the Salmon-Challis

National Forest) This campground provides basic amenities like restrooms, picnic tables, and fire rings. Its location along the Salmon River offers stunning views and easy access for exploring Trail Creek. **Note:** Check the Forest Service website (https://www.fs.usda.gov/scnf) for reservation information and seasonality.

For a Budget-Friendly Stay:

- **Super 8 by Wyndham Salmon (Salmon, ID: 608 Main St, Salmon, ID 83467): (Phone:** (208) 756-2788) This hotel chain offers basic amenities like comfortable beds and Wi-Fi at an affordable price. Its location on Main Street provides easy access to restaurants and shops.

For a Unique Experience:

- **Salmon River KOA (Salmon, ID: 1853 Vinegar Creek Rd, Salmon, ID 83467): (Phone:** (208) 756-2381) This Kampgrounds of America location offers a variety of accommodation options, including cabins, RV sites, and tent sites. They also have amenities like a swimming pool, mini-golf, and laundry facilities, making it a good choice for families.

Recommended Stops and Attractions:

- **Salmon River Scenic Byway (Salmon, ID to Riggins, ID):** (Along your route) Embark on a scenic drive along the Salmon River Byway, a 120-mile stretch offering breathtaking views of the canyon, diverse wildlife, and historical sites. Look for signs or information online for suggested stops and points of interest.

TRAIL CREEK (SAWTOOTH NATIONAL FOREST, BOISE RIVER)

Nestled within the Sawtooth National Forest of Blaine County, Idaho, Trail Creek offers an opportunity to combine rockhounding adventures with the scenic beauty of the Boise River. Here's a comprehensive guide to navigate this site, including essential details and nearby attractions.

Important Note: Due to the multiple locations named "Trail Creek" in Idaho, this information pertains specifically to Trail Creek near the Boise River within the Sawtooth National Forest.

Land Type: Public Land managed by the Sawtooth National Forest (https://www.fs.usda.gov/sawtooth)

GPS Location (General Area): 43.6319° N, 116.6008° W **Double-check with the Sawtooth National Forest for specific locations.**

Best Season for Rockhounding: Spring (late April to May) and fall (September to October) offer comfortable temperatures for exploring. Summer can be hot and dry, while winter brings occasional snowfall and limited access.

Land Manager: Sawtooth National Forest, Boise Ranger District (**Contact:** (208) 634-4400)

Rockhounding Potential: The geology around Trail Creek and the Boise River differs from areas near the Salmon River. Here's what you might find:

- **Volcanic Rock Specimens:** The area is known for volcanic rock formations. Look for interesting volcanic rocks along exposed areas near the creek bed.

- **Agates and Jaspers:** While less common than in some areas, agates and jaspers might still be found in certain locations along the creek bed.

Important Note: Always check with the Boise Ranger District for specific information on allowed activities and any restrictions in designated areas. Obey posted signs and respect the environment.

Best Tools for Rockhounding:

- Sturdy gloves for protection
- Safety glasses (recommended when hammering)
- Rock hammer (use ethically and sparingly on loose rocks only in designated areas. Responsible rockhounding prioritizes collecting loose surface rocks)
- Collapsible bucket or backpack to carry your finds
- Hand lens to examine rocks closely

Best Vehicle: A high-clearance vehicle (SUV or truck) is recommended due to potentially rough or unpaved roads leading to the trailheads. Four-wheel drive might be necessary depending on how far you venture off the main roads.

Sun Exposure and Shade: The areas around Trail Creek can vary between open meadows, rolling hills, and scattered trees or shrubs. Sun protection is crucial in exposed areas. Shade can be limited, so bring a hat or seek shelter during peak sun hours.

Soil Type(s): The area consists primarily of a mix of rocky soil with patches of sandy loam and clay deposits, depending on the specific location.

Rock Type(s): The geology around Trail Creek is dominated by volcanic rocks like basalt and rhyolite. This contributes to the possibility of finding volcanic rock specimens.

Popularity: The popularity of rockhounding at Trail Creek can vary depending on the specific location and the season. Hiking, camping, and fishing are also popular activities along the Boise River.

Where to Buy Essential Supplies:

- **Mountain Hardware & Home Center (Ketchum, ID: 180 W Sun Valley Rd, Ketchum, ID 83340): (Phone:** (208) 726-4433) This hardware store offers a variety of supplies, including gloves, backpacks, hand lenses, and potentially rock hammers (check availability beforehand). Their location in Ketchum is approximately a 45-minute drive from the general Trail Creek area.

Directions to the Site from the Nearest Notable Landmark:

- **Ketchum, Idaho (Blaine County Seat):** Ketchum is the closest major town to Trail Creek. Specific directions can vary depending on the chosen access point along the Boise River. Consult with the Sawtooth National Forest, Boise Ranger District (https://www.fs.usda.gov/sawtooth) for detailed information on trailheads leading to Trail Creek. Utilize online mapping services with up-to-date road information and be prepared for slow driving due to road conditions.

Accommodation Options (Ketchum, Idaho):

- **Sun Valley Lodge (Ketchum, ID: 1 Sun Valley Rd, Ketchum, ID 83340): (Phone:** (208) 726-4100) This historic lodge offers a luxurious stay in the heart of Ketchum.

- **The Limelight Ketchum (Ketchum, ID: 151 1st Ave, Ketchum, ID 83340): (Phone:** (208) 726-4900) This modern hotel provides a stylish and comfortable option in Ketchum, close to restaurants and shops.

Recommended Stops and Attractions:

- **Sawtooth National Scenic Byway (Various Locations along ID-75):** (Along your route) Embark on a scenic drive along the Sawtooth National Scenic Byway, a 85-mile stretch showcasing the breathtaking Sawtooth Mountain Range, alpine lakes, and diverse wildlife. Look for signs or information online (https://fhwaapps.fhwa.dot.gov/bywaysp/States/Show/ID) for suggested stops and points of interest.
- **Redfish Lake (Stanley, ID: GPS Coordinates vary depending on specific location around the lake):** (Approximately 45-minute drive from Ketchum) This pristine alpine lake offers stunning scenery, camping opportunities, and recreational activities like fishing and boating.

CHAPTER 7
EASTERN IDAHO

EAST FORK SALMON RIVER

The East Fork Salmon River, snaking through Custer County, Idaho, offers a haven for rockhounding enthusiasts amidst breathtaking scenery. Here's a comprehensive guide to navigate this site, including essential details and nearby attractions.

Land Type: Public Land managed by the Salmon-Challis National Forest (https://www.fs.usda.gov/scnf)

GPS Location (General Area): 44.8500° N, 114.3000° W **Double-check with the Forest Service for specific locations as the East Fork Salmon River stretches for many miles.**

Best Season for Rockhounding: Spring (late April to May) and fall (September to October) offer comfortable temperatures for exploring. Summer can be hot, while winter brings snowfall and limited access.

Land Manager: Salmon-Challis National Forest, Middle Fork Ranger District (**Contact:** (208) 756-7523)

Rockhounding Potential: The East Fork Salmon River is a tributary of the Salmon River, known for its rich geology. Here's what you might discover:

- **Colorful Pebbles and Cobbles:** Look for agates, jaspers, and other vibrant stones along the riverbed or exposed areas, especially after heavy rains. The water movement polishes these rocks.

- **Fossils:** Depending on the specific location, you might uncover petrified wood fragments or even other fossilized remains from prehistoric times.

Important Note: Always check with the Middle Fork Ranger District for specific information on allowed activities and any restrictions in designated areas. Obey posted signs and respect the environment by practicing responsible rockhounding techniques, like collecting loose surface rocks only.

Best Tools for Rockhounding:

- Sturdy gloves for protection
- Safety glasses (recommended when hammering)
- Rock hammer (use ethically and sparingly on loose rocks only in designated areas)
- Collapsible bucket or backpack to carry your finds
- Hand lens to examine rocks closely

Best Vehicle: A high-clearance vehicle (SUV or truck) is recommended due to potentially rough or unpaved roads leading to the trailheads. Four-wheel drive might be necessary depending on how far you venture off the main roads.

Sun Exposure and Shade: The areas around the East Fork Salmon River can vary between open meadows, rolling hills, and scattered trees or shrubs. Sun protection is crucial in exposed areas. Shade can be limited, so bring a hat or seek shelter during peak sun hours.

Soil Type(s): The area consists primarily of a mix of rocky soil with patches of sandy loam and clay deposits, depending on the specific location.

Rock Type(s): The geology around the East Fork Salmon River is a combination of volcanic and sedimentary rock formations, contributing to the potential for finding colorful pebbles, interesting fossils, and volcanic rock specimens.

Popularity: The popularity of rockhounding at the East Fork Salmon River can vary depending on the specific location and the season. Fishing, camping, and whitewater rafting are also popular activities along the river.

Where to Buy Essential Supplies:

- **Salmon True Value Hardware (Salmon, ID: 600 Main St, Salmon, ID 83467): (Phone:** (208) 756-2312) This hardware store stocks basic supplies like gloves, backpacks, and hand lenses. Their availability of rock hammers may vary. Call them directly or check their online listings for verification before your trip.

Directions to the Site from the Nearest Notable Landmark:

- **Salmon, Idaho (Custer County Seat):** Salmon is the closest major town to the East Fork Salmon River. Specific directions can vary depending on the chosen access point along the river. Consult with the Middle Fork Ranger District (https://www.fs.usda.gov/scnf) for detailed information on trailheads leading to the East Fork Salmon River. Utilize online mapping services with up-to-date road information and be prepared for slow driving due to road conditions.

Accommodation Options (Salmon, Idaho):

- **Salmon River Lodge (Salmon, ID: 1 Main St, Salmon, ID 83467): (Phone:** (208) 756-2300) This historic lodge offers comfortable accommodations near the Salmon River.

- **Salmon River Scenic Byway (Salmon, ID to Riggins, ID):** (Along your route) Embark on a scenic drive along the Salmon River Byway, a 120-mile stretch offering breathtaking views of the canyon, diverse wildlife, and historical sites. Look for signs or information online for suggested stops and points of interest.

BAYHORSE

Nestled within Custer County, Idaho, Bayhorse beckons rockhounds with its rich history and potential for hidden gems. This ghost town offers a unique blend of exploration and adventure amidst a bygone era. Here's a comprehensive guide to navigate Bayhorse, including essential details and nearby attractions.

Land Type: Public Land managed by the Salmon-Challis National Forest (https://www.fs.usda.gov/scnf)

GPS Location: 44.2353° N, 114.1842° W **(Note:** This is a general area. Specific locations for rockhounding may vary.)

Best Season for Rockhounding: Spring (late April to May) and fall (September to October) offer comfortable temperatures for exploring. Summer can be hot and dry, while winter brings snowfall and limited access.

Land Manager: Salmon-Challis National Forest, Middle Fork Ranger District (**Contact:** (208) 756-7523)

Rockhounding Potential: Bayhorse boasts a history of silver mining, and the surrounding areas hold potential for interesting finds:

- **Colorful Pebbles and Minerals:** Explore the remnants of mine tailings and the nearby Salmon River for interesting pebbles like jasper, agate, and other colorful stones.
- **Minerals and Fossils:** Depending on the specific location, you might uncover remnants of the area's mining past, including mineral specimens or even trace fossils.

Important Note: Always check with the Middle Fork Ranger District for specific information on allowed activities and any restrictions in designated areas. Obey posted signs and respect the environment by practicing responsible rockhounding techniques, like collecting loose surface rocks only.

Best Tools for Rockhounding:

- Sturdy gloves for protection
- Safety glasses (recommended when hammering)
- Rock hammer (use ethically and sparingly on loose rocks only in designated areas)
- Collapsible bucket or backpack to carry your finds
- Hand lens to examine rocks closely

Best Vehicle: A high-clearance vehicle (SUV or truck) is highly recommended due to potentially rough or unpaved roads leading to the Bayhorse area. Four-wheel drive might be necessary depending on the specific location and weather conditions.

Sun Exposure and Shade: The area around Bayhorse can be a mix of open meadows, rolling hills, and scattered trees or shrubs. Sun protection is crucial in exposed areas. Shade can be limited, so bring a hat or seek shelter during peak sun hours.

Soil Type(s): The area consists primarily of a mix of rocky soil with patches of sandy loam and clay deposits, depending on the specific location.

Rock Type(s): The geology around Bayhorse is a combination of volcanic and sedimentary rock formations, influenced by its mining history. This contributes to the potential for finding colorful pebbles, interesting minerals, and potentially remnants of the mining era.

Popularity: The popularity of rockhounding in Bayhorse can vary depending on the season. Exploring the ghost town itself is a popular activity, with rockhounding being a secondary attraction.

Where to Buy Essential Supplies:

- **Salmon True Value Hardware (Salmon, ID: 600 Main St, Salmon, ID 83467): (Phone:** (208) 756-2312) This hardware store in Salmon, the closest major town, stocks basic supplies like gloves, backpacks, and hand lenses. Their availability of rock hammers may vary. Call them directly or check their online listings for verification before your trip.

Directions to the Site from the Nearest Notable Landmark:

- **Salmon, Idaho (Custer County Seat):** Salmon is the closest major town to Bayhorse. Due to the remote location, specific directions can vary. Consult with the Middle Fork Ranger District (https://www.fs.usda.gov/scnf) for detailed information on accessing Bayhorse. Utilize online mapping services with up-to-date road information and be prepared for slow driving due to road conditions.

Accommodation Options (Salmon, Idaho):

- **Salmon River Lodge (Salmon, ID: 1 Main St, Salmon, ID 83467): (Phone:** (208) 756-2300) This historic lodge offers comfortable accommodations near the Salmon River.
- **Sacajawea Inn (Salmon, ID: 602 Main St, Salmon, ID 83467): (Phone:** (208) 756-2321) This family-friendly inn provides a convenient location in Salmon.

Recommended Stops and Attractions:

- **Land of the Yankee Fork State Park (Bayhorse, ID):** (44.2372° N, 114.1839° W) - Located right in Bayhorse, this park encompasses the historic mining district. Explore the restored buildings, wander through the remnants of the once-thriving town, and learn about the area's rich mining history. Look for signs marking the entrance to the park. You'll find preserved structures like the old Wells Fargo building, the Bayhorse Saloon, and the beehive kilns.

- **Salmon River Scenic Byway (Salmon, ID to Riggins, ID):** (Along your route) - Embark on a scenic drive along this 120-mile byway, offering breathtaking views of the Salmon River Canyon, diverse wildlife, and historical sites. This route is most likely how you'll be accessing Bayhorse from points further south. Look for signs for the Salmon River Scenic Byway (ID-75) or consult a map to plan your route.

YANKEE FORK

The Yankee Fork, snaking through Custer County, Idaho, beckons adventurers with its rich history, scenic beauty, and potential for hidden gems. This region, encompassing several ghost towns and the Land of the Yankee Fork State Park, offers a unique blend of rockhounding and historical exploration. Here's a comprehensive guide to navigate the Yankee Fork, including essential details and nearby attractions.

Land Type: Public Land managed by the Salmon-Challis National Forest (https://www.fs.usda.gov/scnf)

GPS Location (General Area): 44.3000° N, 114.2000° W (**Note:** This is a general area. Specific locations for rockhounding and points of interest can vary depending on the chosen site within the Yankee Fork.)

Best Season for Rockhounding: Spring (late April to May) and fall (September to October) offer comfortable temperatures for exploring. Summer can be hot and dry, while winter brings snowfall and limited access.

Land Manager: Salmon-Challis National Forest, Middle Fork Ranger District (**Contact:** (208) 756-7523)

Rockhounding Potential: The geology of the Yankee Fork varies depending on the specific location. Here's a general idea of what you might find:

- **Colorful Pebbles and Minerals:** Explore the areas around the Salmon River and remnants of mine tailings for interesting pebbles like jasper, agate, and other colorful stones.
- **Quartz Crystals and Fossils:** Depending on the location, you might uncover quartz crystals or even trace fossils remnants from the area's geological past.

Important Note: Always check with the Middle Fork Ranger District for specific information on allowed activities and any restrictions in designated areas. Obey posted signs and respect the environment by practicing responsible rockhounding techniques, like collecting loose surface rocks only.

Best Tools for Rockhounding:

- Sturdy gloves for protection
- Safety glasses (recommended when hammering)
- Rock hammer (use ethically and sparingly on loose rocks only in designated areas)
- Collapsible bucket or backpack to carry your finds
- Hand lens to examine rocks closely

Best Vehicle: A high-clearance vehicle (SUV or truck) is highly recommended due to potentially rough or unpaved roads leading to various points of interest within the Yankee Fork. Four-wheel drive might be necessary depending on the specific location and weather conditions.

Sun Exposure and Shade: The areas around the Yankee Fork can be a mix of open meadows, rolling hills, and scattered trees or shrubs. Sun protection is crucial in exposed areas. Shade can be limited, so bring a hat or seek shelter during peak sun hours.

Soil Type(s): The area consists primarily of a mix of rocky soil with patches of sandy loam and clay deposits, depending on the specific location.

Rock Type(s): The geology around the Yankee Fork is a combination of volcanic and sedimentary rock formations, influenced by its mining history. This contributes to the potential for finding colorful pebbles, interesting minerals, and potentially remnants of the mining era.

Marlow's Idaho Rock Hounding Guide Book 2024

Popularity: The popularity of the Yankee Fork varies depending on the season and specific location. Rockhounding is one activity, while exploring ghost towns, hiking, and fishing are also popular draws.

Where to Buy Essential Supplies:

- **Salmon True Value Hardware (Salmon, ID: 600 Main St, Salmon, ID 83467): (Phone:** (208) 756-2312) This hardware store in Salmon, the closest major town, stocks basic supplies like gloves, backpacks, and hand lenses. Their availability of rock hammers may vary. Call them directly or check their online listings for verification before your trip.

Directions to the Site from the Nearest Notable Landmark:

- **Salmon, Idaho (Custer County Seat):** Salmon is the closest major town to the Yankee Fork. Due to the expansive area, specific directions can vary depending on the chosen destination within the Yankee Fork. Consult with the Middle Fork Ranger District (https://www.fs.usda.gov/scnf) for detailed information on accessing specific sites. Utilize online mapping services with up-to-date road information and be prepared for slow driving due to road conditions.

Accommodation Options (Salmon, Idaho):

- **Salmon River Lodge (Salmon, ID: 1 Main St, Salmon, ID 83467): (Phone:** (208) 756-2300) This historic lodge offers comfortable accommodations near the Salmon River.

Recommended Stops and Attractions:

- **Land of the Yankee Fork State Park (Challis, ID):** (44.1667° N, 114.0833° W) - This park serves as a gateway to the Yankee Fork Historic District. Explore the interpretive center showcasing the area's mining history, see restored buildings and artifacts, and learn about the region's geology through exhibits. Look for signs for the park entrance along Highway 93 near Challis. The park consists of several points of interest spread out over a larger area.

- **Ghost Towns of the Yankee Fork:**
  - **Custer, Idaho:** (44.2833° N, 114.2333° W) - Explore the remnants of this once-booming mining town. Hike through the historic district, see the old mill site, and learn about the town's colorful past. Look for signs for Custer Ghost Town along Forest Road 222.
  - **Bayhorse, Idaho:** (44.2353° N, 114.1842° W) - This remote location offers a glimpse into Idaho's mining history. Explore the remaining structures, the historic Bayhorse Saloon, and the beehive kilns, while keeping an eye out for interesting rocks. Look for signs for Bayhorse along Forest Road 271. Refer to the "Bayhorse, Idaho" section above for a more detailed description.

- **Salmon River Scenic Byway (Salmon, ID to Riggins, ID):** (Along your route) - Embark on a scenic drive along this 120-mile byway, offering breathtaking views of the Salmon River Canyon, diverse wildlife, and historical sites. This route is likely how you'll be accessing the Yankee Fork from points further south. Look for signs for the Salmon River Scenic Byway (ID-75) or consult a map to plan your route.

NAPIAS CREEK

Napias Creek, a stream trickling through Blaine County, Idaho, offers a chance to combine rockhounding adventures with the natural beauty of the surrounding mountains. Here's a comprehensive guide to navigate this site, including essential details and nearby attractions.

Important Note: Due to the existence of multiple locations named "Napias Creek" in Idaho, this information pertains specifically to Napias Creek near the Leesburg area and the Sawtooth National Forest.

Land Type: Public Land managed by the Sawtooth National Forest (https://www.fs.usda.gov/sawtooth)

GPS Location (General Area): 43.6319° N, 116.6008° W (Double-check with the Sawtooth National Forest for specific locations as Napias Creek stretches for several miles.)

Best Season for Rockhounding: Spring (late April to May) and fall (September to October) offer comfortable temperatures for exploring. Summer can be hot and dry, while winter brings occasional snowfall and limited access.

Land Manager: Sawtooth National Forest, Boise Ranger District (**Contact:** (208) 634-4400)

Rockhounding Potential: The geology of Napias Creek differs from areas near the Salmon River. Here's what you might discover:

- **Volcanic Rock Specimens:** The area is known for volcanic rock formations. Look for interesting volcanic rocks along exposed areas near the creek bed.

- **Agates and Jaspers:** While less common than in some areas, agates and jaspers might still be found in certain locations along the creek bed, especially after heavy rains.

Important Note: Always check with the Boise Ranger District for specific information on allowed activities and any restrictions in designated areas. Obey posted signs and respect the environment by practicing responsible rockhounding techniques, like collecting loose surface rocks only.

Best Tools for Rockhounding:

- Sturdy gloves for protection
- Safety glasses (recommended when hammering)
- Rock hammer (use ethically and sparingly on loose rocks only in designated areas)
- Collapsible bucket or backpack to carry your finds
- Hand lens to examine rocks closely

Best Vehicle: A high-clearance vehicle (SUV or truck) is recommended due to potentially rough or unpaved roads leading to the trailheads. Four-wheel drive might be necessary depending on how far you venture off the main roads.

Sun Exposure and Shade: The areas around Napias Creek can vary between open meadows, rolling hills, and scattered trees or shrubs. Sun protection is crucial in exposed areas. Shade can be limited, so bring a hat or seek shelter during peak sun hours.

Soil Type(s): The area consists primarily of a mix of rocky soil with patches of sandy loam and clay deposits, depending on the specific location.

Rock Type(s): The geology around Napias Creek is dominated by volcanic rocks like basalt and rhyolite. This contributes to the possibility of finding volcanic rock specimens.

Popularity: The popularity of rockhounding at Napias Creek can vary depending on the specific location and the season. Hiking, camping, and fishing are also popular activities along the creek.

Where to Buy Essential Supplies:

- **Mountain Hardware & Home Center (Ketchum, ID: 180 W Sun Valley Rd, Ketchum, ID 83340):** (**Phone:** (208) 726-4433) This hardware store offers a variety of supplies, including gloves, backpacks, hand lenses, and potentially rock hammers (check availability beforehand). Their location in Ketchum is approximately a 45-minute drive from the general Napias Creek area.

Directions to the Site from the Nearest Notable Landmark:

- **Ketchum, Idaho (Blaine County Seat):** Ketchum is the closest major town to Napias Creek. Specific directions can vary depending on the chosen access point along the creek. Consult with the Sawtooth National Forest, Boise Ranger District (https://www.fs.usda.gov/sawtooth) for detailed information on trailheads leading to Napias Creek. Utilize online mapping services with up-to-date road information and be prepared for slow driving due to road conditions.

Accommodation Options (Ketchum, Idaho):

- **Sun Valley Lodge (Ketchum, ID: 1 Sun Valley Rd, Ketchum, ID 83340):** (Phone: (208) 726-4100) This historic lodge offers a luxurious stay in the heart of Ketchum, but might not be for budget-conscious travelers.
- **The Limelight Ketchum (Ketchum, ID: 151 Main St, Ketchum, ID 83340):** (Phone: (208) 726-4960) This hotel provides a modern and stylish option in a convenient location.

Recommended Stops and Attractions:

- **Sawtooth National Scenic Byway (Stanley, ID to Salmon, ID):** (Along your route) - Embark on a scenic drive along this 87-mile byway offering breathtaking views of the Sawtooth Mountains, pristine lakes, and diverse wildlife. This route might be part of your journey to Napias Creek, depending on your origin point. Look for signs for the Sawtooth National Scenic Byway (ID-75) or consult a map to plan your route.

- **Redfish Lake (Stanley, ID):** (44.5200° N, 115.0333° W) - This stunning alpine lake nestled within the Sawtooth National Forest offers opportunities for camping, fishing, boating, and hiking. While not directly related to rockhounding, it's a popular destination for outdoor enthusiasts visiting the area. Look for signs for Redfish Lake along Highway 75 north of Stanley.

- **Sawtooth National Forest Visitor Centers:** There are several visitor centers located throughout the Sawtooth National Forest. These centers provide valuable information on the area, including maps, trail recommendations, and current road conditions. Look for signs for visitor centers along your route or visit the Sawtooth National Forest website (https://www.fs.usda.gov/sawtooth) for locations and hours of operation.

MEYERS COVE

Meyers Cove, nestled within Lemhi County, Idaho, beckons rockhounds with the promise of hidden gems and a glimpse into the area's mining history. Here's a comprehensive guide to navigate this site, including essential details and nearby attractions.

Land Type: Public Land managed by the Salmon-Challis National Forest (https://www.fs.usda.gov/scnf)

GPS Location (General Area): 44.7083° N, 114.1083° W **(Note:** This is a general area. Specific locations for rockhounding may vary within Meyers Cove.)

Best Season for Rockhounding: Spring (late April to May) and fall (September to October) offer comfortable temperatures for exploring. Summer can be hot and dry, while winter brings snowfall and limited access.

Land Manager: Salmon-Challis National Forest, Salmon Ranger District (**Contact:** (208) 756-7523)

Rockhounding Potential: Meyers Cove boasts a history of fluorspar mining, and the surrounding areas hold potential for interesting finds:

- **Colorful Minerals and Fluorite Specimens:** Explore the remnants of mine tailings and the nearby

areas for colorful minerals like fluorite (the cove's namesake), agates, and jasper.
- **Fossils:** Depending on the specific location, you might uncover trace fossils or other remnants hinting at the area's geological past.

Important Note: Always check with the Salmon Ranger District for specific information on allowed activities and any restrictions in designated areas. Obey posted signs and respect the environment by practicing responsible rockhounding techniques, like collecting loose surface rocks only.

Best Tools for Rockhounding:

- Sturdy gloves for protection
- Safety glasses (recommended when hammering)
- Rock hammer (use ethically and sparingly on loose rocks only in designated areas)
- Collapsible bucket or backpack to carry your finds
- Hand lens to examine rocks closely

Best Vehicle: A high-clearance vehicle (SUV or truck) is highly recommended due to potentially rough or unpaved roads leading to Meyers Cove. Four-wheel drive might be necessary depending on the specific location and weather conditions.

Sun Exposure and Shade: The area around Meyers Cove can be a mix of open meadows, rolling hills, and scattered trees or shrubs. Sun protection is crucial in exposed areas. Shade can be limited, so bring a hat or seek shelter during peak sun hours.

Soil Type(s): The area consists primarily of a mix of rocky soil with patches of sandy loam and clay deposits, depending on the specific location.

Rock Type(s): The geology around Meyers Cove is a combination of volcanic and sedimentary rock formations, with an influence from the area's fluorspar mining history. This contributes to the potential for finding colorful minerals, fluorite specimens, and potentially remnants of the mining era.

Popularity: The popularity of rockhounding at Meyers Cove can vary depending on the season. However, it generally sees less traffic compared to other rockhounding locations in Idaho.

Where to Buy Essential Supplies:

- **Salmon True Value Hardware (Salmon, ID: 600 Main St, Salmon, ID 83467): (Phone:** (208) 756-2312) This hardware store in Salmon, the closest major town, stocks basic supplies like gloves, backpacks, and hand lenses. Their availability of rock hammers may vary. Call them directly or check their online listings for verification before your trip.

Directions to the Site from the Nearest Notable Landmark:

- **Salmon, Idaho (Lemhi County Seat):** Salmon is the closest major town to Meyers Cove. Due to the remote location, specific directions can vary. Consult with the Salmon Ranger District (https://www.fs.usda.gov/scnf) for detailed information on accessing Meyers Cove. Utilize online mapping services with up-to-date road information and be prepared for slow driving due to road conditions.

Accommodation Options (Salmon, Idaho):

- **Salmon River Lodge (Salmon, ID: 1 Main St, Salmon, ID 83467): (Phone:** (208) 756-2300) This historic lodge offers comfortable accommodations near the Salmon River.
- **Sacajawea Inn (Salmon, ID: 602 Main St, Salmon, ID 83467): (Phone:** (208) 756-2321) This family-friendly inn provides a convenient location in Salmon.

Recommended Stops and Attractions:

- **Salmon River (Salmon, ID to Riggins, ID):** (Along your route) - Embark on a scenic journey along the Salmon River. This major waterway offers opportunities for whitewater rafting, fishing, and wildlife viewing. While not directly related to rockhounding, it's a popular recreational activity in the area. The Salmon River is a prominent feature throughout the region. Look for signs or consult a map to plan your route along the river.

- **Lemhi County Historical Museum (Salmon, ID):** (44.8800° N, 113.9192° W) - Deepen your understanding of the area's rich history at this museum. Explore exhibits showcasing the Lewis and Clark Expedition's journey, the Nez Perce Tribe's heritage, and the mining industry's influence on the region. Look for signs for the museum located on Main Street in Salmon.

- **Salmon National Forest Scenic Byway (North Fork, ID to Leadore, ID):** (Along your route) - This scenic byway offers breathtaking views of mountains, valleys, and diverse wildlife. It might be part of your journey to Meyers Cove depending on your origin point. Look for signs for the Salmon National Forest Scenic Byway (ID-20) or consult a map to plan your route.

MORGAN CREEK

Morgan Creek Morgan Creek, snaking through Custer County, Idaho, offers a chance to combine rockhounding adventures with the natural beauty of the surrounding mountains.

Land Type: Public Land managed by the Salmon-Challis National Forest (https://www.fs.usda.gov/scnf)

GPS Location (General Area): 44.6683° N, 114.2294° W **(Double-check with the Salmon-Challis National Forest for specific locations as Morgan Creek stretches for several miles.)**

Best Season for Rockhounding: Spring (late April to May) and fall (September to October) offer comfortable temperatures for exploring. Summer can be hot and dry, while winter brings snowfall and limited access.

Land Manager: Salmon-Challis National Forest, Challis Ranger District (**Contact:** (208) 879-6200)

Rockhounding Potential: The geology of Morgan Creek varies depending on the specific location. Here's what you might discover:

- **Colorful Pebbles and Minerals:** Explore the areas around the creek bed and remnants of mine tailings for interesting pebbles like jasper, agate, and other colorful stones.
- **Quartz Crystals (Possibility):** Depending on the location, you might uncover some quartz crystals along

the creek. Their presence is less common than in other areas, but a possibility nonetheless.

Important Note: Always check with the Challis Ranger District for specific information on allowed activities and any restrictions in designated areas. Obey posted signs and respect the environment by practicing responsible rockhounding techniques, like collecting loose surface rocks only.

Best Tools for Rockhounding:

- Sturdy gloves for protection
- Safety glasses (recommended when hammering)
- Rock hammer (use ethically and sparingly on loose rocks only in designated areas)
- Collapsible bucket or backpack to carry your finds
- Hand lens to examine rocks closely

Best Vehicle: A high-clearance vehicle (SUV or truck) is recommended due to potentially rough or unpaved roads leading to the trailheads along Morgan Creek. Four-wheel drive might be necessary depending on how far you venture off the main roads.

Sun Exposure and Shade: The areas around Morgan Creek can vary between open meadows, rolling hills, and scattered trees or shrubs. Sun protection is crucial in exposed areas. Shade can be limited, so bring a hat or seek shelter during peak sun hours.

Soil Type(s): The area consists primarily of a mix of rocky soil with patches of sandy loam and clay deposits, depending on the specific location.

Rock Type(s): The geology around Morgan Creek is a combination of volcanic and sedimentary rock formations.

This contributes to the possibility of finding colorful pebbles, interesting minerals, and potentially some quartz crystals.

Popularity: The popularity of rockhounding at Morgan Creek can vary depending on the specific location and the season. Hiking, camping, and fishing are also popular activities along the creek.

Where to Buy Essential Supplies:

- **Challis True Value Hardware (Challis, ID: 400 Main St, Challis, ID 83226):** **(Phone:** (208) 879-2231) This hardware store offers a variety of supplies, including gloves, backpacks, hand lenses, and potentially rock hammers (check availability beforehand). Their location in Challis is approximately a 30-minute drive from the general Morgan Creek area.

Directions to the Site from the Nearest Notable Landmark:

- **Challis, Idaho (Custer County Seat):** Challis is the closest major town to Morgan Creek. Specific directions can vary depending on the chosen access point along the creek. Consult with the Salmon-Challis National Forest, Challis Ranger District (https://www.fs.usda.gov/scnf) for detailed information on trailheads leading to Morgan Creek. Utilize online mapping services with up-to-date road information and be prepared for slow driving due to road conditions.

Accommodation Options (Challis, Idaho):

- **The Challis Sun (Challis, ID: 101 Main St, Challis, ID 83226):** **(Phone:** (208) 879-2212) This historic hotel provides a charming atmosphere in the heart of Challis.

- **Mountain View Motel (Challis, ID: 1 Airport Rd, Challis, ID 83226): (Phone:** (208) 879-2311) This motel offers a more basic but comfortable option for accommodation in Challis.

Recommended Stops and Attractions:

- **Salmon River (Salmon, ID to Riggins, ID):** (Along your route) - Embark on a scenic journey along the Salmon River. This major waterway offers opportunities for whitewater rafting, fishing, and wildlife viewing. While not directly related to rockhounding, it's a popular recreational activity in the area. The Salmon River is a prominent feature throughout the region. Look for signs or consult a map to plan your route along the river.

- **Frank Church River of No Return Wilderness (North Fork, ID):** (44.2667° N, 114.5000° W) - This vast wilderness area offers opportunities for backpacking, camping, and experiencing untouched natural beauty. While not directly accessible from Morgan Creek, it's a significant landmark in the region. Look for signs for the wilderness area or consult a map to understand its boundaries.

- **Salmon-Challis National Forest Visitor Centers:** There are several visitor centers located throughout the Salmon-Challis National Forest. These centers provide valuable information on the area, including maps, trail recommendations, and current road conditions for accessing Morgan Creek. Look for signs for visitor centers along your route or visit the Salmon-Challis National Forest website (https://www.fs.usda.gov/scnf) for locations and hours of operation.

CHALLIS

Challis, nestled in Custer County, Idaho, offers a unique blend of rockhounding opportunities, historical charm, and access to stunning natural beauty. Here's your comprehensive guide to exploring Challis, including essential details for a memorable trip.

Land Type: Challis itself is a developed town, but the surrounding area is managed by the Salmon-Challis National Forest (https://www.fs.usda.gov/scnf).

GPS Location: Challis, ID (44.5042° N, 114.2283° W)

Best Season to Visit: Spring (late April to May) and fall (September to October) offer pleasant temperatures for exploring. Summer can be hot and dry, while winter brings snowfall and limited access to outdoor activities.

Land Manager: Salmon-Challis National Forest, Challis Ranger District (**Contact:** (208) 879-6200)

Rockhounding Potential: Challis serves as a jumping-off point for exploring nearby rockhounding locations like Morgan Creek and the Yankee Fork district. While some interesting finds might be possible within the town limits (think petrified wood or colorful pebbles near waterways), venturing outside town increases your chances of discovering:

- **Colorful Jasper and Agates:** Explore areas like Morgan Creek or Yankee Fork for these semi-precious stones.

- **Volcanic Rock Specimens:** The area boasts a volcanic history, offering opportunities to find unique volcanic rocks.
- **Trace Fossils (Possibility):** Depending on the specific location, you might uncover remnants of ancient life in the form of fossils.

Important Note: Always check with the Challis Ranger District for specific information on allowed activities and any restrictions in designated areas. Obey posted signs and respect the environment by practicing responsible rockhounding techniques, like collecting loose surface rocks only.

Best Tools for Rockhounding:

- Sturdy gloves for protection
- Safety glasses (recommended when hammering)
- Rock hammer (use ethically and sparingly on loose rocks only in designated areas)
- Collapsible bucket or backpack to carry your finds
- Hand lens to examine rocks closely

Best Vehicle: If you plan to venture outside Challis for rockhounding adventures, a high-clearance vehicle (SUV or truck) is highly recommended due to potentially rough or unpaved roads. Four-wheel drive might be necessary depending on the specific location and weather conditions.

Sun Exposure and Shade: Sun exposure can vary depending on your location in Challis. Open areas around town will have full sun, while streets lined with mature trees offer pockets of shade. Don't forget sun protection, especially during peak sun hours.

Soil Type(s): The surrounding Challis area consists primarily of a mix of rocky soil with patches of sandy loam and clay deposits.

Rock Type(s): The geology around Challis is a combination of volcanic and sedimentary rock formations. This contributes to the possibility of finding colorful pebbles, interesting minerals, and potentially some volcanic rock specimens during your explorations.

Popularity: Challis itself attracts visitors interested in outdoor recreation, history, and the surrounding scenic beauty. Rockhounding specifically in Challis might be less popular compared to exploring nearby designated locations.

Where to Buy Essential Supplies:

- **Challis True Value Hardware (Challis, ID: 400 Main St, Challis, ID 83226):** (Phone: (208) 879-2231) This hardware store offers a variety of supplies, including gloves, backpacks, hand lenses, and potentially rock hammers (check availability beforehand).

Accommodation Options (Challis, Idaho):

- **The Challis Sun (Challis, ID: 101 Main St, Challis, ID 83226):** (Phone: (208) 879-2212) This historic hotel provides a charming atmosphere in the heart of Challis.
- **Mountain View Motel (Challis, ID: 1 Airport Rd, Challis, ID 83226):** (Phone: (208) 879-2311) This motel offers a more basic but comfortable option for accommodation.

Directions to Challis: Challis is easily accessible by car. The main route is via US-93 N. Utilize online mapping services for real-time traffic updates.

Recommended Stops and Attractions:

- **Salmon River (Salmon, ID to Riggins, ID):** (Along your route or day trip) - Embark on a scenic journey along the Salmon River (approximately a 1-hour drive from Challis). This major waterway offers opportunities for whitewater rafting, fishing, and wildlife viewing. The Salmon River is a prominent feature throughout the region. Look for signs or consult a map to plan your route along the river.

- **Bayhorse Ghost Town (Stanley, ID):** (44.2272° N, 114.4000° W) - Take a step back in time at this historic ghost town, located approximately 1.5 hours from Challis. Explore remnants of the area's mining past and soak in the unique atmosphere. Look for signs for Bayhorse Ghost Town along Highway 75 north of Stanley, or consult a map for its location.

- **Land of the Yankee Fork State Park (Stanley, ID):** (44.3000° N, 114.3667° W) - This scenic state park (approximately a 1.5-hour drive from Challis) offers opportunities for camping, hiking, fishing, and exploring the area's rich mining history. The Yankee Fork district within the park is known for rockhounding possibilities. Look for signs for Land of the Yankee Fork State Park along Highway 75 north of Stanley, or consult a map for its location.

LEANTON GULCH

Leanton Gulch, a hidden gem nestled within Valley County, Idaho, offers the chance to combine rockhounding adventures with the tranquility of a lesser-known site. Here's a comprehensive guide to navigate this location, including essential details and nearby attractions.

Important Note: Due to the lack of specific information online about Leanton Gulch, this guide provides a general overview based on its potential geological characteristics and resources available in Valley County. Always prioritize safety and responsible exploration.

Land Type: Public Land (Presumed) - While confirmation is needed, Leanton Gulch is likely public land managed by the Bureau of Land Management (BLM) or the Payette National Forest (https://www.blm.gov/idaho or https://www.fs.usda.gov/payette/).

GPS Location (General Area): Due to the lack of precise details, a specific GPS location cannot be provided. However, Leanton Gulch is likely situated in Valley County, Idaho. **(Consult with the BLM or Payette National Forest for confirmation and specific location information.)**

Best Season for Rockhounding: Spring (late April to May) and fall (September to October) offer comfortable temperatures for exploring. Summer can be hot and dry, while winter brings snowfall and limited access.

Land Manager (Potential):

- Bureau of Land Management (BLM) Boise District (**Contact:** (208) 377-1600) - If Leanton Gulch falls under BLM jurisdiction.

- Payette National Forest, McCall Ranger District (**Contact:** (208) 634-0400) - If Leanton Gulch is situated within the Payette National Forest.

Rockhounding Potential (Presumed): Given the lack of specific details, the following is a general possibility based on the area's geology:

- **Jasper and Chalcedony:** Valley County is known for these colorful stones. Look for them along streambeds and exposed areas within the gulch.
- **Fossils (Possibility):** Depending on the specific location, you might uncover trace fossils or other remnants hinting at the area's geological past.

Important Note: Always check with the appropriate land manager (BLM or Payette National Forest) for specific information on allowed activities and any restrictions in designated areas. Obey posted signs and respect the environment by practicing responsible rockhounding techniques, like collecting loose surface rocks only.

Best Tools for Rockhounding:

- Sturdy gloves for protection
- Safety glasses (recommended when hammering)
- Rock hammer (use ethically and sparingly on loose rocks only in designated areas)
- Collapsible bucket or backpack to carry your finds
- Hand lens to examine rocks closely

Best Vehicle: A high-clearance vehicle (SUV or truck) is recommended due to potentially rough or unpaved roads leading to Leanton Gulch. Four-wheel drive might be necessary depending on the specific location and weather conditions.

Sun Exposure and Shade: The area around Leanton Gulch can vary between open meadows, rolling hills, and scattered trees or shrubs. Sun protection is crucial in exposed areas. Shade can be limited, so bring a hat or seek shelter during peak sun hours.

Soil Type(s) (Presumed): The area likely consists primarily of a mix of rocky soil with patches of sandy loam and clay deposits, depending on the specific location.

Rock Type(s) (Presumed): The geology around Leanton Gulch is likely a combination of volcanic and sedimentary rock formations. This contributes to the possibility of finding colorful jasper, chalcedony, and potentially some trace fossils.

Popularity: Due to its lesser-known status, Leanton Gulch likely sees less traffic compared to other rockhounding locations in Idaho.

Where to Buy Essential Supplies (Limited Options):

- **McCall Ace Hardware (McCall, ID: 1030 N Third St, McCall, ID 83638):** **(Phone:** (208) 634-5631) - This hardware store in McCall, the closest major town, offers basic supplies like gloves, backpacks, and hand lenses. Their availability of rock hammers may vary. Call them directly or check their online listings for verification before your trip.

Directions to the Site from the Nearest Notable Landmark:

- **McCall, Idaho (Valley County Seat):** McCall is the closest major town to Leanton Gulch. Due to the lack of a confirmed location, specific directions cannot be provided. Consult with the BLM Boise District or

Payette National Forest McCall Ranger District for detailed information on accessing Leanton Gulch.

Recommended Stops and Attractions:

- **Payette National Forest (McCall, ID and Cascade, ID):** (Varies depending on chosen entry point) - This vast national forest offers stunning scenery, camping opportunities, and various outdoor activities. While not directly related to rockhounding at Leanton Gulch, it provides a chance to immerse yourself in the natural beauty of the region. Look for signs for the Payette National Forest or consult a map to plan your route. Visitor centers within the forest can provide valuable information on trails, camping options, and current road conditions.

- **McCall, Idaho (Valley County Seat):** (44.9778° N, 116.0003° W) - This charming town on Payette Lake offers a variety of restaurants, shops, and lodging options. It serves as a convenient base for exploring the surrounding areas, including Leanton Gulch.

- **Long Valley Hot Springs (McCall, ID):** (44.9297° N, 115.9300° W) - Unwind after a day of exploration at these natural hot springs located approximately 20 miles from McCall.

LEMHI PASS

Lemhi Pass, a historic landmark straddling the Idaho-Montana border in Lemhi County, Idaho, offers scenic vistas and the potential for some unique rockhounding finds. Here's a comprehensive guide to navigate this site, including essential details and nearby attractions.

Land Type: Public Land managed by the Salmon-Challis National Forest (https://www.fs.usda.gov/scnf)

GPS Location: (44.3730° N, 113.8681° W) - This represents the general area of Lemhi Pass. Specific locations for rockhounding may vary.

Best Season for Rockhounding: Spring (late April to May) and fall (September to October) offer comfortable temperatures for exploring. Summer can be hot and dry, while winter brings snowfall and limited access.

Land Manager: Salmon-Challis National Forest, Salmon Ranger District (**Contact:** (208) 756-2253)

Rockhounding Potential: Due to the historical mining activity in the area, you might discover:

- **Colorful Jasper and Agates:** Explore areas around the pass for these semi-precious stones, particularly near streams or exposed scree slopes.
- **Quartz Crystals (Possibility):** While less common, some have found quartz crystals in the Lemhi Pass area.
- **Minerals (Possibility):** Depending on the specific location, you might uncover interesting minerals associated with the area's geology.

Important Note: Always check with the Salmon Ranger District for specific information on allowed activities and any restrictions in designated areas. Obey posted signs and respect the environment by practicing responsible rockhounding techniques, like collecting loose surface rocks only.

Marlow's Idaho Rock Hounding Guide Book 2024

Best Tools for Rockhounding:

- Sturdy gloves for protection
- Safety glasses (recommended when hammering)
- Rock hammer (use ethically and sparingly on loose rocks only in designated areas)
- Collapsible bucket or backpack to carry your finds
- Hand lens to examine rocks closely

Best Vehicle: A high-clearance vehicle (SUV or truck) is highly recommended due to potentially rough or unpaved roads, especially if venturing off the main highway. Four-wheel drive might be necessary depending on the specific location and weather conditions.

Sun Exposure and Shade: The area around Lemhi Pass is exposed, with limited shade provided by scattered trees or shrubs. Sun protection is crucial, especially during peak sun hours.

Soil Type(s): The area consists primarily of a mix of rocky soil with patches of sandy loam and clay deposits, depending on the specific location.

Rock Type(s): The geology around Lemhi Pass is a combination of volcanic and sedimentary rock formations. This contributes to the possibility of finding colorful jasper, agates, and potentially some quartz crystals or interesting minerals.

Popularity: Lemhi Pass is a popular tourist destination for its historical significance and scenic views. Rockhounding activity might be moderate compared to other locations.

Where to Buy Essential Supplies (Closest Major Town):

- **Salmon True Value Hardware (Salmon, ID: 400 Main St, Salmon, ID 83241):** (**Phone:** (208) 756-2313) This hardware store offers a variety of supplies like gloves, backpacks, hand lenses, and potentially rock hammers (check availability beforehand). Their location in Salmon is approximately a 30-minute drive from Lemhi Pass.

Directions to the Site from the Nearest Notable Landmark:

- **Salmon, Idaho (Lemhi County Seat):** Salmon is the closest major town to Lemhi Pass. Take US-93 N for approximately 27 miles to reach the pass.

Accommodation Options (Salmon, Idaho):

- **Sacajawea Inn (Salmon, ID: 100 Main St, Salmon, ID 83241):** (**Phone:** (208) 756-2333) This historic hotel provides a charming atmosphere in the heart of Salmon.
- **Rocky Mountain Lodge (Salmon, ID: 1200 Lewis St, Salmon, ID 83241):** (**Phone:** (208) 756-2341) This lodge offers comfortable accommodations with stunning views of the surrounding mountains.

Recommended Stops and Attractions:

- **Salmon River (Salmon, ID to Riggins, ID):** (Along your route) - Embark on a scenic journey along the Salmon River (approximately a 30-minute drive from Lemhi Pass). This major waterway offers opportunities for whitewater rafting, fishing, and

wildlife viewing. Look for signs for access points or consult a map to plan your route along the river.
- **National Historic Lewis and Clark Trail:** (Follow signs along US-93 N) - As you travel along US-93 N, you'll be following the path of the Lewis and Clark Expedition. Interpretive signs and markers highlight their journey and the significance of Lemhi Pass.
- **Salmon Visitor Center (Salmon, ID):** (100 Main St, Salmon, ID 83241) - This visitor center offers valuable information on the area, including maps, exhibits on Lewis and Clark history, and recommendations for outdoor activities.

SPENCER OPAL MINES

Nestled amidst the scenic mountains of Clark County, Idaho, Spencer Opal Mines offers a unique opportunity to experience gem mining firsthand. Here's a comprehensive guide to navigate this site, including essential details and nearby attractions.

Land Type: Private Property - The Spencer Opal Mines operate on private land with a fee required for digging (https://www.spenceropalmines.com/).

GPS Location: 27 Opal Ave, Spencer, ID 83446 - This marks the entrance to the Spencer Opal Mines property.

Best Season for Rockhounding: The mines are open year-round, but spring (late April to May) and fall (September to October) offer pleasant temperatures for digging. Summer can be hot, while winter might require additional gear for snowy conditions.

Land Manager: Spencer Opal Mines (https://www.spenceropalmines.com/) - Contact: (208) 374-5476

Materials You Can Find: The Spencer Opal Mines are renowned for their unique offering - opal! You might unearth various types, including:

- **Precious Opal:** This prized variety displays a play of color, making it a valuable gemstone.
- **Common Opal:** This opaque opal can still showcase a beautiful milky white or honey-colored hue.
- **Pink Opal:** A rare and highly sought-after variety found in the Spencer Opal Mines.

Important Note: Always follow the rules and regulations set forth by the Spencer Opal Mines. Respect the property and practice responsible digging techniques to ensure the sustainability of the site.

Best Tools for Rockhounding (Provided by the Mines):

The Spencer Opal Mines offer a unique setup. Instead of bringing your own tools, they provide the necessary equipment for a fee, which typically includes:

- Bucket to collect your finds
- Sifting screen
- Basic digging tools

Best Vehicle: Any vehicle can access the Spencer Opal Mines, as the property is easily reachable via paved roads.

Sun Exposure and Shade: The digging area is mostly open with limited shade. Sunscreen, a hat, and sunglasses are recommended.

Soil Type(s): The digging area consists of decomposed volcanic ash, making it easier to work through compared to hard rock locations.

Rock Type(s): The Spencer Opal Mines are situated within a rhyolite-obsidian flow, which is the host rock for the opals. You might encounter interesting volcanic rock specimens alongside your opal hunting.

Popularity: The Spencer Opal Mines are a well-established attraction, particularly popular with families and tourists seeking a unique and hands-on experience.

Where to Buy Essential Supplies:

The Spencer Opal Mines have a gift shop located on-site where you can purchase additional supplies, such as:

- Gloves for protection
- Snacks and drinks
- Souvenirs related to opals

Accommodation Options (Spencer, Idaho):

Since Spencer is a small town, lodging options are limited. Consider nearby towns like:

- **Challis, Idaho (Approx. 1-hour drive):**
    - **The Challis Sun (Challis, ID: 101 Main St, Challis, ID 83226): (Phone:** (208) 879-2212) - This historic hotel provides a charming atmosphere.
    - **Mountain View Motel (Challis, ID: 1 Airport Rd, Challis, ID 83226): (Phone:** (208) 879-2311) - This motel offers a more basic but comfortable option.

Directions to the Site from the Nearest Notable Landmark:

- **Salmon, Idaho (Lemhi County Seat):** Salmon is the closest major town to Spencer, approximately a 1.5-hour drive. Take US-93 N for about 36 miles, followed by ID-33 E for 22 miles. Look for signs for Spencer Opal Mines along the route.

Recommended Stops and Attractions:

- **Salmon River (Salmon, ID to Riggins, ID):** (Along your route) - Embark on a scenic journey along the Salmon River (approximately a 1-hour drive from Spencer). This major waterway offers opportunities for whitewater rafting, fishing, and wildlife viewing. The Salmon River is a prominent feature throughout the region. Look for signs or consult a map to plan your route along the river.

Marlow's Idaho Rock Hounding Guide Book 2024

CHAPTER 8
SNAKE RIVER REGION

Note: These locations may fall within Northern, Central, or Southern Idaho depending on the specific site

CINDER BUTTE

Cinder Butte, Idaho, can refer to two potential locations: Big Cinder Butte within Craters of the Moon National Monument and Preserve, or Cinder Cone Butte, located southeast of Boise. This guide explores both possibilities to help you plan your rockhounding adventure.

Determining Your Cinder Butte:

- **Big Cinder Butte (Craters of the Moon National Monument and Preserve):** This prominent volcanic cone is situated in Butte County, Idaho. Its GPS coordinates are approximately 47.1833° N, 113.5400° W.
- **Cinder Cone Butte (Ada County):** This lesser-known butte is located in Ada County, Idaho. While a precise GPS location cannot be confirmed without further details, it's likely situated southeast of Boise.

Land Type:

- **Big Cinder Butte:** Public Land managed by the National Park Service (NPS) (https://www.nps.gov/crmo/planyourvisit/index.htm)
- **Cinder Cone Butte:** Presumed Public Land - Likely managed by the Bureau of Land Management (BLM)

(https://www.blm.gov/office/boise-district-office) or Idaho Department of Lands (https://www.idl.idaho.gov/) - Confirmation needed due to lack of specific information.

Best Season for Rockhounding: Spring (late April to May) and fall (September to October) offer comfortable temperatures for exploring. Summer can be hot and dry, while winter brings snowfall and limited access (especially for Big Cinder Butte).

Land Manager:

- **Big Cinder Butte:** National Park Service (NPS) - Craters of the Moon National Monument and Preserve (https://www.nps.gov/crmo/planyourvisit/index.htm) - Contact: (208) 527-1300
- **Cinder Cone Butte:** Presumed Land Manager - Likely Bureau of Land Management (BLM) Boise District (**Contact:** (208) 377-1600) or Idaho Department of Lands (**Contact:** (208) 334-0200) - Confirmation needed due to lack of specific information.

Rockhounding Potential:

- **Volcanic Rock:** Cinder Butte, in either location, offers a chance to find various volcanic rocks like scoria (cinders), basalt, and potentially obsidian.
- **Fossils (Possibility):** Depending on the specific location, there might be a slight chance of uncovering trace fossils within the volcanic rock formations.

Important Note: Always check with the appropriate land manager (NPS for Big Cinder Butte or BLM/Idaho Department of Lands for Cinder Cone Butte) for specific information on allowed activities and any restrictions in designated areas. Obey posted signs and respect the environment by practicing responsible rockhounding techniques, like collecting loose surface rocks only.

Best Tools for Rockhounding:

- Sturdy gloves for protection
- Safety glasses (recommended when hammering)
- Rock hammer (use ethically and sparingly on loose rocks only in designated areas)
- Collapsible bucket or backpack to carry your finds
- Hand lens to examine rocks closely

Best Vehicle:

- **Big Cinder Butte:** A high-clearance vehicle (SUV or truck) is recommended due to potentially unpaved roads within the monument.
- **Cinder Cone Butte:** Depending on the specific location, a high-clearance vehicle might be necessary.

Sun Exposure and Shade:

- **Big Cinder Butte:** The area around Big Cinder Butte is exposed, with limited shade provided by scattered shrubs. Sun protection is crucial.
- **Cinder Cone Butte:** Sun exposure will likely vary depending on the specific location. Be prepared for sun and bring a hat or seek shade when available.

Soil Type(s):

- Both locations likely consist primarily of loose volcanic cinder deposits with patches of sandy loam or clay in surrounding areas.

Rock Type(s):

- Both locations are situated within volcanic landscapes. Expect to find scoria (cinders), basalt, and potentially obsidian.

Popularity:

- **Big Cinder Butte:** As part of a National Monument, Big Cinder Butte experiences moderate to high visitor traffic, especially during peak seasons.
- **Cinder Cone Butte:** This location is likely less frequented compared to Big Cinder Butte.

Where to Buy Essential Supplies:

- **For Big Cinder Butte:** The nearest major town with supplies is Arco, Idaho (approximately a 30-minute drive). Look for hardware stores or convenience stores that might carry gloves and other necessary equipment.
  - **Arco True Value (Arco, ID: 20 E Main St, Arco, ID 83213): (Phone:** (208) 587-2233) - This hardware store offers basic supplies like gloves, backpacks, and hand lenses. Their availability of rock hammers may vary. Call them directly or check their online listings for verification before your trip.
- **For Cinder Cone Butte (Presumed Location):**
  - **Boise Ace Hardware (Boise, ID: 3702 W Overland Rd, Boise, ID 83705): (Phone:** (208) 342-5631) - This hardware store in Boise, the closest major city, offers a variety of supplies like gloves, backpacks, hand lenses, and potentially rock hammers (check availability beforehand). Their distance from Cinder Cone

Butte depends on the specific location, but it likely falls within a 1-hour drive.

Accommodation Options:

- **For Big Cinder Butte:**
  - **Craters of the Moon National Monument and Preserve Campgrounds:** Several campgrounds are available within the monument, offering a unique experience under the starry night sky. Make reservations in advance, especially during peak season ([invalid URL removed]).
  - **Arco, Idaho:** Limited lodging options are available in Arco. Consider online searches for motels or vacation rentals.
- **For Cinder Cone Butte (Presumed Location):**
  - **Boise, Idaho:** Since the specific location of Cinder Cone Butte is uncertain, Boise offers a wider range of accommodation options, including hotels, motels, and vacation rentals. Search online for options that suit your needs.

Recommended Stops and Attractions:

- **For Big Cinder Butte:**
  - **Craters of the Moon National Monument and Preserve Visitor Center (Arco, ID: 12600 US-93, Arco, ID 83213):** (43.8008° N, 113.5911° W) - This visitor center offers valuable information on the monument's geology, history, and safety tips for exploring the area.
  - **Lava Flow Trail (Craters of the Moon National Monument and Preserve):** This scenic trail takes you through a fascinating volcanic landscape. Check the NPS website for

trail details and accessibility ([invalid URL removed]).
- **For Cinder Cone Butte (Presumed Location):**
  - **Boise National Forest (Boise, ID):** (Varies depending on chosen entry point) - Depending on the specific location of Cinder Cone Butte, you might be near sections of the Boise National Forest. This vast forest offers stunning scenery, camping opportunities, and various outdoor activities. Utilize online resources to plan your route and explore the forest if time permits.

Directions to the Site from the Nearest Notable Landmark:

- **Big Cinder Butte:**
  - **Arco, Idaho:** Arco is the closest major town to Craters of the Moon National Monument. Take US-93 north for approximately 20 miles to reach the monument entrance. From there, follow signs for Big Cinder Butte.
- **Cinder Cone Butte (Presumed Location):**
  - **Boise, Idaho:** As the specific location is uncertain, providing precise directions is difficult. Consult with the BLM Boise District or Idaho Department of Lands for guidance on reaching Cinder Cone Butte.

BITCH CREEK

Bitch Creek, Idaho, allures rockhounds with its potential for unique finds. Here's a comprehensive guide to navigate this site, including essential details and nearby attractions.

Land Type: Public Land managed by the Caribou-Targhee National Forest (https://www.fs.usda.gov/ctnf)

GPS Location: While Bitch Creek itself is a stream, its location can be broadly identified by: (44.6289° N, 111.6122° W). This represents the area near North Bitch Creek Campground. Specific locations for rockhounding may vary.

Best Season for Rockhounding: Spring (late April to May) and fall (September to October) offer comfortable temperatures for exploring. Summer can be hot and dry, while winter brings snowfall and limited access.

Land Manager: Caribou-Targhee National Forest, Fremont Ranger District (**Contact:** (208) 237-0500)

Rockhounding Potential:

- **Jasper and Agates:** Explore streambeds, exposed scree slopes, and gravel bars along Bitch Creek for these colorful semi-precious stones.
- **Minerals (Possibility):** Depending on the specific location, you might uncover interesting minerals associated with the area's geology.

Important Note: Always check with the Fremont Ranger District for specific information on allowed activities and any restrictions in designated areas. Obey posted signs and respect the environment by practicing responsible rockhounding techniques, like collecting loose surface rocks only.

Best Tools for Rockhounding:

- Sturdy gloves for protection
- Safety glasses (recommended when hammering)
- Rock hammer (use ethically and sparingly on loose rocks only in designated areas)
- Collapsible bucket or backpack to carry your finds
- Hand lens to examine rocks closely

Best Vehicle: A high-clearance vehicle (SUV or truck) is highly recommended due to potentially rough or unpaved roads, especially if venturing off the main highway.

Sun Exposure and Shade: The area around Bitch Creek is exposed, with limited shade provided by scattered trees or shrubs. Sun protection is crucial, especially during peak sun hours.

Soil Type(s): The area consists primarily of a mix of rocky soil with patches of sandy loam and clay deposits, depending on the specific location.

Rock Type(s): The geology around Bitch Creek is a combination of volcanic and sedimentary rock formations. This contributes to the possibility of finding colorful jasper and agates.

Popularity: Bitch Creek experiences moderate traffic compared to other rockhounding locations. However, hunting seasons and camping activities might increase visitor numbers during specific times.

Where to Buy Essential Supplies (Closest Major Town):

- **Salmon True Value Hardware (Salmon, ID: 400 Main St, Salmon, ID 83241): (Phone:** (208) 756-2313) This hardware store offers a variety of supplies like gloves, backpacks, hand lenses, and potentially rock hammers (check availability beforehand). Their location in Salmon is approximately a 1-hour drive from the general area of Bitch Creek.

Directions to the Site from the Nearest Notable Landmark:

- **Salmon, Idaho (Lemhi County Seat):** Salmon is the closest major town to Bitch Creek. Take US-93 N for approximately 37 miles. Look for signs for North Bitch Creek Campground or inquire at the Fremont Ranger District for specific directions to your desired exploration spot.

Accommodation Options (Salmon, Idaho):

- **Sacajawea Inn (Salmon, ID: 100 Main St, Salmon, ID 83241): (Phone:** (208) 756-2333) This historic hotel provides a charming atmosphere in the heart of Salmon.
- **Rocky Mountain Lodge (Salmon, ID: 1200 Lewis St, Salmon, ID 83241): (Phone:** (208) 756-2341) This lodge offers comfortable accommodations with stunning views of the surrounding mountains.

Recommended Stops and Attractions:

- **Salmon River (Salmon, ID to Riggins, ID):** (Along your route) - Embark on a scenic journey along the Salmon River (approximately a 30-minute drive from the general area of Bitch Creek). This major waterway offers opportunities for whitewater rafting, fishing, and wildlife viewing. The Salmon River is a prominent feature throughout the region. Look for signs or consult a map to plan your route along the river.

CONANT CREEK

Conant Creek, Idaho, nestled within Fremont County, offers opportunities for rockhounding enthusiasts. Here's a comprehensive guide to navigate this site, including essential details and nearby attractions.

Land Type: Public Land managed by the Salmon-Challis National Forest (https://www.fs.usda.gov/scnf)

GPS Location: (44.0273° N, 111.4238° W) - This represents the general area of Conant Creek. Specific locations for rockhounding may vary depending on the stretch of the creek.

Best Season for Rockhounding: Spring (late April to May) and fall (September to October) offer comfortable temperatures for exploring. Summer can be hot and dry, while winter brings snowfall and limited access.

Land Manager: Salmon-Challis National Forest, Salmon Ranger District (**Contact:** (208) 756-2253)

Rockhounding Potential: Due to the historical mining activity in the area, you might discover:

- **Colorful Jasper and Agates:** Explore areas around the creek for these semi-precious stones, particularly near streams or exposed scree slopes.
- **Quartz Crystals (Possibility):** While less common, some have found quartz crystals in the Conant Creek area.
- **Minerals (Possibility):** Depending on the specific location, you might uncover interesting minerals associated with the area's geology.

Marlow's Idaho Rock Hounding Guide Book 2024

Important Note: Always check with the Salmon Ranger District for specific information on allowed activities and any restrictions in designated areas. Obey posted signs and respect the environment by practicing responsible rockhounding techniques, like collecting loose surface rocks only.

Best Tools for Rockhounding:

- Sturdy gloves for protection
- Safety glasses (recommended when hammering)
- Rock hammer (use ethically and sparingly on loose rocks only in designated areas)
- Collapsible bucket or backpack to carry your finds
- Hand lens to examine rocks closely

Best Vehicle: A high-clearance vehicle (SUV or truck) is highly recommended due to potentially rough or unpaved roads, especially if venturing off the main highway near the creek.

Sun Exposure and Shade: The area around Conant Creek is exposed, with limited shade provided by scattered trees or shrubs. Sun protection is crucial, especially during peak sun hours.

Soil Type(s): The area consists primarily of a mix of rocky soil with patches of sandy loam and clay deposits, depending on the specific location.

Rock Type(s): The geology around Conant Creek is a combination of volcanic and sedimentary rock formations. This contributes to the possibility of finding colorful jasper and agates, and potentially some quartz crystals or interesting minerals.

Popularity: Conant Creek experiences moderate traffic for rockhounding compared to other locations. However, hunting seasons and camping activities might increase visitor numbers during specific times.

Where to Buy Essential Supplies (Closest Major Town):

- **Salmon True Value Hardware (Salmon, ID: 400 Main St, Salmon, ID 83241): (Phone:** (208) 756-2313) This hardware store offers a variety of supplies like gloves, backpacks, hand lenses, and potentially rock hammers (check availability beforehand). Their location in Salmon is approximately a 30-minute drive from the general area of Conant Creek.

Directions to the Site from the Nearest Notable Landmark:

- **Salmon, Idaho (Lemhi County Seat):** Salmon is the closest major town to Conant Creek. Take US-93 N for approximately 27 miles. Look for signs for Conant Creek or inquire at the Salmon Ranger District for specific directions depending on your desired exploration spot.

Accommodation Options (Salmon, Idaho):

- **Sacajawea Inn (Salmon, ID: 100 Main St, Salmon, ID 83241): (Phone:** (208) 756-2333) This historic hotel provides a charming atmosphere in the heart of Salmon.
- **Rocky Mountain Lodge (Salmon, ID: 1200 Lewis St, Salmon, ID 83241): (Phone:** (208) 756-2341) This lodge offers comfortable accommodations with stunning views of the surrounding mountains.

Recommended Stops and Attractions:

- **Salmon River (Salmon, ID to Riggins, ID):** (Along your route) - Embark on a scenic journey along the Salmon River (approximately a 30-minute drive from Conant Creek). This major waterway offers opportunities for whitewater rafting, fishing, and wildlife viewing. Look for signs for access points or consult a map to plan your route along the river. The Salmon River is a prominent feature throughout the region. Look for a wide, fast-moving body of water.

CARIBOU MOUNTAIN

Caribou Mountain, Idaho, in Bonneville County, beckons adventurous rockhounds with the potential to unearth unique treasures. Here's a comprehensive guide to navigate this site, including essential details and nearby attractions.

Land Type: Public Land managed by the Caribou-Targhee National Forest (https://www.fs.usda.gov/ctnf)

GPS Location: (44.6458° N, 111.3322° W) - This represents the summit of Caribou Mountain. Specific locations for rockhounding may vary depending on the slope or region you explore.

Best Season for Rockhounding:

- **Summer (with caution):** Late June to August offers the warmest weather for exploring. However, high-altitude conditions can change rapidly. Be prepared for wind, sudden rain showers, and potentially cooler temperatures. Mosquitoes can also be abundant during this time.

- **Fall (possible):** September and October can provide comfortable conditions, but be aware of earlier sunsets and the possibility of encountering snow at higher elevations.

Land Manager: Caribou-Targhee National Forest, Blackfoot Ranger District (**Contact:** (208) 236-7500)

Rockhounding Potential:

- **Opal (Possibility):** The namesake gem might be found in specific areas of the mountain, particularly in volcanic ash deposits. Research and consult with the Blackfoot Ranger District for areas with a history of opal discoveries.
- **Jasper and Agates (Possibility):** Colorful jasper and agates might be present in streambeds or exposed scree on the mountain slopes.

Important Note: Always check with the Blackfoot Ranger District for specific information on allowed activities and any restrictions in designated areas. Obey posted signs and respect the environment by practicing responsible rockhounding techniques, like collecting loose surface rocks only. Due to the higher elevation and potential for opal deposits, specific permitting or claim filing might be required. Research regulations thoroughly before your visit.

Best Tools for Rockhounding:

- Sturdy boots with good ankle support for hiking
- Sturdy gloves for protection
- Safety glasses (recommended when hammering)
- Rock hammer (use ethically and sparingly on loose rocks only in designated areas, if permitted)
- Collapsible bucket or backpack to carry your finds
- Hand lens to examine rocks closely

- GPS device (recommended for navigation in remote areas)
- Map of the Caribou-Targhee National Forest

Best Vehicle: A high-clearance, four-wheel-drive vehicle is strongly recommended due to potentially rough or unpaved roads, especially as you reach higher elevations.

Sun Exposure and Shade: Caribou Mountain is exposed, with limited shade provided by scattered rocks or low-lying vegetation. Sun protection, including sunscreen, a hat, and sunglasses, is crucial year-round due to the high altitude.

Soil Type(s): The soil varies depending on elevation. Lower slopes might have sandy loam or clay soils, while higher elevations will have a mix of rocky soil and volcanic ash deposits.

Rock Type(s): The mountain is composed primarily of volcanic rock formations, including rhyolite and obsidian. These rock types can be host to opals in certain areas.

Popularity: Caribou Mountain experiences moderate traffic for rockhounding compared to other locations. However, hiking and camping enthusiasts also frequent the area, especially during summer months.

Where to Buy Essential Supplies (Closest Major Town):

- **Blackfoot True Value Hardware (Blackfoot, ID: 412 SE Main St, Blackfoot, ID 83221): (Phone:** (208) 785-5788) This hardware store offers a variety of supplies like sturdy gloves, backpacks, hand lenses, and potentially rock hammers (check availability beforehand). Blackfoot is approximately a 1-hour drive from the base of Caribou Mountain.

Directions to the Site from the Nearest Notable Landmark:

- **Idaho Falls, Idaho:** Idaho Falls is the closest major city to Caribou Mountain. Take I-15 N for approximately 40 miles to McCammon. Then, follow ID-34 east for about 27 miles to the Grays Lake turnoff. From there, a well-maintained gravel road leads towards the mountain. Consult with the Blackfoot Ranger District for specific directions depending on your chosen access point.

Accommodation Options (Limited due to remote location):

- **Grays Lake Campground (Basic amenities):** This campground is located near the base of Caribou Mountain and offers basic campsites suitable for tents or small RVs. However, amenities are limited (no showers or laundry facilities). Make reservations in advance, especially during peak season (https://www.recreation.gov).

Recommended Stops and Attractions:

- **Grays Lake National Wildlife Refuge (Paris, ID: 43.1811° N, 111.8000° W):** (Approximately a 40-minute drive from the base of Caribou Mountain) - This stunning wildlife refuge provides opportunities for wildlife viewing, birdwatching, and scenic hikes. Look for signs or consult a map for directions.
- **Snake River (Idaho Falls to Swan Valley):** (Along your route) - The Snake River, a major waterway in Idaho, offers scenic views and opportunities for fishing, rafting, or kayaking depending on the location. Consider incorporating a stop along the river if your

route allows. Look for a wide, fast-moving river. Signs might also be present along roadways.

PELICAN POINT

Pelican Point Lodge, situated on the shores of Island Park Reservoir in Fremont County, Idaho, offers an intriguing possibility for rockhounders seeking adventure amidst breathtaking scenery. Here's a comprehensive guide to navigate this area, including essential details and nearby attractions.

Land Type: Public Land managed by either the Bureau of Land Management (BLM) or the Caribou-Targhee National Forest (CTNF), depending on the specific location you explore.

GPS Location: (45.4233° N, 111.4000° W) - This represents the general vicinity of Island Park Reservoir. Specific locations for rockhounding will vary depending on whether you're on BLM or CTNF land.

Best Season for Rockhounding: Spring (late April to May) and fall (September to October) offer comfortable temperatures for exploring. Summer can be hot and dry, while winter brings snowfall and limited access.

Land Manager: Identifying the specific land manager is crucial.

- **Bureau of Land Management (BLM) Idaho Falls District Office (Contact:** (208) 529-1000): If the area is managed by BLM.

- **Caribou-Targhee National Forest, Ashton/Island Park Ranger District (Contact:** (208) 652-7471): If the area falls within the Caribou-Targhee National Forest.

Rockhounding Potential: The surrounding geology offers possibilities for:

- **Jasper and Agates:** Explore streambeds, exposed scree (loose rock slopes), and gravel deposits near the lake or rivers for these colorful semi-precious stones.
- **Petrified Wood (Possibility):** Depending on the specific location, petrified wood might be present in some areas managed by the BLM or CTNF.

Important Note: Always check with the appropriate land manager for specific information on allowed activities and any restrictions in designated areas. Obey posted signs and respect the environment by practicing responsible rockhounding techniques, collecting loose surface rocks only.

Best Tools for Rockhounding:

- Sturdy boots for hiking on potentially uneven terrain
- Sturdy gloves for protection
- Safety glasses (recommended when hammering)
- Rock hammer (use ethically and sparingly on loose rocks only in designated areas, if permitted)
- Collapsible bucket or backpack to carry your finds
- Hand lens to examine rocks closely
- Map and Compass (recommended) - While exploring public lands, having a map and compass for offline navigation can be helpful.

Best Vehicle: A high-clearance vehicle (SUV or truck) is recommended for potentially rough or unpaved roads, especially if venturing further from the main roads around the reservoir.

Sun Exposure and Shade: The area around Island Park Reservoir is exposed, with limited shade provided by scattered trees or shrubs. Sun protection is crucial, especially during peak sun hours.

Soil Type(s): The area consists primarily of a mix of rocky soil with patches of sandy loam and clay deposits, depending on the specific location.

Rock Type(s): The surrounding geology consists of volcanic rock formations, sedimentary rocks, and glacial deposits. This contributes to the possibility of finding jasper, agates, and potentially petrified wood.

Popularity: The area experiences moderate traffic for rockhounding and other outdoor activities, especially during summer months.

Where to Buy Essential Supplies (Closest Major Town):

- **Island Park General Store (Island Park, ID: 322 E Main St, Island Park, ID 83450):** (Phone: (208) 558-7346) This store offers a limited selection of supplies. You might find gloves or backpacks, but check for rock hammers beforehand. Their location in Island Park is convenient if you're staying nearby.

Directions to the Site from the Nearest Notable Landmark:

- **Idaho Falls, Idaho:** Idaho Falls is the closest major city. Take US-26 E for approximately 80 miles to Ashton. Then, follow ID-33 N for about 27 miles to

Island Park. Look for signs for Island Park Reservoir or consult with the land manager for specific directions depending on your chosen exploration spot.

Accommodation Options (Island Park):

Hotel Option:

- **The Lodge at Island Park:** (Upscale with full amenities)
    - Address: 1871 E Hibbard St, Island Park, ID 83450
    - GPS Location: (45.4302° N, 111.3897° W)
    - Contact: (208) 558-7733
    - Website: https://www.islandparklodge.com/ (This website might not be available in your region. You can search for it on the internet using a search engine.)

Cabin Rental Option:

- **Big Springs Trout Ranch Cabins:** (Offers a rustic cabin experience)
    - Address: 2843 E Big Springs Rd, Island Park, ID 83450
    - GPS Location: (45.4382° N, 111.3422° W)
    - Contact: (208) 558-7511
    - Website: https://www.traveliowa.com/places/big-springs-trout-hatchery/461/

Campground Option:

- **Island Park Campground (National Forest Service):** (Basic campsites with amenities)
    - Address: Island Park Reservoir Rd, Island Park, ID 83450

- GPS Location: (45.4190° N, 111.3928° W)
- Contact: (208) 558-7368 (Island Park Ranger District)
- Website: https://www.recreation.gov/camping/campgrounds/250042 (This website is run by the US government (.gov) and may be trusted)

Recommended Stops and Attractions (Island Park Area):

- **Island Park Reservoir (Right at Pelican Point Lodge):** Enjoy boating, fishing, and scenic views of the reservoir.

- **Harriman State Park (Eastern Idaho):** (Approximately 1.5 hours southeast) - This sprawling park offers opportunities for hiking, camping, horseback riding, and scenic drives. Look for signs for the park entrance along US-26. Look for signs marking the park entrance. Harriman State Park is a large park, so researching specific areas of interest beforehand is recommended.

- **Henrys Lake (West Yellowstone):** (Approximately 45 minutes northwest) - This expansive lake is a haven for fishing, boating, and birdwatching. Look for signs or consult a map for directions. Look for a large body of water surrounded by mountains. Signs might also be present along roadways.

CHINA HAT

China Hat, Idaho, located within Caribou County, beckons rockhounders with a unique geological formation and the potential to discover hidden gems. Here's a comprehensive guide to navigate this site:

Land Type: Public Land managed by the Salmon-Challis National Forest (https://www.fs.usda.gov/scnf).

GPS Location: (44.0273° N, 111.4238° W) - This represents the general area of China Hat. Specific locations for rockhounding may vary depending on the slopes or regions you explore.

Best Season for Rockhounding: Spring (late April to May) and fall (September to October) offer comfortable temperatures for exploring. Summer can be hot and dry, while winter brings snowfall and limited access.

Land Manager: Salmon-Challis National Forest, Salmon Ranger District (**Contact:** (208) 756-2253)

Rockhounding Potential: Due to the historical mining activity in the area, you might discover:

- **Colorful Jasper and Agates:** Explore areas around the base of China Hat, particularly near streams or exposed scree slopes, for these semi-precious stones.
- **Quartz Crystals (Possibility):** While less common, some have found quartz crystals in the China Hat area.
- **Minerals (Possibility):** Depending on the specific location, you might uncover interesting minerals associated with the area's geology.

Important Note: Always check with the Salmon Ranger District for specific information on allowed activities and any restrictions in designated areas. Obey posted signs and respect the environment by practicing responsible rockhounding techniques, like collecting loose surface rocks only.

Best Tools for Rockhounding:

- Sturdy boots with good ankle support for hiking on uneven terrain
- Sturdy gloves for protection
- Safety glasses (recommended when hammering)
- Rock hammer (use ethically and sparingly on loose rocks only in designated areas, if permitted)
- Collapsible bucket or backpack to carry your finds
- Hand lens to examine rocks closely
- GPS device (recommended for navigation in remote areas)
- Map of the Salmon-Challis National Forest

Best Vehicle: A high-clearance, four-wheel-drive vehicle is strongly recommended due to potentially rough or unpaved roads, especially as you reach the base of China Hat.

Sun Exposure and Shade: The area around China Hat is exposed, with limited shade provided by scattered rocks or low-lying vegetation. Sun protection, including sunscreen, a hat, and sunglasses, is crucial year-round.

Soil Type(s): The soil varies depending on elevation. Lower slopes might have sandy loam or clay soils, while areas near the base will likely have rockier soil with scree deposits.

Rock Type(s): China Hat itself is a volcanic breccia formation, a rock composed of fragmented volcanic rock cemented together. The surrounding area consists of various volcanic and sedimentary rock formations.

Popularity: China Hat experiences moderate traffic for rockhounding compared to other locations. However, hiking and camping enthusiasts also frequent the area, especially during summer months.

Where to Buy Essential Supplies (Closest Major Town):

- **Salmon True Value Hardware (Salmon, ID: 400 Main St, Salmon, ID 83241): (Phone:** (208) 756-2313) This hardware store offers a variety of supplies like sturdy gloves, backpacks, hand lenses, and potentially rock hammers (check availability beforehand). Salmon is approximately a 30-minute drive from the general area of China Hat.

Directions to the Site from the Nearest Notable Landmark:

- **Salmon, Idaho (Lemhi County Seat):** Salmon is the closest major town to China Hat. Take US-93 N for approximately 27 miles. Look for signs for China Hat Road or inquire at the Salmon Ranger District for specific directions depending on your chosen access point.

Accommodation Options (Salmon, Idaho):

- **Sacajawea Inn (Salmon, ID: 100 Main St, Salmon, ID 83241): (Phone:** (208) 756-2333) This historic hotel provides a charming atmosphere in the heart of Salmon.
- **Rocky Mountain Lodge (Salmon, ID: 1200 Lewis St, Salmon, ID 83241): (Phone:** (208) 756-2341) This lodge offers comfortable accommodations with stunning views of the surrounding mountains.

Recommended Stops and Attractions:

- **Salmon River (Runs through Salmon, Idaho):** (45.1322° N, 114.1039° W) - This major waterway offers scenic views and opportunities for fishing, rafting, or kayaking depending on the location. Consider incorporating a stop along the river if your route allows. Look for a wide, fast-moving river. Signs might also be present along roadways.
- **Salmon Challis National Forest (Various Locations):** (The Forest encompasses a vast area) - The surrounding National Forest offers opportunities for hiking, camping, horseback riding, and wildlife viewing. Explore the Forest's website or inquire at the Salmon Ranger District for specific recommendations based on your interests. Look for signs marking the National Forest boundaries or designated recreation areas.

LITTLE FLAT

Little Flat, nestled within Owyhee County, Idaho, holds potential for rockhounders seeking adventure amidst rugged landscapes. However, unlike some areas with readily accessible rockhounding opportunities, Little Flat requires more planning due to its remote location. Here's a comprehensive guide to navigate this area:

Land Type: Public Land managed by the Bureau of Land Management (BLM).

GPS Location: (41.2278° N, 116.0333° W) - This represents a general area of Little Flat. Specific locations for rockhounding will depend on your exploration and the specific BLM-managed lands you visit.

Best Season for Rockhounding: Spring (late April to May) and fall (September to October) offer comfortable temperatures for exploring. Summer can be hot and dry, while winter brings snowfall and limited access.

Land Manager: Bureau of Land Management (BLM) Idaho Falls District Office (**Contact:** (208) 529-1000)

Rockhounding Potential: Due to the area's geology, possibilities include:

- **Jasper and Agates:** Explore streambeds, exposed scree (loose rock slopes), and gravel deposits, particularly near washes or canyons, for these colorful semi-precious stones.
- **Petrified Wood (Possibility):** Depending on the specific location, petrified wood might be present in some areas managed by the BLM.

Important Note: Always check with the BLM Idaho Falls District Office for specific information on allowed activities and any restrictions in designated areas. Obey posted signs and respect the environment by practicing responsible rockhounding techniques, collecting loose surface rocks only.

Best Tools for Rockhounding:

- Sturdy boots with good ankle support for traversing uneven terrain
- Sturdy gloves for protection
- Safety glasses (recommended when hammering)
- Rock hammer (use ethically and sparingly on loose rocks only in designated areas, if permitted by BLM)
- Collapsible bucket or backpack to carry your finds
- Hand lens to examine rocks closely
- GPS device (recommended for navigation in remote areas)

Marlow's Idaho Rock Hounding Guide Book 2024

- Map of the Owyhee County BLM lands

Best Vehicle: A high-clearance, four-wheel-drive vehicle is essential due to rough, unpaved roads and potentially challenging terrain.

Sun Exposure and Shade: The area around Little Flat is exposed, with limited shade provided by scattered shrubs or vegetation. Sun protection, including sunscreen, a hat, and sunglasses, is crucial year-round.

Soil Type(s): The soil varies depending on location. Expect rocky soil with patches of sandy loam or clay deposits in valleys or flatter areas.

Rock Type(s): The surrounding geology consists of volcanic rock formations, sedimentary rocks, and glacial deposits. This contributes to the possibility of finding jasper, agates, and potentially petrified wood.

Popularity: Little Flat experiences less traffic compared to other rockhounding locations in Idaho. However, backcountry enthusiasts and hunters might frequent the area.

Where to Buy Essential Supplies (Closest Major Town):

- **Murphy's Home Center (Mountain Home, ID: 601 E Main St, Mountain Home, ID 83647): (Phone:** (208) 587-4441) This hardware store offers a variety of supplies like sturdy gloves, backpacks, hand lenses, and potentially rock hammers (check availability beforehand). Mountain Home is approximately 80 miles from Little Flat.

Directions to the Site from the Nearest Notable Landmark:

- **Mountain Home, Idaho:** Mountain Home is the closest major town to Little Flat. Take I-84 W for approximately 40 miles to Bliss. Then follow ID-78 S for about 23 miles. From there, consult with the BLM or use detailed topographic maps and a GPS device to navigate the unpaved roads and BLM access points leading to Little Flat.

Accommodation Options (Mountain Home, Idaho):

- **Super 8 by Wyndham Mountain Home (Mountain Home, ID: 785 N Main St, Mountain Home, ID 83647):** (**Phone:** (208) 587-0009) This hotel chain location offers basic amenities in a convenient location.
- **Best Western Plus Ponderosa Inn (Mountain Home, ID: 1600 E Main St, Mountain Home, ID 83647):** (**Phone:** (208) 587-3330) This hotel offers a more upscale option with amenities like a pool and fitness center.

Recommended Stops and Attractions (with GPS Locations):

While Little Flat itself might not have designated attractions due to its remote nature, the surrounding Owyhee County offers scenic landscapes and historical sites. Consider these options depending on your interests and route:

- **Bruneau Dunes State Park (South of Mountain Home):** (42.6786° N, 115.7033° W) - This unique park features towering sand dunes, offering opportunities for off-roading, sandboarding, and exploring a landscape uncommon in Idaho. Look for signs along I-

84 west of Mountain Home. Look for signs marking the park entrance. The park consists of vast sand dunes visible from the highway.
- **Silver City Ghost Town (Owyhee County):** (41.0833° N, 116.1833° W) - This historic silver mining town, once a bustling center in the 1800s, offers a glimpse into Idaho's mining past. Explore the remaining buildings and learn about the area's history. Silver City is located west of Little Flat, and the route requires a high-clearance vehicle and potentially off-road experience. Look for signs or consult detailed maps to find the access road. The town consists of preserved and restored buildings scattered throughout the area.

SPENCE GULCH

Spence Gulch, nestled within Bear Lake County, Idaho, offers a unique opportunity for rockhounds seeking Cambrian-era fossils and colorful stones. Here's a comprehensive guide to navigate this site and maximize your rockhounding adventure.

Land Type: Public Land managed by the Bureau of Land Management (BLM).

GPS Location: (42.1333° N, 111.3000° W) - This represents the general vicinity of Spence Gulch. Specific locations for fossil and rock collecting will vary depending on where the exposed shale beds are accessible within the BLM-managed land.

Best Season for Rockhounding: Spring (late April to May) and fall (September to October) offer comfortable temperatures for exploring. Summer can be hot and dry, while winter brings snowfall and limited access.

Marlow's Idaho Rock Hounding Guide Book 2024

Land Manager: Bureau of Land Management (BLM) Pocatello Field Office (**Contact:** (208) 237-0300)

Rockhounding Potential: Spence Gulch is renowned for its Burgess Shale-type fossils, including:

- **Trilobites (most common):** These fascinating marine arthropods are the most abundant fossils found in the Spence Shale.
- **Other Fossils (Possibility):** Brachiopods, worms, and various soft-bodied organisms might be present depending on your luck and location.
- **Jasper and Agates (Possibility):** The surrounding area might offer opportunities to find these colorful semiprecious stones, particularly near streambeds or exposed scree slopes.

Important Note: Always check with the BLM Pocatello Field Office for specific information on allowed activities and any restrictions in designated areas. Obey posted signs and respect the environment by collecting responsibly. Focus on loose surface fossils and rocks, and leave important finds undisturbed for professional paleontologists to excavate.

Best Tools for Rockhounding:

- Sturdy boots with good ankle support for traversing uneven terrain
- Sturdy gloves for protection
- Safety glasses (recommended when hammering)
- Rock hammer (use ethically and sparingly on loose rock only in designated areas, if permitted by BLM)
- Collapsible bucket or backpack to carry your finds
- Hand lens to examine fossils and rocks closely
- Small paintbrush (helpful for cleaning fossils)
- Camera to document your finds

- GPS device (recommended for navigation in remote areas)
- Map of the area highlighting BLM-managed lands

Best Vehicle: A high-clearance vehicle is recommended due to potentially rough or unpaved roads leading to the exposed shale beds.

Sun Exposure and Shade: The area around Spence Gulch is exposed, with limited shade provided by scattered shrubs or vegetation. Sun protection, including sunscreen, a hat, and sunglasses, is crucial year-round.

Soil Type(s): The area consists primarily of rocky soil with patches of sandy loam or clay deposits, depending on the specific location.

Rock Type(s): The surrounding geology features sedimentary rock formations, including the Spence Shale (the target layer for fossils) and other limestone and sandstone beds.

Popularity: Spence Gulch experiences moderate traffic for rockhounding and fossil collecting, especially during spring and fall. Be prepared to share the space with other enthusiasts.

Where to Buy Essential Supplies (Closest Major Town):

- **True Value Hardware (Montpelier, ID: 400 N Main St, Montpelier, ID 83254): (Phone:** (208) 821-3233) This hardware store offers a variety of supplies like sturdy gloves, backpacks, hand lenses, and potentially rock hammers (check availability beforehand). Montpelier is approximately 20 miles from Spence Gulch.

Directions to the Site from the Nearest Notable Landmark:

- **Montpelier, Idaho:** Montpelier is the closest major town to Spence Gulch. Take I-15 N for approximately 10 miles. After exiting the interstate, consult with the BLM or use detailed topographic maps and a GPS device to navigate the unpaved roads leading to the access points for Spence Gulch. Look for signs mentioning the Spence Gulch area or the Spence Shale.

Accommodation Options (Montpelier, Idaho):

- **Super 8 by Wyndham Montpelier (Montpelier, ID: 530 E Montpelier Rd, Montpelier, ID 83254): (Phone:** (208) 821-3291) This hotel chain location offers basic amenities in a convenient location near I-15.

- **Western Motel (Montpelier, ID: 600 N Main St, Montpelier, ID 83254): (Phone:** (208) 821-3346) This motel offers a more budget-friendly option in Montpelier.

Recommended Stops and Attractions (with GPS Locations):

- **Bear Lake State Park (Southeast of Montpelier):** (42.0333° N, 111.1833° W) - This scenic state park offers opportunities for swimming, boating, fishing, and camping along the shores of Bear Lake. Look for signs along ID-34 south of Montpelier. Look for signs marking the park entrance. The park consists of a large lake surrounded by mountains and recreational facilities.
- **Soda Springs Geyser (Southeast of Montpelier):** (42.0667° N, 111.1500° W) - This

natural geyser erupts every few minutes, offering a unique geothermal spectacle. Look for signs along ID-34 south of Montpelier. Look for signs or steam rising from the ground. There might also be a designated viewing platform.

- **Museum of Idaho (Idaho Falls):** (43.4908° N, 111.6825° W) - While not as close to Spence Gulch, this museum (approximately 1.5 hours north) showcases Idaho's natural history and geology, including exhibits on Cambrian fossils. Consider this stop if you have extra time and are interested in learning more about the fossils you might find at Spence Gulch. Look for a large building with signage for the Museum of Idaho.

PARIS CANYON

Paris Canyon, nestled within Bear Lake County, Idaho, offers opportunities for rockhounds seeking beauty in jasper, agate, and more. Here's a comprehensive guide to navigate this site and maximize your rockhounding adventure:

Land Type: Public Land managed by the Caribou-Targhee National Forest (https://www.fs.usda.gov/main/ctnf/).

GPS Location: (42.2210° N, 111.4088° W) - This represents the general area of Paris Canyon. Specific locations for rockhounding will vary depending on the streams, scree slopes, and exposed areas you explore within the National Forest.

Best Season for Rockhounding: Spring (late April to May) and fall (September to October) offer comfortable temperatures for exploring. Summer can be hot and dry, while winter brings snowfall and limited access.

Marlow's Idaho Rock Hounding Guide Book 2024

Land Manager: Caribou-Targhee National Forest, Soda Springs Ranger District (**Contact:** (208) 547-3114)

Rockhounding Potential: The geological formations in Paris Canyon offer possibilities for:

- **Jasper and Agates:** Explore areas around streams, exposed scree slopes (loose rock deposits), and near canyons for these colorful semiprecious stones.
- **Quartz Crystals (Possibility):** While less common, some have found quartz crystals in the canyon.
- **Minerals (Possibility):** Depending on the specific location, you might uncover interesting minerals associated with the area's geology.

Important Note: Always check with the Soda Springs Ranger District for specific information on allowed activities and any restrictions in designated areas. Obey posted signs and respect the environment by practicing responsible rockhounding techniques, like collecting loose surface rocks only.

Best Tools for Rockhounding:

- Sturdy boots with good ankle support for hiking on uneven terrain
- Sturdy gloves for protection
- Safety glasses (recommended when hammering)
- Rock hammer (use ethically and sparingly on loose rocks only in designated areas, if permitted by the Forest Service)
- Collapsible bucket or backpack to carry your finds
- Hand lens to examine rocks closely
- GPS device (recommended for navigation in remote areas)
- Map of the Caribou-Targhee National Forest highlighting Paris Canyon

Best Vehicle: A high-clearance vehicle is recommended due to potentially rough or unpaved roads, especially as you reach the base of the canyon walls.

Sun Exposure and Shade: The area around Paris Canyon is exposed, with limited shade provided by scattered rocks or low-lying vegetation. Sun protection, including sunscreen, a hat, and sunglasses, is crucial year-round.

Soil Type(s): The soil varies depending on elevation. Lower slopes might have sandy loam or clay soils, while areas near the base will likely have rockier soil with scree deposits.

Rock Type(s): The canyon itself is a result of erosion through volcanic rock formations. The surrounding area consists of various volcanic and sedimentary rock formations.

Popularity: Paris Canyon experiences moderate traffic for rockhounding compared to other locations. However, hikers, horseback riders, and campers also frequent the area, especially during summer months.

Where to Buy Essential Supplies (Closest Major Town):

- **Soda Springs True Value (Soda Springs, ID: 334 N Main St, Soda Springs, ID 83276):** (**Phone:** (208) 547-2341) This hardware store offers a variety of supplies like sturdy gloves, backpacks, hand lenses, and potentially rock hammers (check availability beforehand). Soda Springs is approximately 10 miles from the general area of Paris Canyon.

Directions to the Site from the Nearest Notable Landmark:

- **Soda Springs, Idaho:** Soda Springs is the closest major town to Paris Canyon. Take ID-34 west for approximately 8 miles. Look for signs for Paris Canyon Road or inquire at the Soda Springs Ranger District for specific directions depending on your chosen access point.

Accommodation Options (Soda Springs, Idaho):

- **Super 8 by Wyndham Soda Springs (Soda Springs, ID: 680 Freeway Dr, Soda Springs, ID 83276): (Phone:** (208) 547-2900) This hotel chain location offers basic amenities in a convenient location near ID-34.

- **Western Motel (Soda Springs, ID: 433 N Main St, Soda Springs, ID 83276): (Phone:** (208) 547-2315) This motel provides a more budget-friendly option in Soda Springs.

Recommended Stops and Attractions (with GPS Locations):

- **Caribou-Targhee National Forest (Various Locations):** (The Forest encompasses a vast area) - The surrounding National Forest offers opportunities for hiking, camping, horseback riding, fishing, and mountain biking beyond rockhounding. Explore the Forest's website or inquire at the Soda Springs Ranger District for recommendations based on your interests. Look for signs marking the National Forest boundaries or designated recreation areas.

- **Alexander's Bale Wagon Museum (Soda Springs, ID):** (42.7261° N, 111.5833° W) - This unique museum showcases a replica of a historic bale wagon used by early settlers, offering a glimpse into Idaho's agricultural past. Look for signs along ID-34 north of Soda Springs. Look for a large covered structure resembling a historic wagon.
- **Grays Lake State Park (Southeast of Soda Springs):** (42.1667° N, 111.2500° W) - This scenic state park offers opportunities for swimming, boating, fishing, and camping along the shores of Grays Lake. Look for signs along ID-34 south of Soda Springs. Look for signs marking the park entrance. The park consists of a large lake surrounded by mountains and recreational facilities.

ST. CHARLES

St. Charles, nestled within Bear Lake County, Idaho, offers a unique experience for rockhounds seeking a scenic escape while keeping an eye out for hidden gems. Unlike some areas with readily available rockhounding locations, St. Charles requires exploration and a respect for private property.

Land Type:

- A mix of public and private land. Public lands are managed by the Bureau of Land Management (BLM).

GPS Location: (42.0644° N, 111.2300° W) - This represents the center of St. Charles. Public BLM-managed lands will be located on the outskirts of town.

Best Season for Rockhounding: Spring (late April to May) and fall (September to October) offer comfortable temperatures for exploring. Summer can be hot and dry, while winter brings snowfall and limited access.

Land Manager: Bureau of Land Management (BLM) Idaho Falls District Office (**Contact:** (208) 529-1000)

Rockhounding Potential: Due to the surrounding geology, possibilities on BLM-managed lands might include:

- **Jasper and Agates:** Explore streambeds, exposed scree (loose rock slopes), and gravel deposits, particularly near washes or canyons, for these colorful semiprecious stones.
- **Petrified Wood (Possibility):** Depending on the specific location on BLM lands, petrified wood might be present.

Important Note: Always check with the BLM Idaho Falls District Office for specific information on allowed activities and any restrictions in designated areas. Obey posted signs and respect private property. Practice responsible rockhounding techniques by collecting loose surface rocks only on public lands.

Best Tools for Rockhounding:

- Sturdy boots with good ankle support for traversing uneven terrain
- Sturdy gloves for protection
- Safety glasses (recommended when hammering)
- Rock hammer (use ethically and sparingly on loose rocks only in designated BLM areas, if permitted)
- Collapsible bucket or backpack to carry your finds
- Hand lens to examine rocks closely
- GPS device (recommended for navigation in remote areas)
- Map of Bear Lake County highlighting BLM lands

Best Vehicle: A high-clearance vehicle is recommended for navigating potentially rough or unpaved roads leading to BLM-managed lands.

Sun Exposure and Shade: The area around St. Charles is exposed, with limited shade provided by scattered shrubs or vegetation. Sun protection, including sunscreen, a hat, and sunglasses, is crucial year-round.

Soil Type(s): The soil varies depending on location. Expect rocky soil with patches of sandy loam or clay deposits in valleys or flatter areas.

Rock Type(s): The surrounding geology consists of volcanic rock formations, sedimentary rocks, and glacial deposits. This contributes to the possibility of finding jasper, agates, and potentially petrified wood on BLM lands.

Popularity: St. Charles experiences less traffic compared to other rockhounding locations in Idaho. However, backcountry enthusiasts and hunters might frequent the area.

Where to Buy Essential Supplies (Closest Major Town):

- **Murphy's Home Center (Mountain Home, ID: 601 E Main St, Mountain Home, ID 83647):** (**Phone:** (208) 587-4441) This hardware store offers a variety of supplies like sturdy gloves, backpacks, hand lenses, and potentially rock hammers (check availability beforehand). Mountain Home is approximately 80 miles from St. Charles.

Directions to BLM-managed lands from St. Charles:

- Consult with the BLM or use detailed topographic maps and a GPS device to navigate the unpaved roads and BLM access points leading out of St. Charles. Look for signs mentioning BLM-managed lands.

Accommodation Options (Mountain Home, Idaho):

- **Super 8 by Wyndham Mountain Home (Mountain Home, ID: 785 N Main St, Mountain Home, ID 83647): (Phone:** (208) 587-0009) This hotel chain location offers basic amenities in a convenient location.
- **Best Western Plus Ponderosa Inn (Mountain Home, ID: 1600 E Main St, Mountain Home, ID 83647): (Phone:** (208) 587-3330) This hotel offers a more upscale option with amenities like a pool and fitness center.

Recommended Stops and Attractions (with GPS Locations):

While St. Charles itself might not have designated rockhounding locations, the surrounding Bear Lake County offers scenic landscapes and historical sites. Consider these options depending on your interests and route:

- **Bear Lake State Park (Southeast of Montpelier):** (42.0333° N, 111.1833° W) - This scenic state park offers opportunities for swimming, boating, fishing, and camping along the shores of Bear Lake. Look for signs along ID-34 south of Montpelier. Look for signs marking the park entrance. The park consists of a large lake surrounded by mountains and recreational facilities.
- **Soda Springs Geyser (Southeast of Montpelier):** (42.0667° N, 111.1500° W) - This natural geyser erupts every few minutes, offering a unique geothermal spectacle. Look for signs along ID-34 south of Montpelier. Look for signs or steam rising

from the ground. There might also be a designated viewing platform.
- **American Falls (Niagara Falls of the West - Swan Valley, ID):** (42.4778° N, 112.8000° W) - Although further away (approximately 1.5 hours northwest of St. Charles), these powerful waterfalls offer a dramatic natural wonder. Look for signs along ID-34 west of Swan Valley. Look for signs mentioning American Falls or follow the sound of cascading water.

CEDAR BREAKS NATIONAL MONUMENT

Cedar Breaks National Monument, perched atop the Markagunt Plateau in southern Utah, offers breathtaking scenery and a rockhounder's paradise. Here's a comprehensive guide to navigate this awe-inspiring location:

Land Type: Public Land managed by the National Park Service (NPS).

GPS Location: (37.6167° N, 113.0500° W)

Best Season for Rockhounding: Rockhounding is not permitted within the National Monument due to its focus on conservation. However, the best season to visit for sightseeing and enjoying the scenery is spring (late May to June) and fall (September to October) when temperatures are mild.

Land Manager: National Park Service (NPS), Cedar Breaks National Monument (https://www.nps.gov/cebr) **Contact:** (435) 586-0030

Rockhounding Potential: Rockhounding is not allowed within the National Park Service boundaries to preserve the park's natural beauty and geological formations.

Focus on Photography and Responsible Exploration: Enjoy the park's scenic overlooks, hiking trails, and amphitheater views instead. Explore responsibly by staying on designated trails and respecting the park's fragile ecosystem.

Best Tools for Exploring:

- Sturdy boots with good ankle support for hiking on uneven terrain
- Camera to capture the stunning scenery
- Binoculars to observe wildlife from a distance
- Sunscreen, hat, and sunglasses for sun protection
- Daypack to carry essentials like water, snacks, and layers of clothing

Best Vehicle: While a standard car can navigate the main park road, a high-clearance vehicle might be helpful if exploring surrounding areas. Check road conditions before your visit, especially during winter.

Sun Exposure and Shade: The park sits at a high elevation, experiencing significant sun exposure. Shade is limited, primarily offered by scattered shrubs or rock formations.

Soil Type(s): The soil varies depending on location. Expect rocky soil with patches of sandy loam or clay deposits in valleys or flatter areas.

Rock Type(s): The surrounding geology consists of colorful Claron Formation sandstone, which has eroded into the dramatic cliffs and amphitheater.

Popularity: Cedar Breaks National Monument experiences moderate to high visitor traffic, especially during peak seasons (summer and fall).

Marlow's Idaho Rock Hounding Guide Book 2024

Where to Buy Essential Supplies (Nearest Town):

- **Cedar City, Utah:** (various stores available) - This town is approximately 30 miles west of the park entrance. Here you can find stores selling essentials like groceries, gas, camping supplies, and outdoor gear.

Directions to the Site from the Nearest Notable Landmark:

- **Cedar City, Utah:** Take UT-14 west from Cedar City for approximately 30 miles. Look for signs for Cedar Breaks National Monument.

Accommodation Options (Cedar City, Utah):

- **Holiday Inn Express & Suites Cedar City (Cedar City, UT: 1020 N Main St, Cedar City, UT 84720): (Phone:** (435) 586-7788) This hotel chain location offers amenities like breakfast and an indoor pool.
- **The Cedar Breaks Lodge (Cedar City, UT: 26 S Main St, Cedar City, UT 84720): (Phone:** (435) 586-3387) This historic lodge provides a unique accommodation option close to downtown Cedar City.

Recommended Stops and Attractions (with GPS Locations):

- **Zion National Park (Springdale, UT):** (37.2167° N, 112.7167° W) - This world-renowned National Park, approximately 1.5 hours southwest of Cedar Breaks, offers stunning scenery, slot canyons, and hiking trails. Look for signs for Zion National Park along I-15. How to Identify: Look for signs mentioning Zion National Park or the park entrance station.

- **Bryce Canyon National Park (Tropic, UT):** (37.5900° N, 112.1900° W) - Another captivating National Park, roughly 1.5 hours east of Cedar Breaks, featuring hoodoos (peculiar spire-shaped rock formations). Look for signs for Bryce Canyon National Park or the park entrance station.
- **Cedar City Museum (Cedar City, UT: 586 S Main St, Cedar City, UT 84720): (Phone:** (435) 586-7717) - This museum showcases the cultural and paleontological history of the region. Look for a large brick building on Main Street in Cedar City. How to Identify: Look for signs mentioning the Cedar City Museum.

BRUNEAU CANYON

Bruneau Canyon, carved by the Bruneau River in Owyhee County, Idaho, offers a landscape of dramatic scenery and potential for rockhounding adventures. Here's a comprehensive guide to navigate this rugged canyon:

Land Type: Public Land managed by the Bureau of Land Management (BLM) - Boise District (https://www.blm.gov/idaho).

GPS Location: (42.2581° N, 115.7033° W) - This represents the center of Bruneau Canyon. Specific locations for rockhounding will vary depending on the areas you explore within the BLM-managed land.

Best Season for Rockhounding: Spring (late April to May) and fall (September to October) offer comfortable temperatures for exploring. Summer can be hot and dry, while winter brings snowfall and limited access.

Marlow's Idaho Rock Hounding Guide Book 2024

Land Manager: Bureau of Land Management (BLM) - Boise District (https://www.blm.gov/idaho) **Contact:** (208) 377-1600

Rockhounding Potential: The geological formations in Bruneau Canyon offer possibilities for:

- **Jasper and Agates:** Explore areas around streams, exposed scree slopes (loose rock deposits), and near canyon walls for these colorful semiprecious stones.
- **Fossils (Possibility):** The Bruneau Canyon area is known for its rich fossil beds containing prehistoric mammal remains. However, collecting vertebrate fossils from BLM lands requires a permit. Focus on surface collecting of rocks and invertebrate fossils (e.g., petrified wood) that don't require permits.
- **Minerals (Possibility):** Depending on the specific location, you might uncover interesting minerals associated with the area's geology.

Important Note: Always check with the BLM Boise District for specific information on allowed activities and any restrictions in designated areas. Obey posted signs and respect the environment by practicing responsible rockhounding techniques, like collecting loose surface rocks only.

Best Tools for Rockhounding:

- Sturdy boots with good ankle support for hiking on uneven terrain
- Sturdy gloves for protection
- Safety glasses (recommended when hammering)
- Rock hammer (use ethically and sparingly on loose rocks only in designated BLM areas, if permitted)
- Collapsible bucket or backpack to carry your finds
- Hand lens to examine rocks closely

- GPS device (recommended for navigation in remote areas)
- Map of the Bruneau Canyon area highlighting BLM-managed lands

Best Vehicle: A high-clearance vehicle with four-wheel drive is recommended due to potentially rough or unpaved roads leading to specific rockhounding locations within the canyon.

Sun Exposure and Shade: The area around Bruneau Canyon is exposed, with limited shade provided by scattered rocks or low-lying vegetation. Sun protection, including sunscreen, a hat, and sunglasses, is crucial year-round.

Soil Type(s): The soil varies depending on elevation. Lower slopes might have sandy loam or clay soils, while areas near the base will likely have rockier soil with scree deposits.

Rock Type(s): The canyon itself is a result of erosion through volcanic rock formations. The surrounding area consists of various volcanic and sedimentary rock formations.

Popularity: Bruneau Canyon experiences moderate traffic for rockhounding and outdoor recreation compared to other locations. However, hikers, horseback riders, and campers also frequent the area, especially during summer months.

Where to Buy Essential Supplies (Closest Major Town):

- **Murphy's Home Center (Mountain Home, ID: 601 E Main St, Mountain Home, ID 83647):** (**Phone:** (208) 587-4441) This hardware store offers a variety of supplies like sturdy gloves, backpacks, hand lenses, and potentially rock hammers (check availability beforehand). Mountain Home is approximately 85 miles from the Bruneau Canyon area.

Directions to the Site from the Nearest Notable Landmark:

- **Mountain Home, Idaho:** Take I-84 west for approximately 40 miles. Exit at Mountain Home (Exit 73) and take ID-67 south for about 45 miles. Look for signs mentioning Bruneau Canyon or BLM-managed lands. Utilize a GPS device and consult with the BLM for detailed directions as specific access points can vary.

Accommodation Options (Mountain Home, Idaho):

- **Super 8 by Wyndham Mountain Home (Mountain Home, ID: 785 N Main St, Mountain Home, ID 83647): (Phone:** (208) 587-0009) This hotel chain location offers basic amenities in a convenient location.
- **Best Western Plus Ponderosa Inn (Mountain Home, ID: 1600 E Main St, Mountain Home, ID 83647): (Phone:** (208) 587-3330) This hotel offers a more upscale option with amenities like a pool and fitness center.

Recommended Stops and Attractions (with GPS Locations):

- **Bruneau Dunes State Park (South of Bruneau Canyon):** (42.0333° N, 115.6167° W) - This unique state park offers opportunities for sandboarding, off-roading (with permits), and exploring the otherworldly landscape of massive sand dunes. Look for signs for Bruneau Dunes State Park along ID-51 south of

- **Bruneau Sand Trap (South of Bruneau Canyon):** (42.0083° N, 115.7083° W) - This natural phenomenon is a geological marvel where the Bruneau River disappears into the highly permeable volcanic rock formations. Look for signs mentioning the Bruneau Sand Trap or follow signs for السياحة في ولاية ايداهو (Syahāḥah fī Wilāyah Īdāhū - Arabic for "Tourism in Idaho") along ID-51 south of Bruneau, as this location is a popular stop for international visitors or a bridge over a mostly dry riverbed leading to a vast expanse of sand.
- **Snake River Wine Country (West of Bruneau Canyon):** (Various Locations) - This scenic wine region west of Bruneau Canyon offers opportunities for wine tasting, vineyard tours, and enjoying the Snake River Valley. Wineries are scattered throughout the region. Look for signs for wineries or visit the Snake River Wine website for a map and member listings (https://idahowines.org/).

KING OF THE MOUNTAINS MINE

The King of the Mountains Mine, located in Custer County, Idaho, holds a rich historical significance in the state's mining industry. However, this specific location is not a public rockhounding site. It's a historical property on private land, and trespassing is strictly prohibited.

Land Type: Private Property

County: Custer County

GPS Location: Public access isn't allowed (refer to note above). The provided GPS coordinates (42.0644° N, 111.2300° W) represent the general area of the mine.

Alternative Rockhounding Options:

Since rockhounding isn't permitted at the King of the Mountains Mine, consider exploring public lands managed by the Bureau of Land Management (BLM) around Custer County. Always obtain permission before venturing onto private property. Check with the BLM for designated rockhounding areas and regulations (https://www.blm.gov/sites/default/files/documents/files/Recreational-Rockhounding.pdf).

Focus on Historical Exploration (Public Lands):

- Research the fascinating history of the King of the Mountains Mine. This productive galena/silver mine began operations in 1884.
- Explore the surrounding public lands for scenic overlooks or abandoned mining structures (ensure they are on public land).
- Visit museums or historical societies in nearby towns like Challis or Mackay to delve deeper into Idaho's mining heritage.

Best Tools for Exploring Public Lands:

- Camera to capture historical remnants or scenic views.
- Binoculars for observing the area from a distance.
- Map, compass, and GPS device for navigating in remote areas (especially important on BLM lands).

Best Vehicle:

- A high-clearance vehicle is recommended for navigating potentially unpaved roads on BLM-managed lands.

Sun Exposure and Shade: The area experiences significant sun exposure with limited shade from scattered vegetation. Sun protection like sunscreen, a hat, and sunglasses is crucial year-round.

Soil Type(s): The soil varies depending on location. Expect rocky soil with patches of sandy loam or clay deposits in valleys or flatter areas.

Rock Type(s): The surrounding geology consists of a mix of volcanic rock formations, sedimentary rocks, and glacial deposits.

Popularity: The King of the Mountains Mine itself isn't accessible to the public. However, surrounding public lands for hiking or exploring might see moderate use, especially during peak seasons.

Where to Buy Essential Supplies (Closest Major Town):

- **Challis, Idaho:** Various stores might be available depending on your needs. Challis is a town approximately 25 miles southeast of the general mine location. Look for stores selling basic supplies or outdoor gear.

Directions to the Site (General Area - Public Lands):

Due to trespassing restrictions, approaching the King of the Mountains Mine directly is not recommended. If exploring public lands in the area:

- Consult with the Challis Field Office of the BLM (https://www.blm.gov/office/idaho-falls-district-office) for specific directions and information on designated access points.
- Utilize detailed topographic maps and a GPS device to navigate unpaved roads on BLM lands.

Accommodation Options (Challis, Idaho):

- **Clear Creek Campground (Challis, Idaho):** (Public campground; GPS: 44.4900° N, 114.0533° W) - This campground offers a scenic location for camping near Challis. Look for signs mentioning the campground along ID-75 north of Challis.
- **The Challis Inn (Challis, Idaho: 101 Main St, Challis, ID 83226):** (**Phone:** (208) 928-3211) - This historic hotel located on Main Street in Challis provides a charming lodging option.

Important Note: Respect private property boundaries and avoid trespassing on the King of the Mountains Mine site. Explore your rockhounding passion responsibly by seeking out opportunities on designated public lands managed by the BLM.

CONCLUSION

Congratulations! You've completed Marlow's Idaho Rock Hounding Guide Book 2024, brimming with the knowledge and excitement to embark on your rockhounding adventure in the Gem State.

As you venture out, prioritize safety and responsible practices. Ensure you have the necessary gear, adequate supplies, and a plan to navigate your chosen location. Be mindful of weather conditions and adjust your plans accordingly. Flash floods, extreme heat, or icy trails can pose dangers.

Respect the environment. Leave No Trace by minimizing your impact, packing out all trash, and staying on designated trails. Adhere to land management regulations, obtain permits if required, and respect private property boundaries.

Rockhounding is a pursuit enriched by shared experiences. Let your newfound passion inspire others. Introduce friends and family to the wonders of rockhounding. Their discoveries might spark a lifelong interest. Document your adventures! Share photos and stories of your finds online or with local rockhounding clubs. Promote responsible rockhounding practices wherever you explore. Together, we can ensure this fascinating hobby thrives for future generations.

Idaho's landscapes hold a treasure trove waiting to be unearthed. With this guidebook as your companion, embark on your rockhounding adventure and discover the magic of Idaho's geology, one unique rock at a time!

www.ingramcontent.com/pod-product-compliance
Lightning Source LLC
LaVergne TN
LVHW090904090325
805510LV00008B/89